The Public Opinion Process:
How the People Speak

The Public Opinion Process: How the People Speak

Irving Crespi
Opinion Research Consultant
Princeton, New Jersey

LEA LAWRENCE ERLBAUM ASSOCIATES, PUBLISHERS
1997   Mahwah, New Jersey   London

Lawrence Erlbaum Associates, Inc., Publishers
10 Industrial Avenue
Mahwah, New Jersey 07430

Library of Congress Cataloging-in-Publication Data

Crespi, Irving.
    The public opinion process : how the people speak / Irving Crespi.
        p.   cm.
    Includes bibliographical references and index.
    ISBN 0-8058-2664-5 (alk. paper). — ISBN 0-8058-2665-3
(pbk. : alk. paper)
    1. Public opinion. I. Title.
HM261.C695   1997
303.3'8—dc21   97–1381
                                                        CIP

Books published by Lawrence Erlbaum Associates are printed on
acid-free paper, and their bindings are chosen for strength and dura-
bility.

Printed in the United States of America
10 9 8 7 6 5 4 3 2 1

Contents

Acknowledgments

I want to express my deep gratitude for the encouragement and assistance I received from friends and colleagues. Without burdening them with any responsibility for the limitations of this work, their critical comments and suggestions helped me rethink and sharpen a number of my initial formulations and also guided me to ideas I might otherwise have missed.

I owe a special debt of gratitude to Leo Bogart for his personal encouragement, his critical reading of an early draft, and for reminding me of early examples of relevant research. Kurt Lang's detailed, perceptive reading of the early draft was particularly helpful in identifying issues that required further development. Harold Mendelsohn's comments on that draft further directed my critical review.

I am indebted to Albert Gollin, whose guidance regarding communications technology was invaluable, and to Juan Linz for his guidance regarding polling in authoritarian states. Similarly, Helene Riffault and Norman Webb provided irreplaceable assistance regarding polling in communist regimes.

Michael Kagay, Samuel Reed, and Cliff Zukin each contributed his extremely helpful familiarity with important developments in their respective areas of expertise. Robert Trulio provided invaluable assistance at various stages in the physical production of the original manuscript.

Introduction

What is public opinion? How can we best study it?

This volume presents a process model that answers these questions by defining public opinion in a way that also identifies an approach to studying it. The model treats public opinion as an interactive, multidimensional, continuously changing phenomenon whose diverse aspects form causally interrelated patternings. This contrasts with the idea that public opinion should be studied as the state of public agreement, or disagreement, about issues that confront a people at various points in time, for example, as might be measured in public opinion polls. The model integrates established general social science theory with (a) what has been learned from empirical research about different aspects of the public opinion process and (b) existing middle-range theories.

THE NEED FOR A DEFINITION
OF PUBLIC OPINION

Public opinion is a phenomenon of significance to all kinds of people. Politicians, political scientists, political journalists, and social philosophers all deal with public opinion as a vital part of a people's political life. Public opinion is also the object of extensive study by social scientists interested in how the opinions of individuals come into being, how they merge into a significant collective force, and how all this relates to the working of government, especially in democratic societies.

Building on the more speculative writings of earlier centuries, during the 20th century, empirical social scientists representing many different disciplines have generated a large body of knowledge about public opinion. Courses on public opinion are offered by many political science, sociology, psychology, and communications departments, and those that do not offer such a course normally include public opinion as a topic in courses of broader scope. Considerable library shelf space is allocated to the topic, there are specialized journals on public opinion, and articles on diverse aspects of public opinion are standard fare in many other social science journals.

With so much attention paid to public opinion by so many different types of people across a long period of time, it is natural to assume that by now there is a general agreement regarding what it is. On the contrary, despite the many definitions that have been offered over the years, there is still no agreement. Sir Henry Maine's comment (cited in Lowell, 1926), "Vox Populi may be Vox Dei, but very little attention shows that there has never been any agreement as to what Vox means or as to what Populi means" (p. 21), is as true today as when he made it more than 100 years ago.

The lack of agreement is due in no small part to the complexity of the phenomenon, a point made by Bryce about 100 years ago when he sought an answer to the question, "What is public opinion?". He noted that some answer this question in terms of the existence and size of a majority view, others in terms of a prevailing or dominant opinion regardless of numbers, and still others by the means or "organs" through which opinions are expressed (Bryce, 1891).

The search for an answer to Bryce's question has been a recurrent theme throughout the 20th century. In 1924, difficulty in reaching an agreed-on definition led a group of social scientists to recommend that the term not be used at all (Childs, 1937). Ten years later, reviewing attempts to reach a common understanding, Childs (1937) noted "there are about as many definitions as there are studies in the field" (p.327). Still later, Key (1961) wrote, "To speak with precision of public opinion is a task not unlike coming to grips with the Holy Grail" (p. 8). In the same spirit, in his subsequent overview of public opinion in the *International Encyclopedia of the Social Sciences*, Davison (1968) observed, "There is no generally accepted definition of public opinion" (p. 188). More recently, Donsbach (1994)echoed Bryce's century-old question in his review of a panel of the 1994 conference of the World Association of Public Opinion Research (WAPOR) without being able to offer an answer: "What's public opinion? This is a question many would like to have an answer to, in and outside WAPOR. We are sorry to say Joohoan Kim [one of the panelists] didn't have the answer either" (p. 6).

The contrasting perspectives from which public opinion is studied impeded the development of a common understanding of public opinion that most observers and analysts will accept. Understandably, politicians seeking office, unelected government authorities, and philosophers in their efforts to justify—or attack—popular involvement in governance, have very different concerns when thinking about public opinion. Also reflecting the complexity of public opinion, public opinion researchers have come from many disciplines, most notably political science, sociology, psychology, and communications—each tends to focus on different aspects of the phenomenon and how it functions. As a result, the study of public opinion is characterized by a congeries of concepts and theories derived from different, and sometimes conflicting, traditions.

Fortunately, the lack of a generally accepted understanding of what we mean by the term *public opinion* has not inhibited its study by social scientists. During the past half century, empirical research generated an extensive body of information and concepts bearing on diverse aspects of the phenomenon. Furthermore, some convergence has taken place, so that—despite the lack of agreement on what public opinion is—by now there exists a considerable body of knowledge and middle-range theory on which there is considerable agreement. The process model presented here serves, therefore, as a solution to continuing controversy as to what public opinion really is by building a new framework out of what, heretofore, was a collection of ideas and facts imperfectly related to each other.

A MULTIDIMENSIONAL PROCESS

The starting point of our proposed process model is the assumption that any workable theory of public opinion cannot restrict itself to a unidimensional perspective. Intellectual rigor requires a theoretical model that defines public opinion in a way that incorporates its multidimensionality. In no other way can the disparate concerns of the different disciplines that study public opinion be dealt with satisfactorily.

A multidimensional process model also enables us to avoid the twin pitfalls of reductionism and reification in a way that integrates the results of a half century of empirical research. By recognizing the separate significance of the individual and collective aspects of the public opinion process, we do not feel compelled, on one hand, to explain collective phenomena solely as the outcome of individual-level processes, nor, on the other hand, to assume the existence of a collective level of existence independent of those processes. Our task is to relate these dimensions to each other and not to explain away one by assuming that only the other represents the underlying reality.

PUBLIC DISAGREEMENT
AND SOCIAL DISSENT

The one definitional point on which there is consensus is that public opinion has to do with conflict or disagreement as to how public issues should be resolved. This consensus exists among students of public opinion whose understandings are otherwise often very different from each other. Blumer (1939) referred to "a group of people ... who are confronted by an issue ... [and] who are divided in their ideas as to how to meet the issue" (p. 245), F. Allport (1937) relates public opinion to "conflict between individuals upon opposing sides," (p. 13), whereas Doob (1948) made "conflict among people" (p. 36) essential to his definition. From a very different perspective, Lippmann (1946) stated that "the symbols of public opinion ... are subject to check and comparison and argument" and that "the symbolism of public opinion usually bears ... this balancing of interest" (p. 7). In accord with this consensus, the process model excludes from consideration the full range of opinions that people hold about the world around them, and focuses instead on opinions that come into play when there is disagreement on how a public issue should be resolved. Furthermore, the process model deals not only with the individual opinions that arise when there is disagreement about some public issue but, equally important, with the collective judging that occurs about the issue.

The model also rejects the notion that public opinion is preeminently a form of social control, a mechanism for enforcing social conformity and discouraging social dissent. Instead, our interest lies in the judging—individual and collective—that occurs when there is disagreement about matters of public concern. Therefore, the model treats any possible social control functions as outcomes of the public opinion process rather than as its essence.

THE IDEA OF PROCESS

The idea that public opinion can best be studied as process and not as a political condition or state of being has been around for a long time. Nonetheless, relatively little attention has been paid to the need for a comprehensive theory of public opinion as process that is rooted in and integrates accepted social science theory. The process model presents such a theory.

Almost a century ago, Cooley (1918) explicitly formulated the principle that public opinion should be understood as process and not merely as a state of agreement, a principle that is today almost universally accepted. A diffuse effect of this principle is that it has served as a corrective against static studies of what the public thinks at given points in time, studies that do little more than correlate opinions with a variety of independent variables without investigating underlying causal processes. A more specific effect has been to generate interest in depicting the stages through which public opinion passes, from the emergence of an issue through the crystallization of a consensus on what to do about it, on to its eventual disappearance as a public concern. Whereas considerable success has been achieved in describing the stages of the process, there has been much less progress in identifying the components of that process as an articulated whole. In particular, there has been little follow-through to Bryce's insight that a major stage of development involved a transition from the individual to the collective level of opinion (see Davison, 1958, and Bryce, 1891).

Any acceptable theory of public opinion as process must meet the following criteria:

1. The theory must specify the components of the process and how they relate to each other and not be satisfied with a general affirmation of the principle that public opinion is process.
2. The process components must relate to general social science theory rather than being ad hoc formulations that are relevant only, or primarily, to public opinion.
3. The theory must be supported by the large body of empirical knowledge and middle-range theories that has been developed during the past half century.
4. The theory must encompass the individual, collective, and political dimensions of the public opinion process rather than focus primarily on one of them.

A theory that meets these criteria will be both familiar and strange. In detail, it will be made up of the usual concepts and research findings to be found in any comprehensive work on public opinion. Nonetheless, the articulation of those details—how they are organized and related to each other—will in some ways differ significantly from what is found in standard treatments. For these reasons, although the process model of public opinion relies on established social science theory and research, its organization deviates from common practice.

SURVEY DATA, HISTORICAL DATA, AND POLITICAL PHILOSOPHY

Inevitably, most of our examination of the public opinion process rests on survey data. The survey method has dominated empirical research on public opinion for the past half century, so that much of what we know about public opinion is based almost exclusively on what we have learned from surveys.

Nonetheless, empiricism does not require us to rely only on the results of quantitative analyses of survey data. Doing so would result in our ignoring historical sources of information pertinent to the public opinion process, as well as information about phenomena, such as the institutional organization of a people, that have barely been touched on in surveys about public opinion. Consequently, on some topics we rely on primarily historical, nonquantitative data. This contrast in data sources is unavoidable if the process model is to be fully explicated. However, at no point is it our purpose to present a history of how public opinion has functioned throughout time. Rather, our intent is to use whatever relevant data are available to develop the process model, whether they be survey data or historical records.

Finally, a full examination of the public opinion process must deal with what political philosophers have said about it. We must emphasize, however, the purpose of our examination is to further our analysis of the public opinion process and not to evaluate the correctness of competing philosophies. For all these reasons, the process model as presented in this volume comprises an examination of, as appropriate, survey data, historical records, and political philosophy.

PLAN OF THE BOOK

The plan of the volume, its content and how it is organized, is driven by the proposed process model of public opinion. The model, as presented in chapter 1, consists of three dimensions—one related to individual-level phenomena, a second to collective phenomena, and a third to political phenomena. The defining subprocess of each dimension, its components, and how it is related to the others are identified. The model is then contrasted with other approaches and its advantages reviewed. The remaining chapters, in a very real sense, are no more than a spelling out in some detail of the dynamics of each dimension of the process model.

A key characteristic of the model is that the three dimensions are interactive, with none having theoretical or empirical priority over the others. Selecting one dimension as the starting point of our exposition is, therefore, to a considerable degree an arbitrary decision. However, given the current orientation of survey research methodology and its dominance in empirical research, it is convenient to begin with individual-level phenomena.

Chapter 2, therefore, focuses on individual opinions, their sources, and dynamics as one dimension of the public opinion process. Opinions are discussed as a product of the individual's transactions with the world in which he or she lives. A crucial aspect of this discussion is the distinction between attitudinal systems as intervening variables in those transactions and opinions as outcomes or end-products.

A transactional analysis of individual opinions in itself cannot explain how they merge to become a significant collective force. To explain that, chapter 3 deals with a second dimension of the public opinion process, namely, the way in which, through communications, collective opinion emerges as an empirically demonstrable social force that is more than the sum of individual opinions. Mutual awareness, participation in shared universes of discourse, and opinion leadership are discussed within this framework.

Although communications technology is exogenous to the process model, it must be dealt with because its interactive relations with the social environment influence the scope, breadth, and structure of collective opinion. With this in mind, utilizing historical rather than survey data, chapter 4 traces the introduction of printing, the rise of long-distance mass communications in the 19th century, and the development of 20th-century electronic media.

The next two chapters deal with the political dimension of the public opinion process, the central subprocess being the extent to which it is accepted as a legitimate basis for governing. Chapter 5 focuses on authoritarian and totalitarian states. Given the sparsity of survey data from such states, historical and anecdotal sources predominate. With respect to authoritarianism, two examples are presented of the role of public opinion in medieval western Europe (selected because that was a time when the principles of authoritarianism were unchallenged by democratic ideas). The role of public opinion under Fascism and communism is then analyzed, with the historical record supplemented by material obtained directly from pollsters who had been active in communist ruled countries.

Chapter 6 deals with the political role of public opinion in democracies. The philosophical opposition between elitist and populist conceptions of what should be the legitimate role of public opinion is contrasted, the light cast on this controversy by recent social science research is reviewed, and strains in the legitimacy of contemporary linkages between government and collective opinion are discussed.

Public opinion polls have been proposed as a new way of linking collective opinion to political institutions in democracies. In chapter 7, we turn to the development of public opinion polls as an influence, both positive and negative, on the democratic linkage of collective opinion to government.

The final, summary chapter briefly discusses the implications of the model. The outcome of the public opinion process is not a state of being that, as in elections and polls, can be summarized by a few numbers. Rather, it is a never-ending kaleidoscopic movement. The implications of the process model are summarized from this point of view.

1

A Public Opinion Model

Public opinion, if we wish to see it as it is, should be regarded as an organic process, and not merely as a state of agreement about some question of the day. (Cooley, 1918, p. 378)

A THREE-DIMENSIONAL
INTERACTIVE SYSTEM

Public opinion on particular issues emerges, expresses itself, and wanes as part of a three-dimensional (3-D) process in which individual opinions are formed and changed, these individual opinions are aroused and mobilized into a collective force expressive of collective judgments, and that force is integrated into the governance of a people. Associated with each dimension is a corresponding subprocess: (a) *transactions* between individuals and their environments, (b) *communications* among individuals and the collectivities they comprise, and (c) the *political legitimation* of the emergent collective force.

These three processes are interactive aspects of the larger, continuous process so that their significance has to be understood in relation to each other. This conceptualization of public opinion as a multidimensional interactive process serves as an anaytical model for studying public opinion.

Three implicit characteristics of this model of public opinion as process that should be made explicit at this time are:

1. None of the three dimensions of public opinion is inherently antecedent to any other.
2. The three dimensions form an interactive system that is not characterized by a unidirectional causal flow.

3. Each dimension is itself modeled around interactions related respectively to the transactional, communicative, and legitimizing dynamics of public opinion.

Each of the three dimensions can be described in terms of how the subprocess associated with it links a particular set of variables, namely:

1. *Transactions*: This subprocess has to do with the interactions among attitudinal systems (consisting of beliefs, affective states, values/interests), controversial situational contexts, and perceived reality worlds that lead to the emergence of individual opinions.

2. *Communications*: This subprocess, which creates collective opinion as a social force by developing mutual awareness of one another's opinions, involves the interactions between the language used in public discourse and the group contexts and roles related to that discourse.

3. *Legitimation*: This subprocess establishes the political role of collective opinion through the interactions between the principles that establish whether collective opinion is politically legitimate and linkages of collective opinion to government.

Figure 1.1 models this understanding of public opinion as process rather than as a condition of or decision by a society. Note that the public opinion process as depicted in Fig. 1.1 forms an interactive system and not a sequence of causally linked stages of development. By way of illustration, part of the situational contexts out of which individual opinions arise in contemporary democracies are the collective opinions which individuals experience—through nonpolitical as well as political contacts—and expectations that opinion should and, in fact, does have a legitimate role in the political life of a society. Both these elements affect the public opinion process at all stages rather than each being characteristic of a particular stage.

Intrinsic to this model of public opinion as process is the realization that public opinion is neither a group, institution, or structural aspect of a society nor the discrete states of mind of a set of individuals. Rather, it refers to continuous interactions and outcomes. Davison (1958) referred "to action or readiness for action with regard to a given issue on the part of members of a public who are reacting in the expectation that others in the public are similarly oriented toward the same issue" (p. 93). He contrasted this perspective with the view that public opinion is the majority view (e. g., as measured in a poll), the ideas that dominate public communications, or that act as an agent of social control. To demonstrate public opinion as process, instead of describing a given state of public opinion, Davison traced a sequence of

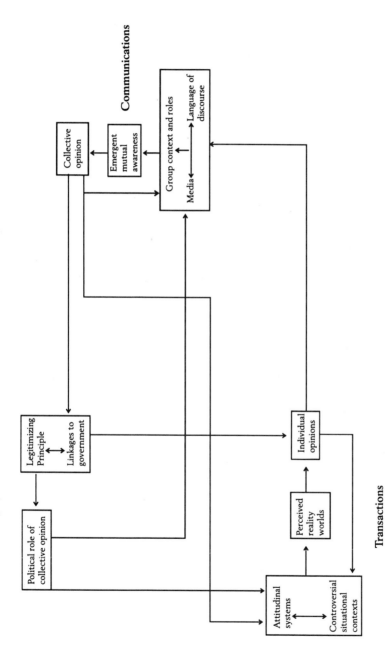

FIG. 1.1. The Public Opinion Process.

Legitimation

Communications

Transactions

Political role of collective opinion

Legitimizing Principle ↔ Linkages to government

Collective opinion

Emergent mutual awareness

Group context and roles
Media ↔ Language of discourse

Individual opinions

Perceived reality worlds

Attitudinal systems ↔ Controversial situational contexts

3

stages, namely: The emergence of a public issue, the role of leadership in gaining public attention, the onset of public debate and discussion, the continued interchange of individual opinions, which leads to awareness and expectations concerning the opinions of others, which, in turn, may result in opinion change and, finally the disappearance of the issue in public thinking. Our model adds to Davison's description the idea that at each stage of development there is a multidimensional interaction of psychological, sociological, and political elements.

The model accommodates existing middle-range theories derived from separate disciplines without reducing the many aspects of public opinion to one dimension. The individual elements of the model, as elaborated in this work, represent the tested output of empirical research. The model's contribution is to explicitly structure the separate dimensions of the public opinion process and their component elements into a multidimensional, integrated, ongoing phenomenon. In doing so, the model resolves the old and ultimately sterile controversy as to whether public opinion is really no more than an aggregate of individual opinions or whether it is a collective phenomenon that is reflected in individual opinions. The model also helps us examine the interrelations among the psychological, sociological, and political dynamics of the public opinion process. Thus, it avoids the twin fallacies of reductionism and reification.

Before turning to the details of the model's three dimensions, it is useful to review briefly how the model affects how we think about public opinion.

THE SIGNIFICANCE
OF MULTIDIMENSIONALITY

There is a long-standing theoretical controversy as to what attribute or quality defines the essence of public opinion, for example, whether it is the majority position or the dominant opinion (Lang & Lang, 1983). Underlying such controversy is the unidimensional assumption that there is one central quality that defines what is truly public opinion, whether that quality refers to individual opinions, some kind of collective structuring of individual opinions, or the political role of opinions. Integral to the assumption of unidimensionality is that there is a single causal flow at work so that, no matter how complex public opinion may be, it is possible to identify a common underlying causal factor, or set of factors, that explains the rise and development of public opinion.

In opposition is the multidimensional stipulation that public opinion exists simultaneously at a number of levels of reality, each characterized by distinctive causal processes. This view has its roots in the realization that public opinion does not merely exist as a summarization of opinions but is in a constant process of emergent development. An early expression of this realization is Bryce's description of the stages through which public opinion must go before opinion begins to affect government (Bryce, 1891). These stages proceed from (a) a rudimentary form characterized by expressions of individual opinion that are in some way representative of general thought on an issue; to (b) a stage at which individual opinions crystallize into a collective force; to (c) a third stage in which after discussion and debate definite sides are taken; and then to (d) the final stage in which action has to be taken, typically as a member of some group or faction.

Our multidimensional process model goes beyond Bryce's formulation in that it does not assume a fixed, unidirectional sequence of transitions. Instead, it recognizes that a complex set of processes are at work at each stage and that these processes are interactional rather than unidirectional. This recognition incorporates the findings of public opinion researchers who have investigated such varied phenomena as the relation of opinion to underlying beliefs and values; socioeconomic position and political leadership; the impact of events and communications on the movement of opinion; political socialization; interaction between opinion leaders and followers; the role of mass media in agenda setting; and personal versus impersonal forms of communication. Without giving up the notion that there is a life history of public opinion on any particular issue, the multidimensional process model requires us to think about all these phenomena as existing at each stage.

INDIVIDUAL VERSUS COLLECTIVE ASPECTS
OF PUBLIC OPINION

A problem inherent in the term *public opinion* is how to differentiate between its individual and collective aspects, and then reconcile them. One impediment to a satisfactory resolution of this problem has been a proclivity to reify the concept of public opinion, that is, to conceptualize the relationship of the public opinion process to collective action in a way that transforms the process into a being or thing that acts in its own right, separate from the individuals who make up the collectivity. The propensity to reify the public opinion process stems from the fact that although opinions are held by individuals, there is a feeling that the process has to do with something more than the thought and behavior of individuals and that "there is some social reality beyond individual attitudes" (Back, 1988, p. 278).

Social scientists have long been sensitive to the danger that asserting that public opinion involves more than individual opinions can lead to the "group mind" fallacy, with public opinion personified as "some kind of being which dwells in or above the group, and there expresses its view upon various issues as they arise" (F. Allport, 1937, p. 8). It is especially important that those who maintain that public opinion involves collective phenomena with a reality distinct from individuals should also recognize that this does not mean that public opinion is a distinct being that, in any meaningful way, can be said to think, feel, decide, or act. Discussing the public opinion process as if it is an acting entity directs attention away from its actual complexity as a collective phenomenon. The reality is that there is a never-ending flux in which the balance of individual opinions and coalitions of opinions shifts back and forth, a flux in which the relevance and importance of different issues continuously change. Reifying the public opinion process muddles our understanding of this reality, even if, when pressed, we hasten to acknowledge the fallacy of reification.

Clarity requires recognizing that when we say, "Public opinion is aroused," "Public opinion has spoken," or "Public opinion has bestowed its mandate," we are using what is little more than a journalistic or literary metaphor. But even as a journalistic metaphor, reifying public opinion can have pernicious effects by leading to misinterpretations of political reality. This is readily evident in news analyses of the meaning of election results, of what mandate has been decreed. The reality is not that the electorate, as a corporate body, has reached a new consensus on issues of the day but that a different balance of political power has come into place. Those who lose an election have not, as components of the larger body, changed their opinions. They may recognize the fact that they are not in power, they may change their strategies and tactics, but in all likelihood, they mostly continue to promote the same basic policies they have in the past.

The fact that election results can have a significant impact on how a democracy is governed does not mean that political cleavages based on conflicting values and interests have somehow been, at least temporarily, resolved. They persist, though sometimes in altered forms. Also, although the losers do not disappear, over time, winning and losing particular elections can affect the ability of contending parties to persist as viable political forces. Metaphorical references to public opinion having reached a decision should not be allowed to confuse thinking on these matters.

Unfortunately, the realization that public opinion is not a superindividual actor often leads to the reverse fallacy of reductionism, that is, analyzing the collective aspects of the public opinion process only in terms of its individual components. Contributing to the reductionist perspective in the study of public opinion is the fact that over 50 years of empirical research have been dominated by survey research methodology. As Back (1988) observed, this is "a very individual oriented method, adding up individual opinion to reach a societal characteristic and corresponds to our individualistic society" (p. 278). He further observed that this extreme individualism has hindered the development of a general definition of public opinion that is not restricted to contemporary American and European society.

Illustrative of the reductionist approach to the study of public opinion is this definition:

> Public opinion refers to people's attitudes on an issue when they are members of the same social group. ... The key psychological word in this definition is that of "attitude" ... (namely), the socially significant, internal response that people habitually make to stimuli (Doob, 1948, p. 35).

Although this definition acknowledges group membership as an aspect of public opinion, there is no question that the essence of public opinion as Doob sees it lies in the expression of individual attitudes.

F. Allport (1937) left open "the possibility that a superior product of group interaction may exist," but nonetheless asserted that "if there is such an emergent product, we do not know where it is, how it can be discovered, identified or tested, or what the standards are by which its value may be judged." (p.11) In accord with this point of view, Allport listed 13 items as constituting the phenomena to be studied under the term public opinion. Of the 13 items, 7 explicitly refer to the individual, although in some cases a collective context is acknowledged:

They are behaviors of human *individuals*.

They are performed by ... many *individuals*.

The object or situation they are concerned with is *important to many*.

They are frequently performed with an *awareness* that *others are reacting to the same situation* in a similar manner.

The attitudes or opinion they involve are expressed or . . . . *individuals* are in readiness to express them.

The *individuals* performing these behaviors, or set to perform them, may or may not be in one another's presence.

Being efforts toward common objectives, they frequently have the character of *conflict between individuals* aligned upon opposing sides. (F. Allport, 1937. p. 13, italics added).

Although Allport's other six points did not stress so explicitly that public opinion refers to the thoughts and behavior of individuals, they related to individual phenomena such as verbalization and action or readiness to action.

Even when individual thoughts and actions are examined as manifesting themselves in aggregations, the reductionist understanding of public opinion will exclude the possibility that collective qualities may emerge that involve more than the thoughts, feelings, and behavior individual (F. Allport, 1937). The following is one illustration of this perspective:

> I do not want to imply that the public is any more than the sum of all its parts. Clearly, as in any assemblage of people such as a town meeting, some will feel the issue is irrelevant, and having no opinions they may not participate. Public opinion in such cases is the opinion of those who have preferences and choose to participate. The saliency of the issue to a given individual and his resulting intense participation might well cause his opinion to weigh more heavily in some linkage processes. (Luttbeg, 1974, p. 1)

In contrast, others who insist that only individuals think and behave, and not collectivities, may still recognize the reality of a collective dimension to the public opinion process. Lasswell (1927) explicitly rejected the idea that "collective attitudes" relate to a superorganic entity that exists "on a plane apart from individual action," (p. 27) but he argued that to avoid confusion we need a concept that connotes uniformity of conduct without also implying a biological or metaphysical unity. He opted to borrow the anthropological term *pattern* in order to designate uniformity in the distribution of individual acts when discussing collective attitudes. Unfortunately, useful as the term pattern is, it is too static to analyze adequately how aggregating individual opinions can create public opinion as a strong social and political force. A more dynamic concept is needed.

Much of the analytical focus of the pioneer studies of voting behavior conducted during the 1940s and 1950s at Columbia University's Bureau of Applied Social Research and later at the University of Michigan's Survey Research Center was on individual psychological processes. For example, the Columbia studies investigated the activation and reinforcement of existing characteristics of individual voters and the effect of cross-pressures created by conflicting characteristics on individual voting decisions (Lazarsfeld, Berelson, & Gaudet, 1948) whereas the motivational impact on voter choice of party identification, issue orientation, and candidate orienta-tion, and importance of individual attitudes such as political efficacy were the focus of the early Michigan studies (Campbell, Gurin, & Miller, 1954).

Nonetheless, in those early studies there was also recognition of the role of collective factors. The structure of the institutional environment and the pattern of group memberships and identifications were important analytical variables in the Sandusky, Ohio and Elmira, New York studies conducted by the Bureau of Applied Social Research. Comparably, in the first national study conducted by the Survey Research Center, superin-dividual factors were specified as exogenous variables, making it possible to focus on the individual level of causation without ignoring the signifi-cance of the collective level. Whether public opinion should be treated as an individual or collective phenomenon is a false issue. The question, rather, is how to integrate the individual and collective aspects of public opinion.

What has been lacking is the systematic and consistent application of existing theory of society as an emergent phenomenon whose nature is more than the sum of its parts. The need to use that theory is often overlooked, as when public opinion is defined equally as "the sum *or* as the resultant" of individual opinions, so that these two very different understandings are treated as equivalent (e.g., Smith, 1947, p. 507, italics added). The problem is not so much the unavailability of an applicable theory but, rather, the failure to apply existing theory of social phenomena as arising out of communications among individuals and groups of individuals. The process model of public opinion, by positing communications as the subprocess associated with the collective dimension of public opinion, seeks to remedy this failure.

Dealing with the individual and collective aspects of public opinion as distinct but interrelated dimensions of the public opinion process is essential to the multidimensional process model. There can be no question as to the relevance of such traditional concerns of individual psychology as learning, perception, and motivation to the study of how individual opinions develop and change. Neglecting these concerns would make it impossible to under-stand the public opinion process. At the same time, superindividual factors of concern to sociology and political science, such as group cohesion and conflict, acceptance and rejection of group standards of behavior, patterns of leadership and authority, and the role of power in governance clearly also have to be taken into account in any analysis of how public opinion affects a society. Leaving them out, or assuming that they are adequately encom-passed by psychological processes, does not work either.

BEYOND REIFICATION AND REDUCTIONISM

Common to both the reification and reductionist perspectives is the propensity to think of public opinion as the product of a being that acts. In the former case, public opinion is the product of some kind of supraindividual actor and in the latter of an aggregation of individual actors. The process model, in contrast, rejects the notion that public opinion is the product of any kind of actor, or actors. Instead, it conceptualizes public opinion as existing in the transactional, communication, and legitimizing processes just outlined. When those processes are expressed through social organizations—which may be informal communal groups such as neighborhoods and networks of friendships, or formal corporate bodies such as political parties and voluntary associations—they impel those organizations to act. That is, the public opinion process is the energizer of corporate activity and not the actor itself.

The failure to make explicit the distinction between public opinion as process versus public opinion as actor accounts for much of the confusion that has characterized attempts to define what public opinion really is. It is not a decorporalized general will; neither is it a statistical construct made up of individual data points. It is an expression of social energy that integrates individual actors into social groupings in ways that affect the polity. This understanding takes the concept of public opinion out of metaphysics and therefore makes it impossible to study empirically and, at the same time, avoids reducing it to a set of discrete individualized observations that cannot account for its composite sociopolitical significance.

With this understanding, we now proceed to a detailed consideration of the three dimensions of the public opinion process.

2

The Emergence
of Individual Opinions

Individual opinions are judgmental outcomes of *transactions* between individuals and the environments in which they live. To discuss the emergence of individual opinions, therefore, it is first necessary to define the transactional process. Once that is done, we must further specify what we mean by the term *opinion*, how opinions and attitudes are related to each other, and what is involved when individual opinions change. We then are prepared to discuss issues related to the quality of individual opinions. That discussion sets the stage for our consideration, in the next chapter, of how individual opinions are mobilized into a social force.

REALITY WORLDS AND TRANSACTIONS

People are active, thinking, and feeling agents whose perceptions and understandings of the world in which they live are always subject to change as a consequence of how they experience an external world that is itself always subject to change. The emergence of individual opinions, and any subsequent changes in them, must be considered in these terms.

A transactional perspective adds to standard interaction formulations by looking at a process of becoming, that is, a continuous, mutual shaping and reshaping of internal and external variables (H. Cantril, 1958, 1988). Adopting this perspective does not mean that we substitute poorly defined qualities for measurable variables, but it does require us to be sensitive to a level of complexity that is often overlooked. Individuals think, feel, and behave in relation to the world as they perceive it to be—their distinctive "reality worlds"—and not only in reaction to objectively definable external stimuli.

These reality worlds are the psychological products of a process involving interdependent variables, a process that is not adequately encompassed if we think only of interactions between independent variables. Individuals relate creatively to the world around them so that the psychologically meaningful environments in which they live do not consist merely of external, objective variables; significantly, those environments consist of interpretive perceptions of those external variables. At the same time, the psychological qualities and neurophysiological characteristics of individuals that influence their perceptions of their surroundings are not simply products of inner biological mechanisms but are themselves, in part, shaped by environmental forces.

Opinions emerge from the mutually creative influence of a set of inner and outer forces on each other. These forces include (a) the circumstances in which individuals find themselves (including their social positions, relationships with others, structure and culture of the groups to which they belong, etc., as well as the specific circumstances surrounding the controversy); (b) individual qualities and characteristics (such as beliefs, values and interests, feelings, goals, standards of judgment, etc.); and (c) the patterning of interactions of all those variables that shape and mold the world as one perceives it to be. Rather than thinking in terms of how one's opinion on a particular issue results from interactions between specific variables such as one's group affiliations, interpersonal relations, beliefs, and so on, we substitute the idea that that opinion is the outcome of how the patterning of interactions of all those variables sets into motion a process of continuous change and development.

SITUATIONAL AND DEMOGRAPHIC CORRELATES OF OPINION

The transactional perspective comes into play when interpreting correlations between opinion on one hand and situational contexts or demographic variables on the other. To understand individual opinions, we have to see the real people behind the categories into which we place them. This requires taking into account the particular situational context about which an opinion is voiced and the individual's social position as it relates to that situation. Situational contexts help explain why individuals sometimes express seemingly contradictory opinions. For example, for humanitarian reasons, opponents of foreign aid may nevertheless support emergency relief to earthquake and drought victims. Similarly, pacifist proponents of support to democratic forces in other countries may oppose armed intervention to implement a policy designed to help those forces.

The nature of an individual's involvement in an issue is a further influence on opinion formation. Some people who oppose legalized abortion as a general principle of public policy might come to support allowing circumstantial exceptions after an experience involving themselves or a member of their family. Unless the effects of situational circumstances such as these are taken into account, expressed opinions can often be incorrectly interpreted as irrational or meaningless.

With regard to demographic variables, despite their seeming objective quality, they can be ambiguous in their meanings. Consequently, correlations between demographics and opinion in themselves typically have little more than descriptive value. To understand linkages between demographics and opinions, one must also consider the sociopsychological meanings of those demographics. Age, education, and income are three cases in point.

Age is a frequent discriminator between holders of different opinions. However, once a difference in opinion by age has been identified, we are often faced with the question as to whether this is an *age cohort* or *age grade difference*. That is why, when there are age differences, we ask ourselves whether these are differences among, for example, the "silent generation" of the 1950s, the "Vietnam generation" of the late 1960s and early 1970s, and the "Yuppie generation" of the 1980s. Or, are they related to aging and to changes in one's life situation as one gets older? This question is significant, not only for interpreting age differences at any given point in time but, perhaps even more importantly, for analyzing trends in opinion across extended periods of time (Evan, 1959). Among other things, long-term trends are often more the result of cohort replacement, with an older generation dying off and being replaced by a younger generation, than of changes in individual opinion. Davis' analysis of trends across a 20-year span, provides a particularly rich demonstration of this phenomenon along with a useful review of the literature (Davis, 1992).

Differences in opinion by level of educational achievement, with those who have attended college holding opinions different from those who have not, are another frequent survey finding. But, is the distinctiveness of the college-educated due to the intellectual consequence of having attended an institution of higher learning, to the predominantly upper- and middle-class origins of most college students, to occupational and income correlations with education, or to socialization into a college subculture? Differences of opinion within the college-educated, for example, between liberal arts versus business administration majors, or graduates of Ivy League universities versus community colleges, sharpen the significance of this question. In any event, number of years of formal schooling in itself has limited explanatory utility in analyses of causation.

Similarly, the explanatory value of income lies not only in its external objectivity but, equally important, in its utility as an indicator of social roles and the meanings and subjective states associated with those roles. It is true that having an annual income of $50,000 has a direct impact on buying power and, therefore, a direct relation to financial interests that can affect opinion. But, the financial interests related to a $50,000 annual income are very different for a married mid-level business manager whose wife does not work outside the home and has one child, a two-income manual worker family with three children, and an unmarried, recently graduated lawyer. In the same vein, support for transfer welfare payments to low-income families is related not merely to income, but to the tax implications of the combination of income and age (Ponza, Duncan, Corcoran, & Groskind, 1988). To understand how the process of opinion formation is related to demographic variables, we must go beyond analyzing their correlations with opinion and deal with their interrelations with psychological processes.

OPINIONS AS JUDGMENTAL OUTCOMES

Individual opinions are *judgmental outcomes* of complex psychological processes, in which the pros and cons of opposing views are considered (see Albig, 1956). When we want to know an individual's opinion about an issue, we ask questions to find out what position he or she has taken, or what conclusion he or she has reached, about that issue. Replying that you do not have an opinion on an issue implies that you have not made a judgment, perhaps because you had never heard of the issue, have not thought much about it, or because you have not been able to reach a conclusion.

In an informal conversation, we might ask a general question such as "What do you think about ... ?" whereas in a survey we might ask such questions as "Do you favor or oppose ... ?", "Do you think it is a good idea or a bad idea to ... ?", "Do you approve or disapprove of ... ?", "How favorably or unfavorably do you rate ... ?", and "With whom do you agree or disagree more ... ?". To define fully the opinion that has been reached, we may also further questions about specific aspects of the controversy. For example, in a poll on approval of a president's performance in office, a question on overall performance might be followed by questions on how the president is handling various problem areas such as foreign policy, the national economy, race relations, and so on, or on specific issues in each area (e. g., the situation in the Mid East or the threat of inflation). A battery of questions like that is needed when the complexity of an issue may lead to complex judgments.

Answers to opinion questions, whether only one or a battery of questions has been asked, seldom give us sufficient information to understand why those opinions are held. In and of themselves they do not tell us much, if anything, about the judging process that went into forming the opinion. Despite the often seeming simplicity and completeness of individual expressions of opinion, the judging process encompasses a complex network of feelings and thoughts. This is why in-depth surveys that seek to go beyond straightforward tallying of individual opinions must probe the elements of those processes. Such surveys seek to find out what personal experience with the issue the individual has had, what information an individual has (or does not have) on a controversy, whether the individual thinks the controversy is important or unimportant, and why he or she feels that way, as well as to investigate individual motivations, fears, expectations, and goals. These are matters that go far beyond the position(s) an individual has taken on the issue per se. In this way, they become more than "opinion polls" but investigations of the transactions that lead to the formation of opinions.

For example, a June 1994 *New York Times*/WCBS-TV Channel 2 Poll that surveyed the opinions of New York City residents regarding the seriousness of crime and the performance of the city's police force also asked the following questions:

> Compared to one year ago, do you see more police officers walking in your neighborhood, fewer, or about the same number?

> In your neighborhood where you live, have you seen people selling drugs in the last few months?

> In the last year or so, have you yourself done anything special to protect yourself or your family from the threat of crime, or not?

> When you think about yourself and crime, what kind of crime do you think is most likely to happen to you?

> When it comes to worries about your children, which worries you more—that they will be the victim of a crime or that they will become involved with drugs?

Although the questions just posed are clearly related to opinions about crime, in and of themselves they do not tell us what those opinions may be. Individuals with similar perceptions of the incidence of drug selling or of police in their neighbohoods may nonetheless hold drastically different opinions as to how good a job the police force is doing or as to what needs to be done to reduce crime. What answers to these questions can do is help us understand the judging process out of which opinions emerge.

Similarly, to comprehend an individual's opinion of the *Roe v. Wade* Supreme Court decision that established a constitutional basis for legal abortion, it helps to find out if approval or disapproval of that decision varies by whether the abortion will take place in the first, second, or third trimester; whether the acceptability of abortion varies in different contexts— if the mother's life is in danger, in cases of rape, if the fetus is deformed, if the parents are unmarried teenagers, if the father is opposed to the abortion, if a woman has two children and does not want any more, and so on. For an even fuller understanding of opinion on abortion, one would also seek to investigate beliefs concerning when life begins or when a fetus begins to experience pain. In other words, we go beyond asking what judgment one has reached—what is one's opinion—and investigate the thought processes that lead a person to hold a particular opinion.

In response to criticism of the limitations of polls that do not probe such matters and are restricted to measuring only opinions, Gallup (1947) proposed an interviewing strategy that he called the quintamensional question design. Although this question design was never widely used by him, or anyone else for that matter, it represents a rare methodological effort to systematically relate opinion polling to the process of opinion formation and is, therefore, worth reviewing briefly. Whatever limitations the quintamensional question design may have, it clearly differentiates between measurements of opinion per se, and aspects of the judging process that lead to opinion positions.

Gallup (1947) posited five attributes to measure, each with a prototypical question.

1. The informational foundation for an opinion, that is, whether the person being interviewed has given any thought or attention to an issue and what is known about it. According to Gallup, question(s) to ask might be, "Have you heard or read about (issue)?" and "What can you tell me about (issue)?"

2. The important viewpoints or perspectives that establish the context in which opinions are formed. For this purpose, open-ended or unstructured questions such as the following might be asked: "What is your feeling about what should be done about (issue)?"

3. Issue position, for example, a positive or negative reaction to specific proposals. In order to tally responses regarding complex issues, they would have to be broken down with separate questions asked concerning each issue component. Standard opinion questions such as those just cited would be asked.

4. The underlying reasoning for holding an opinion—the reasons "why." A typical question might be, "Why do you feel this way?" (in reference to the endorsed position in the third step).

5. Intensity of feeling or commitment to one's opinion. A structured or "closed" question would be asked, for example, "How strongly do you feel about that?"

From a transactional perspective, Gallup's proposed questioning strategy can be described as an attempt to operationalize the distinction between opinion as output and some of the input variables that must be taken into account if we are to understand the processes through which opinions emerge. Rather than letting us conceptualize opinion as little more than an overt expression of latent attitudes, the transactional perspective requires us to think about the judging process that intervenes between and links external conditions, pre-existing psychological variables, and emergent opinion.

OPINIONS AND ATTITUDES

It is unfortunately common to conceptualize opinions and attitudes as virtually equivalent phenomena (see Price, 1992, for a summary of how opinions and attitudes have been differentiated over time). Often, they are either not differentiated or, at most, treated as classifications based on different ways of looking at the same thing. McGuire (cited in Keissler, Collins, & Miller, 1969) asserted that the distinction between attitude and opinion is a "situation involving names in search of a distinction, rather than a distinction in search of a terminology" (p. 4). Similarly, in tracing the history of attitude research, McGuire (1986) treated opinion and attitude as interchangeable concepts.

Thurstone (1928), one of the first to attempt a precise differentiation between opinions and attitudes, defined attitudes as latent psychological states that cannot be directly observed but are inferred from overt verbalized opinions and behavior. Nonetheless, according to Fleming, he repeatedly ignored even this small distinction, often using the term *attitude* when his own precepts required *opinion* (cited in Price, 1992). Similarly, G. Allport, even as he recognized a difference between opinion and attitude, nonetheless discussed opinion measurement as one way of measuring the strength and nature of personal attitudes (G. Allport, 1967). Rokeach largely followed Thurstone's lead by defining opinion as the verbalization of attitudes, sentiments, and values (Rokeach, 1968). A more substantive distinction describes attitudes as enduring global orientations as contrasted with the situational specificity of opinions (Wiebe, 1953; Hovland, Janis, & Kelley, 1953). Another distinction emphasizes the affective content of attitudes as contrasted with the more cognitive quality of opinions that involve reaching conscious judgments (Fleming, 1967).

Although verbalization, situational specificity, and cognitive quality may be meaningful attributes of opinion when used descriptively, they contribute little to an understanding of how individual opinions develop. In contrast, the transactional perspective leads to our making a distinction between emergent opinion and antecedent attitudinal variables that focuses on development. To establish that distinction, however, our definition of attitudes must be clarified.

The concept of *attitude* has been called "the most distinctive and indispensable concept in contemporary American social psychology. ... In fact several writers ... define social psychology as the scientific study of attitudes" (G. Allport, in Fishbein, 1967, p. 3; see also Green, 1954). Nonetheless, attitudes have been defined in many, often conflicting ways. There is general agreement on the meaning of attitudes with respect to one characteristic, namely, persistent affect (feeling tone): "Attitudes refer to persistent and affectively charged psychological states that enable individuals to relate to their surroundings and to 'objects' (people and/or things) that comprise their surroundings in ways that make for behavioral consistency." (G. Allport, 1967, p. 3–13; see also G. Allport, 1954; Beninger, 1987, pp. S52–S53; Doob, 1948, p. 39; Fishbein & Raven, 1967, pp. 183–189; Green, 1954, pp. 335–336; Krech & Crutchfield, 1948, p. 152; Rosenberg, 1960, p. 320; Rosenberg & Hovland, 1960, p. 3; Sherif, Sherif, & Nebergal,1965, p. 4; Thomas & Znaniecki, 1958, pp. 23–24). Beyond that, the many definitions of attitude that have been proposed can be placed, with minimal distortion, on a behaviorist/cognitive–functional continuum.

At the behaviorist pole of this continuum is the view that attitudes are learned mental or neural states of readiness that predispose the individual to behave in specified ways (e.g., F. Allport, 1954; Doob, 1947). So defined, attitudes are latent behavior whereas opinions are little more than overt verbalizations of those latencies. In that case, the analysis of individual opinion ultimately becomes a special case of attitude analysis. However, if one adopts the behaviorist conceptualization, attitudes are virtually indistinguishable from other forms of learned behavior, a point that has led some to recommend abandoning the concept completely (Doob, 1947; see also Chein, 1948). Even more disturbing is research demonstrating the often tenuous relation between measured attitudes and subsequent behavior (e.g., Festinger, 1964). The behaviorist position clearly does not offer a usable theoretical frame for investigating the formation of individual opinion as judgments on issues.

In contrast, as becomes evident in our further discussion, conceptualizing attitudes functionally simplifies the task of relating opinion to underlying psychological processes. At the functional pole of the continuum, attitudes are conceptualized as persistent evaluative tendencies and not as behavioral predispositions. Thus, a succinct definition of attitude in the functionalist tradition is, "Attitude is defined at the individual level, namely, the specific organization of feelings and beliefs according to which a given person evaluates an object or symbol positively or negatively" (D. Katz, 1972, p. 13). More fully elaborated, attitudes consist of integrated systems of cognitive, affective, and conative response modes. Moreover, they are supported motivationally by helping individuals learn how to cope with their surroundings as well as with internal emotions and conflicts, express their values, and know their worlds in structured, meaningful ways (D. Katz, 1960; Krech & Crutchfield 1948; Rokeach 1968, p. 18; Rosenberg & Hovland, 1960; see also Blumler & Katz, 1974). Adopting the functional perspective, therefore, leads to thinking about systems of response modes that constitute attitudes, rather than to a behavioral predisposition that we call "an attitude."

Accordingly, henceforth we do not use the term *attitude* by itself (except when quoting others). Instead, we substitute the phrase *attitudinal system*, and define attitudinal systems as comprised of four types of components:

1. Evaluative frames of reference (values and interests).
2. Cognition (knowledge and beliefs).
3. Affection (feelings). Because many use the term attitude as referring only or primarily to the affective mode whereas others use attitude more generally, an added benefit of adopting this nomenclature is that it avoids confusing the affective response mode with the entire system.
4. Conation (behavioral intentions).

Finally, we posit that attitudinal systems influence behavior indirectly, as an intervening variable that mediates perception, thereby establishing evaluative predispositions (see Beninger, 1987).

This functional understanding of attitudinal systems provides a compatible theoretical foundation for our earlier discussion of individual opinions as judgmental outcomes of an individual's transactions with the surrounding world. The system components—values and interests, beliefs, feelings, and behavioral intentions—influence opinion formation through their interactive effects on how the external world is perceived and then judged.

Unfortunately, the distinction between opinion and the components of attitudinal systems is easily blurred. One reason for this is that similar questioning techniques are typically used to measure them all. As noted in the earlier discussion of opinions as judgments, when opinion surveys seek to go beyond the mere tallying of opinions, they invariably ask batteries of questions that investigate values, interests, beliefs, and feelings along with related opinions. Although they differ substantively, the various questions are usually stylistically similar and are administered as part of a common instrument. To understand the process of opinion formation, therefore, it is essential to specify the differences between the system components and how they interact with each other in the judging process.

Values and Interests.   What individuals think is important, either intrinsically (values) or instrumentally (interests), creates a frame of reference for judging issues. In this way, they help define the standards of judgment that are employed when thinking about issues and forming opinions (Cantril, 1941). When reaching an opinion as to whether the nation's military budget should be increased or decreased, it matters very much if the frame of reference is fear of foreign military threats, availability of funding for desired domestic programs, desire to reduce the national deficit, or dependence of one's job on arms production.

Holding apparently contradictory values and interests is not inherently irrational. An individual may be concurrently concerned about both military threats and domestic welfare programs. In such instances, how individuals prioritize their values and interests becomes decisive. This is why two individuals who agree that more funding is needed for domestic programs may nonetheless have conflicting opinions regarding the desirability of reducing the military budget.

Priorities may change under changing circumstances, such as the easing of international tension or the onset of economic recession. And, it is often the case that an individual may endorse conflicting values at the same time, for example, the injunction not to kill and the right to go to war to resist an aggressor nation. Differences regarding what frame of reference is appropriate in a given situation underlie opinion conflict related to such issues as the freedom of bigoted faculty members to voice their biases on campus and the right of groups such as the Ku Klux Klan (KKK) to parade in a southern community on Martin Luther King, Jr.'s birthday or in a town like Skokie, Illinois, which has a large Jewish population.

Cognition.   Beliefs (including what one knows or thinks one knows, misinformation, and ignorance) can exert a powerful influence opinion formation. They define the perceptual field in ways that give direction to and set limits to the judging process. Thus, the more information an individual has about a subject, and the more detailed that information, the more likely it is that the individual has made an evaluative judgment about it (Einseidel, 1994). Also, in a study of reaction to the 1980 Carter–Reagan presidential debates, less knowledgeable voters used the debates to gain information and were the most likely to be influenced by them. In comparison, among the more knowledgable voters, their existing knowledge screened out inconsistent new ideas so the debates had little effect on them (Lanoue, 1992). Performing this function, however, does not mean that the judgments that are reached flow directly from beliefs. For example, a person who believes that life begins at conception might still think that first trimester abortions should be legal in cases of rape or incest.

A June 1963 Gallup Poll (conducted at a time of intense civil rights activism) illustrates the extent to which opinion cannot be predicted directly from beliefs. In answer to a question that asked about the prevalence of discriminatory treatment of African Americans in hiring, almost half (48%) felt that "Negroes do not have as good a chance as white people in your community to get any kind of job for which they are qualified," and 43% said their chances were as good. But, these beliefs were not in themselves expressions of support for or opposition to government action to reduce racial discrimination: 41% thought the Kennedy Administration was pushing racial integration too fast, 14% felt the administration did not push fast enough, and 31% felt the push toward integration was about right (14% voiced no opinion; Gallup 1972b; pp. 1828–1829).

For a variety of reasons, individuals may come to hold inconsistent or contradictory beliefs. Whatever the reason, a strain to consistency develops as a reaction to the resultant stress. Although questions regarding the specific processes through which consistency is achieved have not been fully resolved, it is clear that they may lead to opinion change (see the following section for an extended discusssion of strain to consistency as a source of opinion change.) On the other hand, exposure to new, potentially stress-inducing knowledge in itself does not assure opinion change. Selective exposure, perception, and retention can inhibit the integration of new information into existing belief systems, thereby militating against change (Klapper, 1960). Public information campaigns that attempt to influence opinion often fail because they assume that exposure to new information will in itself be sufficiently persuasive to make for opinion change.

Affect. Whether one's feelings concerning some behavior, individual, or other object are positive or negative plays a decisive role in the process of opinion formation. However, it is not the direction of feeling considered by itself that is important but how it is associated with relevant beliefs, values, and interests. Only then can their combined influence on opinion formation be properly understood.

For example, whether one approves or disapproves of a legislative proposal for changing how the Social Security system is financed will be influenced by whether one likes or dislikes Social Security in principle as opposed to other means for providing for retirement income. Similarly, how one feels in general toward the persons or political party making the proposal may influence whether one supports or opposes it—for no reason other than that feeling. How one feels about the purpose of the proposed change—for example, whether the purpose is to balance the federal budget, to strengthen Social Security's finances, or to reduce the financial burden on the active labor force—also plays a role in how one judges this issue.

Nonetheless, an individual's opinion is not a direct projection of the affect associated with an issue. Consider the opinions of three hypothetical individuals as to what should be done about the rioting that followed the 1993 acquittal of four Los Angeles police officers accused of unjustifiably beating an African American, Rodney King. Let us assume that two of them agree that the jury was wrong, and the third accepts the jury's verdict. The two who agree may nonetheless differ markedly in their feelings about that acquittal and the rioting that followed, with one of them reaching an opinion similar to the third person's. The first may be deeply shocked by the verdict and feel that, regardless of the rioting, drastic measures to eradicate racism among police must have the highest priority. The second may feel that, however wrong the verdict was, the most disturbing development was the rejection of due process and recourse to lawless violence. For that reason, the second person might agree with the third person (who feels that the verdict was correct) that the highest priority must be to prevent any recurrence of rioting.

Affect differs in strength as well as direction. Five dimensions of strength have been differentiated (Krosnick & Abelson, 1994; Scott, 1968), namely:

1. Extremity: The degree of favorableness or unfavorableness, for example, completely versus partially favorable.
2. Intensity: The strength of feelings, for example, strong versus mild feeling.
3. Certainty: The degree of conviction that one is correct, for example, very sure versus not so sure.
4. Importance: The degree of personal involvement, for example, personally very important versus not so important.

5. Complexity: Amount of information held about the issue, for example, quite a bit versus only a little.

It is evident that affect does not lead directly to opinion. For example, the relative strength of one's committment to the right of free speech and academic freedom versus one's opposition to racism or religious bias, in conjuction with how certain one feels it is that each value is being threatened, will define the saliency of relevant values and beliefs when reaching an opinion about such issues as allowing KKK demonstrations, granting tenure to racist professors, or imposing sanctions against racist or inflammatory speech.

Behavioral Intentions. Opinions can be considered analogs of behavioral intentions in that both are outcomes of transactions between pre-existing psychological states and particular situations. Opinions differ from intentions in that the latter imply a behavioral consequence whereas opinions do not. An individual may favor passage of clean air legislation without having any specific intention to act on that opinion, for example, to write his congressman to vote for that legislation, to contribute money to environmental action groups or, as a way of protecting air quality, to use public transit rather than drive to work.

Individual opinion is also comparable to behavioral intention as an attitudinal output in that it is a conditional outcome. Opinions are conditional in the sense that particular combinations of factors unique to various situations will evoke different configurations of any individual's values and interests, beliefs, and feelings. And, as different configurations are evoked, different opinions will arise. Furthermore, in a feedback loop comparable to the effect that behavior can have on attitude, forming and expressing an opinion can lead to modifications in specific values, interests, beliefs, and feelings.

The failure explicitly to distinguish opinions as judgmental outcomes that have been influenced by antecedent attitudinal variables does not mean that those variables will necessarily be ignored by someone attempting to analyze opinions. There is widespread recognition among survey researchers that frames of reference, beliefs, and feelings that are built into the wordings of questions asked in polls can significantly influence poll results. For example, in Adamek's (1994) assessment of what poll results on abortion have revealed as to how many adult Americans approve or disapprove of the Supreme Court's *Roe v. Wade* decision, he placed great emphasis on the fact that the proportion expressing approval varies considerably according to how different polling organizations specified the frame of reference and factual assumptions in their question wordings. However, nowhere in his discussion is there any indication that either he, or the organizations that conducted the polls he reviewed, systematically considered the underlying processes that would account for these variations. Instead, Adamek (1994) confined himself to the admonition, "Even carefully crafted questions can be rendered less than adequate by changing circumstances and must continually be assessed for current validity" (p.417). The gain in specifying opinions as judgmental outcomes of a process in which beliefs, feelings, values, and interests are inputs, is that we then have a theoretical model that deals specifically with the problem of how to analyze these attitudinal components in relation to judgmental outputs (see Bishop, 1980).

THE PROCESS OF OPINION CHANGE

It is a truism to observe that once individuals form opinions, they may still change their minds. At the same time, individuals can also be tenacious about their opinions, so that one cannot assume that opinions are inherently volatile. However, to say that in some cases opinions are volatile and subject to seemingly overnight shifts whereas in other cases opinions are set as if in concrete is saying little. We need to be able to specify when and why opinions do, or do not, change. Why is it, for example, that among politically active individuals we are more likely to find persistence rather than change of opinion (Marwell, Aiken, & Demerath, 1987)? To cast light on why such a relationship, surprising to some, should exist, we need to examine how opinions change.

Opinion change is more than a unidirectional process in which one rethinks an issue and comes to a new judgment. It involves the effects of situational influences on individuals in conjunction with the interactions among an individual's values, beliefs, and the affective states associated with them. Also, newly formed opinions can feed back into and modify existing beliefs, values, and feelings, thereby initiating further change. Understanding how opinion changes, therefore, requires us to consider interactions that involve all these variables.

Two factors have hampered the study of opinion change. One is the fact that, as has been discussed, many do not differentiate between opinions and attitudes. The failure to do so leads to the treatment of opinion change as identical with, or no more than an aspect of, attitudinal change. In contrast, treating opinions as judgmental outcomes requires us to think about how changes in values, beliefs, or feelings are related to consequent changes in the judgments people make. Studies of how attitudinal changes occur can do no more than provides us with guides for thinking about how opinions change. We therefore briefly outline some highlights of what has been learned from research on attitudinal change that are pertinent to opinion change, without attempting to deal in any depth with the substantial theoretical and methodological issues that are involved. We then discuss what light that might cast on how individual opinions change.

The other hampering factor is that empirical research on opinion and attitudinal change has to a considerable degree been dominated by concern with communication and persuasion, that is, how opinions and attitudes change in response to messages disseminated through the mass media. In comparison, the question of how opinions change in response to events and personal experience—for example, changing economic circumstances, crime rates, and school performance—has been relatively neglected. It is true that public opinion polls that repeat the same questions, either periodically or in reponse to unfolding events, and continuing academic surveys such as NORC's General Social Survey (GSS) and the Monitoring the Future series conducted by the Michigan Survey Research Center, have tracked changing opinions, beliefs, values, and feelings across time. However, all too often the connection between change as measured by such time series and specific events has been inferential rather than demonstrated. The result is that we have learned a lot about how efforts to influence the way people think about some topic can affect their beliefs, values, and feelings but less about how opinion change occurs in the context of day-to-day living. Nonetheless, enough has been learned about attitudinal change in response to direct experience to draw some reasonable inferences about how opinions change through direct experience.

APPROACHES TO STUDYING
ATTITUDINAL CHANGE

We will consider two basic pathways for attitudinal change—through the *learning* of new information and behaviors and through the *reconfiguration* of attitudinal systems and their components. These very different psychological processes have been studied by two very different and conflicting theoretical approaches—learning theory and systemic–cognitive psychology. Learning theory examines attitudinal change in terms of the role of reward and punishment in establishing, reinforcing, and inhibiting positive or negative feelings about or toward some object. In contrast, system–cognitive psychology looks at attitudinal change as a response to tensions among and within components of attitudinal systems.

Despite major theoretical and methodological controversies that swirl around these two approaches, it is difficult, even impossible, to ignore the fact that the empirical findings of each research tradition have significantly contributed to our understanding of how and why attitudinal change occurs. We must also recognize that, despite the real distinctions that exist between these approaches, research conducted by given individuals associated with each is not always easily classified, so that insisting on drawing a hard and fast line between the two approaches is not productive for our purposes. We restrict ourselves to drawing whatever implications we can from what has been learned about attitudinal change from both traditions as they pertain to opinion change, without attempting to resolve the underlying controversies.

Even without an exhaustive (and exhausting) discussion of the intricacies of attitudinal change and the comparative merits of alternative theories, we can draw one general conclusion, namely: Opinion change cannot be properly understood solely as a matter of persuasion as that term is commonly understood, that is, inducing change through the force of one's argument. Rather, opinion change is the outcome of complex psychological processes in which the weight of sound logic as applied to empirical fact is often limited. This quality of opinion change is the basis for the effectiveness of many opinion manipulators—from the rhetoricians of ancient Athens to the "spin doctors" of contemporary politics. A brief review of this idea demonstrates the point.

Although in some ways outdated by theoretical and methodological developments that have been made in light of ongoing research, Kiesler, Collins, and Miller, 1969, is still an outstanding detailed, critical analysis of alternative theories of attitudinal change (see also Hovland, Janis, & Kelley, 1953; Jahoda & Warren, 1966; Petty & Cacioppo, 1981; Rosenberg, Hovland, McGuire, Abelson, & Brehm, 1960; Uleman & Bargh, 1989).

Learning Theory

A standard formula for studying attitudinal change and communications is to answer the question, "Who says what to whom with what effect?". This question directs our attention to four sets of variables to examine. The first two sets have to do with the stimuli that trigger the learning process—characteristics of the communicator and characteristics of the message that is communicated. With respect to communicators, we are concerned with variables that influence their credibility, for example, their trustworthiness and knowledgability (Hovland, Janis, & Kelley, 1953). As for the messages themselves, variables of relevance relate both to (a) how they are organized—for example, the comparative effectiveness of opening versus closing arguments (primacy versus recency) and of introducing or excluding opposing arguments (Hovland et al., 1953); and (b) what kinds of motivating appeals are most effective—for example, fear, altruism, social acceptance, and the like (Hovland et al., 1953).

Another important set of variables relate to the "whom " in the question just posed. They measure audience characteristics that affect predispositions to accept or resist any given message. These include group memberships that establish norms to which individuals feel they should conform and personality factors such as a general readiness to pay attention to various viewpoints and also existing beliefs and feelings that are relevant to the issue at hand. Finally, with respect to communications effect, variables that measure conviction and retention need to be considered (Hovland et al., 1953). These variables must be dealt with in order to determine whether any change that may occur in response to any communication is superficial and transitory or whether it results in conversion to a new way of looking at things.

Despite theoretical controversy, there is no doubt that the above four sets of variables touch on fundamental aspects of attitudinal change. Furthermore, these aspects of change have an immediate, reasonable implication specifically with respect to opinion change as part of transactions between individuals and their environments; we cannot expect opinions to change merely in response to the factual content and logical coherence of messages. Perceived characteristics of who conveys a message are as important as the message itself. Similarly, the psychological organization of a message and its motivational strength may have more to do with its effect on how an issue is judged than does the validity of its claims and the logical quality of its presentation. Additionally, messages are not received on a "clean slate" as it were, but in the context of a welter of predispositions that can significantly alter its intended meaning. And finally, we must ask not only whether any opinion change has occurred but, more importantly, about the quality of that change—whether the change is only temporary acquiescence or is a convinced conversion.

Systemic–Cognitive Psychology

As an alternative to some form of conditioning as the mechanism through which change occurs, this approach provides the idea that what must be studied is the dynamics of attitudinal systems as *systems*. That is to say, we must look at the organization of beliefs, values, and feelings into interdependent, mutually supporting, and integrated wholes. Although there is no one system theory—in fact, there are a number of theories that in some ways disagree with each other—they have in common an emphasis on system dynamics. Three concepts—strain to consistency, coping with change and newness, and conservation of psychological energy—capture much of the essence of the system approach.

Other important contributions that should be mentioned include the idea that attitudinal change may perform the function of satisfying an individual's motivational needs (Kelman, 1961; Smith, Bruner, & White, 1956) and that change involves a judging process as to whether, for example, any attitudinal element falls within an individual's lattitude of what is acceptable, what is clearly rejected, and what is in an intermediate range of noncommittment (Sherif et al., 1965; see also Cohen, 1960; McGuire, 1960, 1966; Osgood, 1960; Zajonc, 1960).

"Strain to consistency" is a form of equilibrium theory. It refers to the tendency of the components of an attitudinal system to adjust to each other in ways that are mutually reinforcing. Any imbalance, inconsistency, or contradiction that may exist among the components of the system creates psychological tension or discomfort. That tension sets off a reaction to restore consistency to the system and thereby reduces psychological tension (Brehm, 1960; Fishbein, 1967; Kiesler, Collins, & Miller, 1969; McGuire, 1967). Whatever the source of inconsistency might be, the essence of that reaction is a reorganization and modification of the system and not a learned response. It must be emphasized that there are a number of specific formulations of how a strain to consistency leads to attitudinal change. However, their common, underlying premise is that striving to achieve consistency or balance is central to attitudinal change. It is not necessary to consider all the varieties of system theory to demonstrate the point that a strain to consistency within an attitudinal system can play a major role in opinion change. For that purpose, a brief review of just two, balance theory and cognitive dissonance should suffice.

Balance theory (Heider, 1958) analyzes interpersonal perceptions in terms of the reciprocity of liking or disliking of each other and some object (e. g., between two individuals with respect to a common object). When these perceptions are consistently positive, or consistently negative, they are in balance and the system is stable. When they are inconsistent, the system is not in balance and change takes place as a consequence of the effort to establish balance. In a hypothetical example given by Heider, Jim, who strongly dislikes Bob, reads a poem that he very much likes. He then discovers that Bob wrote the poem. To resolve this imbalance, Jim may either change his feeling about Bob or about the poem, or he may change his belief that Bob wrote the poem. If, for some reason, Jim finds it impossible to follow either of these strategies, he can withdraw from the field, that is, simply stop thinking about the matter. Although this simple illustration does not encompass all the complexities of balance theory, the basic principle that an imbalanced system of interpersonal perceptions, in and of itself, can act as an impetus to change provides a model for analyzing opinion change.

First, however, we must note that balance theory has been expanded to deal with cognition and related affect, so that it is not restricted only to interpersonal perceptions (Rosenberg & Abelson, 1960). Cognition and affect are always associated with each other; some feeling tone (whether it be positive, negative, or neutral) is always associated with any particular belief. It follows that balance or imbalance involves the relations of a number of beliefs and their associated affects and not only the relations between beliefs and affect considered separately (see Anderson and Fishbein, 1965). That is, for balance to be achieved, there must be consistency within a system of linked beliefs and associated feelings.

We now consider a hypothetical example of opinion change that follows the formal structure used by Heider, although the elements are not perceptual: An individual feels that society has a transcendant, moral obligation to provide financial assistance to the poor and, therefore, endorses the opinion that the government should fund a public welfare system. But this same person also feels that it is morally degrading to accept charity, so that he or she experiences tension from the resultant imbalance. In accord with Heider's formulation, that tension can be eased by deciding that it is not morally degrading to accept charity, that the obligation to help the poor is subject to possible mitigating circumstances (such as a heavy personal tax burden), or by ignoring the issue of what should be done about the financial needs of the poor. Depending on which way of easing tension is adopted, the individual may change his or her opinion that the government should fund a public welfare system. In such a case, the mechanism through which opinion changes is system dynamics and not learning.

Cognitive dissonance theory also makes a strain to consistency the lever of attitudinal change, in this case avoiding psychological tension that is generated when two elements of a belief system are not in accord with each other. However, it has some distinctive properties as compared with balance theory (Brehm, 1960; Festinger, 1957; see also Kiesler et al., 1969; Petty & Cacioppo, 1981, for critical reviews of the theory). These properties include: (a) considering dissonance only between cognitive elements, (b) thinking in terms of degree of dissonance rather than a consonant–dissonant dichotomy, and (c) relating dissonance to choices the individual must make and not simply to preference.

By way of summary and simplification, we can say that cognitive dissonance has to do with the extent to which an individual experiences psychological discomfort when having to make a decision because one of two relevant beliefs does not follow from the other. To avoid, or at least minimize, that discomfort, the individual may follow a number of strategies, such as changing one of the beliefs related to the behavioral choice to be made or to the situational context in which the choice is to be made, or by accepting new beliefs that mitigate the initial dissonance. Which strategy is followed by any one individual in any specific situation is not predictable from this formulation. However, some kind of cognitive change is clearly predicted. Once some cognitive change occurs, of whatever sort, we would expect it to affect the individual's judgment concerning the issue at stake. That is, we would expect his or her opinion to change accordingly.

The implications of cognitive dissonance theory for opinion change can be seen when we consider a *New York Times*/CBS News Poll on welfare reform conducted during December 6 to 9, 1994. In that poll, 71% believed that there are jobs available for most welfare recipients who really want to work, and only 34% felt that most welfare recipients really want to work. In that same poll, 87% favored the creation of work programs by the government in which welfare recipients would be required to participate. The fact that an overwhelming majority was in favor of mandatory work programs can be seen as being in large part a consequence of the consonant beliefs that jobs are available for those who want to work but that most welfare recipients do not want to. However, in times of widespread, persistent unemployment, we would anticipate that there would also be a sharp reduction in the number of people who believe that jobs are available for welfare recipients who want to work. As a way of resolving the otherwise inevitable cognitive dissonance, we would also anticipate a comparable change in the proportion who think most welfare recipients really do not want to work. Under those circumstances, we would predict a sharp decrease in support for mandatory work programs for welfare recipients. That is to say, cognitive dissonance theory leads us to expect opinions to change as a result of efforts to resolve discordant beliefs even if there has not been any "persuasion" to convert to an opposing opinion.

Coping with change can lead to opinion change through alternative routes, depending on how one copes with that change. Casual observation alone indicates that, regardless of the issues involved, some individuals are typically willing to reconsider their opinions in the light of new information, new experience, and exposure to other points of view, whereas others tend to be unyielding in their opinions and highly resistant to change. These differences in readiness to cope with new or different ideas and experiences are neither idiosyncratic nor haphazard; rather, they stem from contrasting closed or open styles of thinking rooted in personality. Personality characteristics that influence individual styles of thinking include: Rigidity versus flexibility in problem solving; concreteness and narrowness versus abstractness and broadness; early versus late closure in perception; and rejection versus tolerance for ambiguity (Rokeach, 1960).

The thinking of those with relatively closed styles is characterized by rigidity and dogmatism. In comparison, others are relatively open to cognitive and affect change in their thinking (Rokeach, 1960). Rigid thinking is characterized by a persistence in holding to particular beliefs that impede the individual's analytical ability when considering an issue. Dogmatic thinking differs somewhat in that it has to do with the preservation of entire belief systems, so that an individual ability to think synthetically, that is, to integrate or deal with new thoughts and ideas in relation to existing cognitive configurations, suffers (Rokeach, 1960).

Dogmatic thinking can be associated with various political colorations, so that doctrinal thinking of either the political left or right is characteristic of closed thinking. What we are dealing with is not the specific opinion positions that an individual takes but, rather, how the route followed in reaching an opinion influences its quality. Similarly, although dogmatists are resistant to new opinions, the contrast between closed versus open thinking should not be confused with frequency of opinion change. Rigid or dogmatic thinking does not preclude changing one's opinion on an issue, nor does open thinking imply that opinions are, as a consequence, easily susceptible to change. Rather, the contrast has to do with what is involved when opinions change. In one case, change is more likely to require a thinking through of issues whereas in the other change is more a matter of substituting or replacing one opinion, or set of opinions, for another. The contrast, therefore, is in the quality of thinking and the quality of the judgmental outcomes.

Conservation of psychological energy—McGuire called humans "lazy organisms" (McGuire, 1969) because they seem to have an aversion to making more of an effort than is necessary when thinking about any matter. This aversion exerts an important influence on the ways in which attitudinal systems process new or alternative cognitive material that can lead to opinion change. This idea is also captured by the economist's concept of *satisficing*, namely, that individuals often stop short of seeking full satisfaction when deciding whether something is acceptable (Simon, 1976). Depending on the extent to which major values or interests are not at stake, solutions that achieve less than what one would most like—the second best—may be acceptable if the cost or effort necessary to achieve the most preferred goal is judged not to be worth the extra effort. On a large scale, satisficing can serve as the basis for political negotiation and compromise. With regard to change of individual opinions, it involves a sort of implicit weighing of costs and benefits: Just how much is it worth to me to think my way through to a considered judgment on this issue, as opposed to endorsing a possibly less satisfying position—so long as I do not feel the latter position is reprehensible or inimical to my interests and I do feel it has redeemable qualities?

The fact is that "attitudes can be changed following either a careful and effortful consideration of a persuasive communication or a less cognitively effortful inference and association process" (Priester & Petty, 1995, p. 637). That is, there are two information-processing routes to change, one that involves considerable effort in an extensive processing of persuasive messages and one that does not (Chaiken, Liberman, & Eagly, 1989; Petty & Cacioppo, 1986).

1. When individuals are sufficiently motivated and are cognitively capable of doing so, they may follow a route that requires careful and thoughtful consideration of the merits of an argument. Applying moderate to high levels of effort, the individual assesses whatever information is available for its usefulness and relevance to some judgmental task. Following this route leads to relatively enduring change that tends to be resistant to further modification and to be predictive of subsequent behavior. It is identified by the depth and intensity of cognitive processing related to reaching a specific judgment. It should not be confused with open-mindedness, which refers to a persistent, personal style of thinking and not to how particular judgments are reached.

2. Often an individual may have limited or no motivation for effortful information processing. Or, the individual for whatever reason may be incapable of adequately grasping the content and meaning of a message, even when there is sufficient motivation. In such circumstances, acceptance or rejection of a message will be induced primarily by following external cues or rules without much thought given to the content of the message itself. Illustrative of these cues and rules are reaching a decision on the basis of the perceived credibility of the communicator, the sheer volume of proferred arguments, and the perceived likability of the communicator. By relying on such cues and rules whose assumed validity derives from remembered experience, the individual short-circuits any need to think through the worth of an argument. Any change that may occur by following this route seems to be relatively likely to be temporary and susceptible to further modification.

This explanation of why opinion change sometimes occurs with limited thought given to the details of an issue provides a theoretical underpinning to Popkin's (1991) observationn that "*low-information rationality*, or 'gut' rationality, best describes the kind of practical reasoning about government and politics in which people actually emerge. ... Gut rationality draws on the information shortcuts and rules of thumb that voters use to obtain and evaluate information and to choose among candidates" (p. 212). Low-information rationality is a phenomenon relevant to the discussion, in chapter 6, of the political significance of individual opinions characterized by limited cognitive content.

In addition to considering which information processing route is followed, we also have to take into account the fact that the two routes to change are not mutually exclusive. When judging any one issue, an individual may employ deep cognitive processing with respect to some aspects of judging, and rule following with respect to others (Chaiken et al., 1989). Furthermore, any one variable can have very different, even opposite, effects depending on which route to change is followed (Petty & Cacioppo, 1986).

An important implication of this picture of opinion change is that the quality of individual opinions stems from the level and quality of related information processing. Furthermore, the same person may form opinions that vary considerably in their quality›depending on the focus and intensity of his or her involvement in one issue as compared with another, and his or her competence in dealing with each. Thus, in some instances, an individual's opinions may be considered after extensive cognitive processing, in other cases adopted through some combination of cognitive processing and cue following, and in still others may represent nothing more than superficial acquiescence after minimal cue following. This issue of opinion quality is one that we deal with in greater detail in a later section.

ATTITUDINAL–OPINION CHANGE AND DIRECT EXPERIENCE

Relatively little empirical research has been conducted regarding the dynamics of how individual beliefs, feelings, and opinions change in the course of everyday living. The difficulties inherent in designing controlled investigations under natural conditions in large part explains why this is so. Nonetheless, the research on this question that has been conducted demonstrates that direct, personal experience is an important source of attitudinal and opinion change, and in a manner that is congruent with what has been learned from studies of communication effects. Although hardly earth shaking, this conclusion needs to be emphasized to counteract any tendency to conclude from the plethora of communications studies that opinion change is only, or primarily, a matter of communication effects. The emergence of individual opinions, and their change, involves transactions between individuals and the totality of their environments, of which communications media constitute only a part. To understand how and why opinions change, we must realize that they are not merely products of exposure to and manipulation by all-powerful communications media. Individuals are active, creative beings whose direct, personal experiences can and do play an important part in what they think and feel.

Evaluation studies of the effects of planned change within controlled institutional settings have, among other things, successfully analyzed attitudinal and opinion changes (see, e.g., Rossi & Freeman, 1993). One historically interesting example of attitudinal and opinion change in an institutional setting is *Project Clear*, a study that dealt with the effects of integrating military units on military performance (Bogart, 1992). That study's findings document how important direct experience can be. The research design called for interviewing Whites and Blacks serving in integrated and segregated units, both in Korea and in the continental United States.

In early 1951, despite President Harry S. Truman's order calling for the racial integration of the military, 80% of Black Army personnel serving in Korea were still in segregated units. There was evidence that the performance of these units was unsatisfactory and that the problem existed at the unit level, not at the individual level. Additionally, disparities in the availability of White and Black replacements, and the need for replacements, were increasingly leading to the de facto integration of hitherto segregated units despite opposition by many.

In considering the research results, it should be remembered that at the time, segregation was legally and socially enforced throughout the South with respect to such matters as marriage, schools, transportation, restaurants, public rest rooms, and drinking water fountains. Interracial social contacts, especially between men and women, were taboo throughout the region. In the rest of the country, despite the prevalence of prejudicial beliefs and feelings at the individual level, discrimination was private and informal and not a matter of legally established public policy. And, for a variety of reasons, including the desire to maintain good relations with local community leaders, the standard practice of military post commanders was to conform to local segregation practices wherever they existed.

As to be expected, White Northerners and Southerners brought contrasting racial beliefs and feelings with them when they entered the U. S. Army.

For example, White Southerners were far more likely to express disapproval of serving in units that included Black troops. But when asked how they would actually behave if Black replacements were assigned to their unit, the predominant response of both White Southerners and Northerners was, to an equal degree, that they would accept integration. Of course, the authoritarian structure of the Army made it unlikely that many would do otherwise (Bogart, 1992). However, the absence of overt resistance to integration was more than enforced conformity. There was a systematic difference in expressions of personal opposition to, or acceptance of, segregation by Whites assigned to racially homogeneous or racially heterogeneous units. For example, the percentage of Whites who said that Blacks should be assigned "as individuals regardless of color" was consistently lower among Whites serving in all-White units than those serving in integrated ones. This difference existed with respect to both personal preference and official policy (Bogart, 1992). This difference was attributable specifically to the experience of serving in segregated or integrated units and not to other influences such as personal demographics (Bogart, 1992).

Interviews with troops in the continental United States produced comparable results: "Contact with Negroes in mixed units in the Continental United States leads White troops to more favorable attitudes toward integration, although the pattern of this relationship is more complex than was found to be the case in Korea" (Bogart, 1992, p. 195). The surrounding civilian environment had a significant independent effect. Acceptance of integration among northern-born Whites assigned to training camps in the North increased by the later stages of training. On the other hand, among both northern and southern White trainees at Southern locations, the reverse was true (Bogart, 1992). It was also discovered that less favorable change occurred when the number of Blacks in integrated units reached a density that led to their being perceived not as individuals but as a socially distinct aggregate. Unfavorable change also occurred among northern Whites whose actual contacts with Blacks did not conform to optimistic expectations. Initial feelings changed markedly in response to experience with integration during the training period and with assignment to integrated or segregated units.

Clearly, changes in acceptance of segregation took place as a product of changes in the ambient social environment that gave individuals new experiences to which they had to adjust. This conclusion should not be interpreted to mean that attitudinal and opinion change can be brought about simply by manipulating institutional and social organizations. For, just as clearly, differences in what individuals bring to a new situation also have their effect. But there can be no doubt that personal experience can be a powerful influence on opinion, one that under some circumstances can override other influences.

THE QUALITY OF INDIVIDUAL OPINION

The judgments people make about issues can differ considerably in their cognitive and affective quality. The fact that opinions are the outcomes of a judging process does not mean that they are necessarily reasoned, rational, and strongly held conclusions drawn from an extensive body of information. Although opinions may be based on considered judgments following careful thought and factual analysis, they may also be based on snap judgments that do no more than express a visceral response to an issue. Or, they may lie between these extremes. Additionally, there is considerable variation among individuals regarding the completeness and correctness of the "facts" they believe to be true. This variation is complicated by differences from issue to issue in the proportion of people who are informed on each. Furthermore, some opinions are associated with strong feelings embedded in deeply held values, vital interests, and ingrained group identifications. In other instances, there is little or no commitment to expressed opinions, so that an individual may do no more than iterate the most recently heard point of view. Attempts to deal systematically with such variations have been hindered by ideological, conceptual, and methodological considerations.

Contradictory distinctions are often made that not only lead to semantic confusion, but that often have more to do with ideological preferences as to whose opinions should be listened to than with testable hypotheses. We return to this point in chapter 6, within the context of a comparison of the justifications elitists and populists give for their views of what should be the proper role of public opinion in a democracy. At this juncture, however, our task is to clarify the concept of opinion at the individual level.

Typical of the contrasting definitions that confuse analysis is the following contrast: There are those who differentiate between "sentiment" and "opinion," that is, between unreasoned feeling and reasoned thought. Others contrast "mere opinion" with "reasoned judgment." Lippmann (1946) contrasted casual opinion, which is the product of partial contact, tradition and personal interest, with realistic opinion, which is characterized by exact records, measurement, analysis, and comparison. Blumer (1939) made a comparable distinction in his statement that any given opinion can be "anywhere between a highly emotional and prejudiced point of view and a highly intelligent and thoughtful opinion" (p.249). Young (1954) differed slightly in that he restricted the term *opinion* to the middle of a continuum of quality: "Opinion means a belief or conviction more verifiable and stronger in intensity than a mere hunch or impression but less valid and strong than truly verifiable or positive knowledge. We thus distinguish between a fact and an opinion " (p. 63).

Common to all the distinctions just discussed is a hypothesized continuum of quality. At one pole of this continuum are judgments that would be reached by anyone who applies reasoned logic to verifiable facts and that, consequently, can be trusted. At the other pole are judgments based on ignorance or misinformation, driven by irrational emotion, and the product of limited and undisciplined thought. Despite its surface reasonableness, this conceptualization has serious weaknesses.

One weakness is that the continuum does not provide for opposing opinions that are equally high in cognitive content but that involve conflicting values and interests. For example, support for or opposition to eliminating a capital gains tax may reflect anticipated effects of such a tax on an individual's income rather than how well-informed the individual is. Similarly, direct experience with an issue, such as rising prices at the supermarket, may constitute a sound cognitive basis for opinions on current inflationary trends even in the absence of knowledge about the most recent Bureau of Labor estimate (which in any event will be subject to revision as data are updated, corrected, and reanalyzed). More generally, instances like the continued controversy over the correctness of United States involvement in Vietnam, after decades of debate and the release of previously classified information, emphasizes the subjectivity of all judgments.

Overall assessments of the cognitive quality of someone's opinion can be useful for political rhetoric, but they have limited analytical utility. For the latter, it is far more productive to relate the depth, extent, and correctness of relevant knowledge that is cited to support a particular opinion to the values, interests, and feelings that are associated with it. That would enable us to analyze how individuals come to hold an opinion, the stability of that opinion, and the prospects for its being expressed in overt action.

Conceptual controversy has focused on the incidence of nonattitudes and nonopinions in survey data. There is a large body of evidence showing that substantial numbers of interviewees express opinions on issues about which they have little knowledge, awareness, or interest, so that to a considerable degree survey data may be contaminated by nonattitudes or nonopinions (Bishop, Tuchfarber, & Oldendick, 1986; Converse, 1970, 1974; Schuman & Presser, 1978). Treating nonattitudes as if they are real not only creates analytical problems, but it also raises the question as to whether they play any meaningful role in the public opinion process. In opposition is the view is that "individual opinion times series are reliable measures of social change and that in the aggregate opinion trends often show a great deal of consistency and cohesion" (Smith, 1994, p. 200; see also chap. 6, this volume; Mayer, 1992; Page & Shapiro, 1992; Smith, 1990; Stimson, 1991).

Smith reviewed 36 large changes of opinion (10 percentage points or more across 1 year or 15 points or more across 2 years) as measured by the General Social Survey. He concluded that, rather than being random or nonsensical, almost all the changes are explainable—the largest number as the result of dramatic events, others as the result of cyclical or secular trends, whereas measurement variation accounted for most of the remaining changes (Smith, 1994). Only two were not readily explicable. In other words, after excluding the influence of measurement variation, the observed changes in opinion make sense as the outcome of transactions between individuals with attitudinal systems that may be very stable but whose environments are undergoing drastic change. As discussed in chapter 6, this finding has significant implications regarding the political role of opinion.

The possibility that many measured opinions are artifacts created by faulty methodology further complicates efforts to analyze the quality of individual opinions. In fact, some have concluded that "there ... is little substantial grain to measure [and] ... opinion change [is] little more than random noise ... largely erratic, inexplicable, and meaningless" (Smith, 1994, p. 187). At issue are the meaning and treatment of "don't know" responses, the effects of filter questions and offering middle responses, and making point estimates of the split of opinion. We must also take into account the fact that survey results are sometimes subject to considerable variation caused by differences in question format or structure. The use of such techniques as open- versus closed-ended questions, offering middle responses rather than yes–no dichotomies, presenting only one or two sides of an issue, and filter questions to differentiate the informed from the uninformed can significantly influence the number of people who select alternative response categories or who reply "don't know" or "no opinion" to a question (Bishop 1987; Bishop, Oldendick, & Tuchfarber, 1982, 1983, 1984; Bishop, Oldendick, Tuchfarber, & Bennet, 1980; Bishop, Tuchfarber, & Oldendick, 1986; Bogart, 1967; Gilliam & Granberg, 1993; Hippler & Schwarz, 1989; Sanchez & Morchio, 1992). Furthermore, "don't know" and "no opinion" responses, frequently treated as synonomous, often have distinct meanings. A "don't know" response may reflect uncertainty even after thought whereas "no opinion" may indicate more the absence of any awareness or thought. Failing to make this distinction muddies attempts to specify the quality of opinions as expressed in a poll (Duncan & Stenbeck, 1988). Finally, estimates of the percentage by which opinion splits on any given issue are significantly affected by analytic techniques and question wording (Sigelman & Presser, 1988). In summary, much of the instability and low cognitive content of opinion as measured in surveys can be ascribed to the methodology that is employed.

Conceptual and methodological issues such as those just reviewed underline the difficulties encountered when trying to assess the quality of individual opinions in terms of some presumably objective scale of goodness. In contrast, the linkages of values and interests, beliefs and feelings, and of situational variables to expressed opinions are measurable without having to reach any conclusions as to the objective quality of those opinions. Then, by eschewing the impossible task of objectively assessing opinion quality in favor of measuring those linkages, we can analyze the processes whereby antecedent attitudinal and situational variables affect the emergence of individual opinions.

THE ROLE OF COMMUNICATIONS MEDIA

The understanding of how attitudinal systems function that is presented here is based on the proposition that they are intervening variables that affect opinions by mediating perceptions. Exemplifying this proposition is the selective nature of communications effects. Selective exposure to communications, selective perception and understanding of message content, and selective retention and integration of those understandings predispose individuals to judge an issue one way rather than another, thereby limiting the extent to which communication campaigns can change opinions (Klapper, 1960). Furthermore, research conducted as early as the 1940s and 1950s indicated that "facts may be successfully communicated without producing the opinion changes which they are intended or expected to produce" (Klapper, 1960, p. 88). Situational circumstances, such as being subject to cross-pressures created by conflicting group memberships and norms and being compelled to overtly endorse a given opinion, also can limit the effectiveness of communications campaigns (Klapper, 1960). Other important limitations on the role of communications media are interpersonal communications, personal influence and opinion leadership (as discussed in chap. 3).

The cumulative effect of research findings such as those just listed led to a challenge to the image of all-powerful mass media that manipulate opinion at will. In place of the assumption that individual opinions could not resist the influence of mass communication campaigns, the "law of minimal effect" was proposed. This law is the proposition that mass communications do not normally have major consequences with respect to changing individual attitudes and opinions (Klapper, 1960). In accord with the law of minimal effects, although individuals may change their opinions in response to external communications, media effects are small and incremental.

Despite the large body of empirical findings that appear to substantiate the law of minimal effects, it has been the target of considerable criticism. To many critics, merely from a commonsense perspective, it does not make much sense that continued exposure to messages transmitted through the mass media (including everything from product advertising to interpersonal violence to political campaigns) does not significantly influence individual thought and behavior. Agenda-setting theory has been presented as an alternative model to the law of minimal effects specifically with respect to opinions. Although it does not accept the discredited image of all-powerful mass media, agenda-setting theory does ascribe a major role to them in the public opinion process.

In a sense, agenda-setting theory can be said to do no more than remind us that the mass media affect the public opinion process by giving saliency to selected issues. Nonetheless, it also directs our attention to aspects of that process that cannot be ignored. The starting point of agenda-setting theory is the propositions that the mass media are increasingly the link between political candidates and voters, that candidates use the mass media to reach the electorate in place of personal contacts, and that voters get most of what they know about the world around them from the mass media. This led to the hypothesis that "the mass media set the agenda for each political campaign, influencing the salience of attitudes toward the political issues" (McCombs & Shaw, 1972, pp. 176–177). An elaboration of this hypothesis is that by deciding what news items to report and, of those, which to highlight, editors are able to dominate what issues people talk and think about. In this way, according to agenda-setting theory, the news media come to play a major role in determining what the public thinks is important (McCombs, 1992; McCombs & Shaw, 1977).

There is a complex patterning of media types and news events that influences agenda setting. For this reason, it would be a mistake to assume that the public's agenda, for example as recorded in answers to poll questions such as "What is the most important problem facing the country today?", is a simple reflection of what is in the headlines. The variety of news media alone makes that impossible. Thus, the effectiveness of agenda setting varies between print and broadcast media as well as between national, regional, and local media (Wanta & Hu, 1994). Comparably, there is variability in the ways in which different sectors of the public respond to news. Some members of the public habitually pay considerable attention to what is in the news, whereas others habitually pay little heed. Paradoxically, at least in the short term, the agenda-setting effect of the news media can be greater on the heedless. Apparently, the former are more likely to have developed their own agenda on the basis of a variety of influences related to their political involvement. The heedless, on the other hand, are more susceptible to immediate situational influences (Singer & Ludwig, 1987). This finding is relevant to the elitist–populist controversy discussed in chapter 6.

Additionally, the flow of issues and events is uneven, interrupted on occasion by "killer issues" that suddenly dominate the news (Brosius & Kepplinger, 1995). Consequently, in the competition between events for saliency in the news media, editorial judgment of what is important reflects a balancing of perceptions of what the public is interested in, what the editor believes is significant, and the drama inherent in an event. The extent to which the news media can set the public agenda is a function of how well editors perform this balancing act, and not a mechanical reflection of what is printed or broadcast.

Implicit in agenda-setting theory is the assumption that the mass media have a direct effect on individual opinion rather than being mediated through interpersonal communications (McCombs & Shaw, 1977). The dynamics of interpersonal versus mass communications are discussed more fully in the next chapter. At this time, we only observe that the weight of evidence is that the interplay of mass and interpersonal communications is complex and cannot be reduced to either–or formulas. For example, there is some evidence that the agenda-setting process may first influence opinion leaders who mediate between the mass media and the public, serving as a source of advice and guidance for the others (Weimann & Brosius, 1994).

Agenda-setting theory stresses the cognitive rather than the affective aspects of mass communications effects on opinion formation by emphasizing level of attention, awareness, and information. These factors become the center of attention rather than levels of support for competing issue positions (McCombs & Shaw, 1977). Also, when media effectiveness is measured along a cognitive-affect continuum, the greatest effectiveness is found at the cognitive end. For example, in an evaluation of the effectiveness of an official campaign designed to generate support for economic reform in China, it was found that the campaign was very effective in disseminating information about economic reform, quite effective in conveying the reasons for reform, somewhat effective in gaining support for the policy, and ineffective in rallying support for the Communist Party (Zhao, Zhu, Li, & Bleske, 1994). This kind of relationship between effectiveness and the cognitive versus affective content of messages undoubtedly underlies the contention of agenda-setting theorists that emphasizing the affective aspects of communications led to the law of minimal consequences

(McCombs & Shaw, 1977). In this context, it should be noted that this finding is also consonant with earlier research showing that successful factual communication does not by itself lead to opinion change.

The cognitive and affective dimensions of attitudinal systems are intimately linked in interaction with each other. We cannot, therefore, adequately evaluate the role of communications media with respect to apparent long-term cognitive agenda-setting effects and minimal short-term affective effects simply in terms of an opposition between the affective and cognitive aspects of their role. We need to make progress in specifying the role of the mass media in a way that integrates the cognitive and affective aspects of opinion change. That can best be accomplished by examining the role of communications media with respect to establishing both the prominence of events and issues in individual thinking and the emotional involvement of individuals in those events and issues.

A TEST CASE: PRESIDENTIAL DEBATES

Empirical research on the reactions of viewers to televised presidential debates provides a test of alternative interpretations of the role of communications media in the opinion process. First, however, we must emphasize that debates are communications events that are experienced by their audiences in their totality and that what each debater says is only part of the event—even if a central part. For example, direct experience through viewing the televised debates had more of an effect than merely reading about them (Graber, 1978).

Although each candidate's remarks are planned and rehearsed, what happens during the debate and what is said consists of more than planned symbol manipulation. Depending on a debate's format, there is room for improvisation on the part of both the debaters and questioners, especially if members of the audience ask questions. Unanticipated occurrences such as equipment breakdowns, the ways in which the debaters respond to the questioners and to the on-site audience, and the overt responses of the on-site audience can and have all affected the content and tone of debates. Also, members of the audience are "primed" in that they know and have thought about it in advance and have anticipated what might happen (Katz & Feldman, 1962). Finally, because they are events, in addition to being experienced directly, debates are experienced indirectly through the coverage they receive from the news media and through conversations with others (Deutschmann, 1962). For these reasons, the effects televised debates have on individual opinions combine elements of both communications and direct experience in complex ways.

Analyses of audience reactions to televised presidential debates document the importance of cognitive input into opinion formation and change that results from exposure to communications media; but, they also confirm many of the basic precepts of the law of minimal effects. With regard to the former, one distinguishing characteristic of presidential debates is that media attention to their existence can make them headline news. A series of forums sponsored by the League of Women Voters during the primaries phase of the 1976 presidential campaign attracted little media attention and minuscule audiences. However, the League's later efforts to organize debates between the major party candidates to be telecast on the major networks during the fall campaign were treated by the news media as important news stories in their own right—if only because of difficulties in getting agreement to hold them (Alexander & Margolis, 1978).

In the fall of 1976, a national audience estimated at 97 million saw or listened to one or more of the four debates that were held (*The Gallup Opinion Index*, October 1976, No. 135). The near monopolization of the airwaves by the networks, in combination with major media attention, undoubtedly generated this huge audience, but the contrast in the audience sizes attracted by the earlier League forums is instructive. When the news media give saliency to presidential debates, this can be an important factor in generating interest in watching them among politically uninformed members of the public, as happened in 1976. However, it should also be noted that whereas the novelty of the 1960 debates and the excitement generated by them may have contributed to the high voter turnout that year (63.8%), in 1976 voter turnout fell to a low of 54.4%. The prominence in the news achieved by presidential debates did not by itself reverse the long-term trend toward declining voter participation.

Televised debates can reduce the effects of selective exposure, the proclivity to hear only messages that come from one's preferred party or candidate (Katz & Feldman, 1962). By helping place the debates high on the public's agenda, the news media can to some degree counteract the usual tendency of the politically uninvolved to ignore all campaign activities, and of the politically partisan to pay attention only to their side's campaigning. Furthermore, and most intriguing, the interpretive function of the news media may even be capable of overriding the effects of direct experience. For example, there is some evidence that in 1976 there was a reversal in viewer reactions to the first debate between Jimmy Carter and Gerald Ford, with Carter faring better in measurements taken immediately after the debate and Ford doing better a week later (Lang & Lang, 1978). Similarly, in 1960 reactions to the Kennedy–Nixon debates were mediated by media interpretations (Deutschmann, 1962). In the latter case, the indications are that personal conversations also mediated immediate, direct effects. In addition to the direct communications effects of viewing the debate, long-term reactions to presidential debates were the outcomes of interactions of those effects with media coverage and interpersonal communications.

Although televised debates bring messages from both sides of a campaign to segments of the electorate that would normally not be aware of them, they do not eradicate the ability of predispositions to minimize the persuasive influence of those messages. To the contrary, in 1960, and again in 1976, although the debates did generate some changes in candidate preferences, their primary effect was to reinforce existing predispositions (Hagner & Rieselbach, 1978). Audience members who went into the debates with established candidate preferences largely remained loyal; whatever change took place was primarily among political independents, that is, among those without strong, integrated predispositions (Tannenbaum, Greenberg, & Silverman, 1962). What was said and what happened during the debates did not have some inescapable, objective meaning, but was selectively perceived and interpreted in accord with predebate beliefs and feelings. Even when they are directly experienced, communication events like presidential debates are subject to the usual selective effects of predispositions that act to minimize attitudinal and opinion change (Deutschmann, 1962; Graber, 1978).

Indications are that the presidential debates have not sparked any major shift in voting intentions or even initiated any significant trends. That is not to say that they did not induce any changes but only that those that did occur were limited. Rather than persuading viewers to change voting intentions, the debates reduced uncertainty about existing intentions by strengthening their cognitive foundations (Becker, Sobowale, Cobbey, & Eyal, 1978). They also influenced candidate imagery, inducing measurable shifts in response to variations in the quality of each candidate's performance (Lang & Lang, 1962), by clarifying and firming up the images viewers already held of the candidates (Nimmo, Mansfield, & Curry, 1978), and by sharpening associations between candidates with particular issues, which enhanced their ability to serve as spokesmen on those issues (Lang & Lang, 1962). A possible long-term "sleeper" effect of these changes in imagery that needs to be confirmed is that, once images are established in a debate, they act as predispositions that influence future judgments (Lang & Lang, 1962). Thus, even though the debates were not very persuasive with respect to voting intentions, they did influence cognitive processing in politically significant ways.

Because they occur in the context of ongoing trends, it is very difficult to distinguish debate effects from the effects of long-term trends. It is not at all clear whether Carter's relatively strong showing in the second 1976 debate halted a pro-Ford trend or merely coincided with a peaking of that trend that was already underway (Graber, 1978). Campaign contexts also need to be dealt with when evaluating the importance of debate effects because they can make even minimal effects politically significant. The political significance of communications effects is very different from their magnitude. This was certainly the case in 1960, when Kennedy's margin of victory over Nixon was measured in tenths of a percent. Whether or not the 1960 debates affected the outcome of that year's election is a very different question from whether communications media have only minimal effects on opinion. To understand fully what happens as a result of viewing televised debates, we must consider how they fit into the total flow of a campaign and not see them solely as encapsulated events.

As this review of the effects of televised presidential debates demonstrates, communications media do not have a unique role in forming and changing individual opinions, functioning in ways that are separate and different from other influences. They can be, and often are, powerful influences on individual opinions, but as part of the daily flow of activity. What matters ultimately is how the media are integrated into that flow, not whether their effects can be measured only in small, incremental bits or as major influences that give form and direction to the cognitive processing out of which individual opinions emerge.

Attitudinal predispositions have a selective, limiting effect on how individuals respond to all influences, not only to communications media. When televised debates do induce change, for example, in clarifying candidate images and reinforcing candidate preferences, they do so in accord with general principles related to maintaining attitudinal systems and to cognitive processing and not in some special way. Agenda setting versus the law of minimal effects is not a media issue per se but a question of the dynamics of individual opinion under any conditions. To understand the role of communications media in the public opinion process, we need to examine how the communications process is influenced by the defining characteristics of various media and how they are organized. This we will do, but only after we first consider (in chap. 3) the communications process itself.

THE COLLECTIVE MOBILIZATION
OF INDIVIDUAL OPINIONS

To recapitulate, individual opinions are outputs of the transactions between internal psychological states and external circumstances. Because they are judgmental outcomes of how individuals relate to their reality worlds, it is a mistake to think of them as no more than overt verbalizations of latent attitudes that have been activated by situational influences. However wise or foolish individual opinions may be, they represent individual efforts to make sense of issues in the experienced world by judging them in relation to one's beliefs, values and interests, and feelings.

When individuals keep their opinions to themselves, those issues do not become socially and politically significant. Not until they tell each other what they think about an issue, or act on them in each other's presence, can privately held opinions enter the public arena. Without some kind of public interchange or acting out, the public opinion process is put on hold, with the still-private opinions of individuals in "storage" as it were. In that case, individual opinions remain no more than potential input for a time when, for whatever reason, they may finally be evoked into public discourse. Of course, even in storage, individual opinions are always subject to change as a consequence of continuing transactions between changing external circumstances and existing attitudinal systems—which themselves may then be modified to some extent in reaction to intervening events. This is an important source of the proverbial fickleness of public opinion.

What cannot be ascertained by applying the transactional perspective just discussed is how individual opinions become significant and effective in social and political life. To do that requires going beyond analyses of the dynamics of individual opinion to a consideration of collective processes. There is a distinct level of collective process through which (a) a problem becomes salient for at least some people, even a small minority; leading to (b) discussion, which results in increased saliency; (c) out of which alternative solutions are formulated and then narrowed down; and (d) culminating in the final mobilization of opinions to affect the collective decision (D. Katz, 1972). This collective level of process must be examined in its own right. Central to such an examination is what happens with the introduction of privately held individual opinions into public discourse.

> Public opinion, or more appropriately the public-opinion process, is a description at the collective level and refers to the mobilization and channeling of individual responses to affect group or national decision-making (D. Katz, 1972, p. 13)

This collective mobilization and channeling of individual opinions cannot be understood if we restrict ourseves to individual-level analysis. For this reason, we next consider, in chapter 3, what happens when there is an interchange of individual opinions.

3

Collective Opinion
as a Social Force

Individual opinions are the building blocks of collective opinion as a social force but in themselves do not, and cannot, create that social force. Even if there is unanimity of individual opinions, not until they are joined together and somehow integrated with each other can opinions have significance beyond the level of individual thought and action. This joining together involves more than what is captured by statistical aggregations of individual opinions.

Election models of public opinion, such as are used in public opinion polls, focus attention almost exclusively on tallies of individual opinions, thereby diverting attention from the processes through which collective opinion emerges as a social force. However, collective opinion is not "the statistical aggregate of the opinions of some public, but rather a social process involving the interactions of publicly expressed opinions" (Mutz, 1989, p. 21; see also Albig, 1956; Blumer, 1939, 1948). To deal with the processes out of which collective opinion emerges, we must answer the following questions: How do individual opinions coalesce into a collective force? What are the processes through which that force integrates individual opinions into group activities? Once opinions coalesce, what is the nature of the resultant force?

COMMUNICATION AND EMERGENT
COLLECTIVE OPINION

The integration of individual opinions into a collective opinion does not take place through some ineffable, mysterious medium somehow permeating the social atmosphere and making itself felt in some mystical manner. Rather, collective opinion emerges and expresses itself through the *commu-*

47

nication of opinions between and among individuals and the groups to which they belong. The outcome is a complex patterning of coalesced individual opinions that then becomes a social reality and force in its own right.

The role of communication in coalescing individual opinions into a collective opinion is a special case of the long-established proposition that communication is the medium for all social processes, the medium through which "human relations exist and develop" (Cooley, 1909, p. 61). From this perspective, institutions, organizations, and groups do not exist as entities but as shared communications networks that link individuals to each other through their participation over time in common or shared behavior. Thus, a political party "as a historic entity is merely abstracted from thousands upon thousands of ... single acts of communication, which have in common certain persistent features of reference" (Sapir, 1931, Vol. 4, p. 78). Comparably, collective opinion emerges from innumerable acts of interindividual and intergroup communication, from "the processes of discussion, debate, and collective decision making" (Price, 1992, p. 91). Above all else, collective opinion is a communications concept.

This emergent conceptualization contrasts with both the view that public opinion as a form of collective action does not exist on a plane separate from individual action and that it is a force that somehow exists separate from individual opinions. In their places, we substitute the following proposition: The coalescence of individual opinions into the social force we call collective opinion is a product of the emergence of mutual awareness among persons who communicate with each other by using a common universe of discourse.

MUTUAL AWARENESS

Intrinsic to the idea of mutual awareness is that the response of one individual to a stimulus can serve as a parallel stimulus to another individual exposed to the same initial stimulus and that this can lead to comparable responses from both. As a result, each person's behavior is continuously adjusted to the other's actual behavior and to resultant expectations of what the other's response will be (see, e.g., G. Mead, 1934). Mutual awareness, therefore, explains why in a baseball game the second baseman's response to a ball hit down the third base line reflects what he expects the third baseman will do—and vice-versa. Playing the game is not merely a sequence of individual acts but, rather, a pattern of interconnected acts linked by shared beliefs and expectations of each other.

Mutual awareness implies the simultaneous and inseparable existence of two or more individual actors and a level of action that is independent of them as individuals. It includes self-awareness, a sense of one's actions as an expression of one's inner thoughts and feelings, plus an awareness of how all that relates to, and in a sense is the consequence of the actions, thoughts, and feelings of others with whom one is interacting. The emergence of mutual awareness, therefore, is the product of complex patternings of perceived agreement and disagreement within a collectivity and not only between individuals, behavioral expectations of oneself and others, and behavioral consequences of these perceptions and expectations. Finally, the quality of mutual awareness can vary, depending on the interactions of these factors.

Mutuality within the public opinion process calls out in each individual expressions of individual opinion that are at the same time responses to the opinions of the others in the collectivity. Rather than contrasting individual opinions with a bodiless supraindividual opinion, mutuality enables us to recognize the simultaneity of the subjective and objective; simultaneity in that awareness of inner self and what one is thinking of necessity involves awareness of external others and what they are thinking.

Without a process in which individuals grasp how their opinions compare with the assumptions, feelings, and beliefs of others—both concordant and discordant, individual opinions can be no more than a hodgepodge of idiosyncrasies. That process is communications. Mutual awareness emerges out of communications. This, in turn, leads to the emergence of a collective opinion (see Bryce, 1891, for an early description of this process).

For individual opinions to beome part of a collective opinion, the individual must have some conception of how his or her opinion fits into and compares with the complexity of the totality of other opinions. They do not become socially significant one by one, but in relation to the perceived patterning of the opinions of others who are involved in the same issue, insofar as that patterning affects the individual's response to that issue (see G. Mead, 1934, for a discussion of the interrelatedness of "self" and "generalized other").

What makes mutual awareness possible is a set of complex interactions among perceived agreement and disagreement on the part of others, expectations of their behaviors, and the behavioral consequences of these perceptions and expectations. Through these interactions, a set of individuals experience each other's views in terms of patterns of consensus and not only as a matter of a number of like-minded individuals developing a sense of solidarity. This is why collective opinion cannot be defined as a group average or norm nor as the dominant opinion. Rather, it exists in a collective representation, a shared understanding of what people are thinking about an issue, in understandings of what are the different likely responses to that issue and of who holds each viewpoint (see Lang & Lang, 1983). An important implication of this perspective is that collective opinion is not a form of social control as such but a force that may energize social control mechanisms. We return to this point later.

Communications is the medium through which emerging mutual awareness, with its implicit recognition of the extent of consensus (or dissensus) within a group, produces collective opinion. In its simplest form, this occurs in conversations in which individuals exchange opinions on various matters of the day, conversations that serve as the crucibles in which collective opinion is forged (see E. Katz, 1992, for an extended discussion of the role of conversation). Two important consequences of conversations are:

1. As individuals articulate and defend their opinions, they come to understand better their own thinking and its implications, to the point that they may even surprise themselves by voicing opinions that they had not previously been aware of but that emerge from the effort to communicate to others.

2. Each individual becomes "more or less aware of the similarity of his judgments with those of others; for if each one thought himself isolated in his evaluation, none of them would feel himself to be (and hence would not be) found in close association with others like himself" (E. Katz, 1992, p. 84).

The confluence of these consequences is experienced as an attribute of the interacting collectivity, with the result that individual opinions are subsumed under a dominant opinion (E. Katz, 1992). The almost ineffable quality of this experience underlies the historical conception of "public opinion as a state of mind, diffuse, shapeless, and shifting as a cloud ... a force like currents of the air or ocean, constantly changing in their contours and directions". It also contrasts with the public opinion poll that "requires that these elusive currents be treated as though they were static," definable, and measurable (Bogart, 1985, p. 15).

The significance of mutual awareness for the rise of collective opinion as a social force is evident in Smith's journalistic account of the measures used by the Soviet government during the 1970s and 1980s to prevent its emergence (Smith, 1990). As he noted, the purpose of Soviet censorship was "not only to block unwanted views, but to keep people who are unhappy from knowing how many millions of others share their unhappiness, to keep the dormant opposition from awakening to its own developing strength". However, small clusters of dissident academicians at places like Academic

City, 2,000 miles east of Moscow and far enough from the nearby city of Novosibirsk "not to fall constantly under the prying eyes of local regional party bosses" (Smith, 1990, 8–16) were able to work privately and clandestinely to exchange the results of their research. The existence of these clusters frustrated government efforts to prevent the emergence of mutual awareness and played a major role in the eventual collapse of the Communist dictatorship.

Mutual awareness can emerge through participation in the larger society, not only through interpersonal communication. In fact, such participation is crucial to the existence of mutual awareness among the general public in large, complex societies that offer geographically dispersed individuals limited opportunities for directly shared experience and for direct communication. The retrospective comment in a newspaper interview of one voter who had voted Republican in the 1994 Congressional election (which had resulted in a decisive Republican victory over the previously dominant Democrats) is illustrative: "I wanted a change in what politicians were doing. I didn't know the whole country felt the same way. I was shocked that I voted the way most Americans were feeling" (Berke, 1995, pp. 1, 7).

Although anecdotal, this comment succinctly illustrates the difference between casting individual ballots in a secret election and collective opinion based on mutual awareness. Secret elections are specifically designed to aggregate the preferences of individuals (whatever the sources of those preferences may be) and not to register a negotiated judgment. The results of a secret election may conform to individual expectations, or they may surprise the electorate, but in any case they serve to create mutual awareness by communicating to the general public some idea of what all the others are thinking. Rather than being merely expressions of collective opinion, elections must also be understood as input. That is, once a sense of mutual awareness develops on the basis of election returns, it becomes part of the situational context to which individuals react, thereby influencing and reinforcing the formation of individual opinions.

If a common sensation of mutual awareness and recognition emerges within a number of groups, especially if those groups are linked in some way, it is no longer a matter of some individuals thinking, for example, that the police should eject homeless people from public parks or subways, whereas others favor allowing the homeless to erect shelters in public places. Instead, previously isolated individuals who agree with each other can now draw on the authority, even the power, that derives from the belief that they are part of a larger entity.

A significant form of mutual awareness also emerges when individual opinions differ. The nature and bases of disagreement are expounded through argument and alliances established among those who do agree with each other in opposition to the others. Understandings of conflicting opinions are often imperfect, but some sense of whose opinions are different, how prevalent disagreement may be, and how intensely conflicting opinions are held can develop through the act of communicating with others. In this way, the emergent collective opinion comes to include a sense of the extent and patterning of social contention and conflict. Thus, starting with disagreement among individuals, communications can establish a basis for conflict between factions that goes far beyond individual disputation.

Collective opinion as a social force is multidimensional in a manner that corresponds to the cognitive, affective, and value–interest dimensions of attitudinal systems that underly individual opinions. Thus, the sharing of beliefs, direction and strength of affect, values, and interests contributes to the conviction and tenacity of a collective opinion's hold on a populace. This helps explain the refusal of many supporters of the Vietnam war to accept Robert McNamara's (1995) assertion that when, as Secretary of Defense, he was publicly defending President Lyndon Johnson's Vietnam War policy, his private judgment, based on information available to him but withheld from the public, he knew that the policy was based on false assumptions and that the war could not be won.

When widely shared individual values, interests, and beliefs are evoked in relation to a highly salient public controversy or crisis, an immediate convergence of individual opinions can occur even with minimum discussion. This can lead to a virtually instant mutual awareness. Illustrative of this is the perceived unanimity of support that followed the Japanese attack on Pearl Harbor on December 7, 1941. This silenced for the moment the bitter debate between interventionists and isolationists that preceded the entry of the United States into World War II.

More typically, extended antecedent communication is necessary to create a common, widespread base of understandings and concerns before much of the collectivity will react similarly to an emergency. An example is the development of the Watergate crisis of 1973–1974 that led to President Richard Nixon's resignation. Antecedent communications had so prepared the ground that individual opinions of the "Saturday Night Massacre," and later of the revelation that 18½ minutes had been erased from Nixon's Oval Office tapes, converged with minimal additional communications (Lang & Lang, 1983). However, the collective response both to Pearl Harbor and to the "Saturday Night Massacre" was not so much the sum of aggregated individual opinions as it was the effect of news reports that revealed to individuals that their opinions were congruent with the larger whole.

THE REALITY OF COLLECTIVE OPINION

Collective opinion as a phenomenon above and beyond the statistical aggregation of individual opinions has been reported both impressionistically and analytically. At the impressionistic level, politicians and journalists often refer to some presumed shared orientation or collective quality—the "climate of opinion" or the public's mood, for example, whether the public is optimistic, satisfied, frustrated, angry, disillusioned, and so on—when trying to explain voting behavior. However, we must go beyond anecdote and metaphor if we are to verify the reality of collective opinion as more than the aggregate of individual opinions. We need measurements that operationalize the concept. Across the years, such measurements have been developed and used successfully in a number of studies. Mood (or climate of opinion), as investigated in these studies, is a common response element that pervades answers to a set of questions that is identified by analyzing aggregated measurements and not from the individual measurements themselves.

An early, ingenious measurement was used by Bogart and his colleagues in their 1951 "Project Clear" study of the effects of racial integration on military performance in Korea (Bogart, 1992). After posing a hypothetical situation that involved interracial contact, they asked three questions. The first question used a form of spontaneous projection to measure individual perceptions of group practices: "What would 'Joe Doakes' (a personalization of the average individual) do in that situation?" The second question measured individual understanding of the applicable group standard: "What should he do?" The third measured how the individual resolved, for himself, the application of group practices and moral standards to the situation: "What would you, yourself, do?" (Bogart, 1992, pp. 293–297). The responses of White personnel who were serving in integrated units differed from those who had served only in all-White units, reflecting different climates of opinion in integrated and segregated units (Bogart, 1992).

Multivariate analyses of survey data in other studies have been successful in identifying and measuring liberalism–conservatism as a collective mood based on "shared feelings that move over time and circumstance," the "idea of changing *general* dispositions" (Stimson, 1991, pp. 17–18). Stimson measured the trend in the liberalism–conservatism of the public mood from 1973–1989 by analyzing responses to six questions from the General Social Survey (GSS) that asked whether the government was spending too much or too little on each of six problem areas. Although responses on each issue area produced distinctive trend lines, further analysis of the trend in the *average* of responses concerning the six issues (after standardizing each series) showed that the six trend lines moved in conjunction with each other. That is, "much of the variation in … spending priorties is shared" (Stimson, 1991, pp. 36–39). A regression analysis added precision and robustness to this conclusion. Furthermore, a principal components analysis identified a first component that accounted for 71% of all the variance within the analyzed series (Stimson, 1991). These analyses provide strong evidence that, over time, there are common movements in collective opinion that cannot be explained by individual-level, "psychology-driven models [that] strive to account for interpersonal similarity and difference" (Stimson, 1991, pp. 124–125).

SELF VERSUS OTHERS

Studies that separately measure individual opinions and perceptions of what "others" or "most people" think consistently demonstrate that individuals can, and do, differentiate between the two. Similarly, individuals can and do distinguish between the quality of their own participation in public discourse and the participation of others. However, the linkages between individual opinions and perceptions of "other opinions" can be complex, so that sometimes there is a close correspondence between them, whereas at other times there is considerable difference. Contributing to this complexity is the fact that the perceived general opinion is not consistently identical with the sum of the opinions of other individuals with whom one comes into contact. Finally, the perceived general opinion exerts an influence, sometimes positive and sometimes negative, both on individual opinions and on the readiness of individuals to express them.

A standard response in opinion surveys is the "looking-glass perception, the belief that others think the same as oneself" (Fields & Schuman, 1976, p. 445). Often, looking-glass perceptions are congruent with actual majority opinion, leading some to conclude that individual endorsements of a given opinion are dependent on looking-glass perceptions. However, on occasion there is considerable discongruity. Whether there is congruity between the looking-glass perception and individual opinions can have important consequences.

One example of discongruity comes from a study of working-class support for communism in France and Italy during the 1950s, in which individual opinions were compared with perceived opinions of others (Cantril, 1958). In a survey of residents of a Roman *borgata* that voted heavily communist, Cantril found that individual perceptions of majority opinion not only differed markedly from tallies of individual opinions, but that these perceptions were influential in their own right. Nineteen percent said that the United States is the foreign country best liked by the people in their *borgata*, marginally lower than the 22% that thought the Soviet Union is liked best. However, when asked what foreign country they personally liked best, four times as many said they liked the United States best as opposed to those who said they liked the Soviet Union best—29% versus 7%. In other words, the perceived atmosphere of this communist-voting *borgata* was much less favorable to the United States than an analysis of individual opinions would suggest (Cantril, 1958). Cantril concluded that the perception of procommunist strength in the borgata led to a greater protest communist vote than would have been expected solely on the basis of individual opinions.

A contrast between individual opinions and beliefs as to what others think was also found in the Detroit Area Study, based on periodic surveys of the adult population living in metropolitan Detroit conducted by Michigan University's Survey Research Center. In the 1969 survey, 76% of Whites said they would consent if their child asked to bring a Negro schoolmate home to play. This contrasted with only 33% who felt that most people in the Detroit area, and 38% in their neighborhood, would agree with this decision (Fields & Schuman, 1976). A comparable contrast is evident in a national 1960s survey in which the proportion of Whites favoring segregation was substantially smaller than the proportion who thought most Whites were in favor and in which White racial opinions were perceived to be more conservative than they actually were (O'Gorman, 1975; O'Gorman and Garry, 1976). This misperception was associated with willingness to legitimize racial discrimination in housing (O'Gorman, 1975).

The frequency and magnitude of incongruencies between the actual distribution of individual opinion and the perceived distribution among the population at large suggest that, whatever else may be involved, these occurrences are not aberrations but the result of a normal social process. In any event, the extent to which the actual distribution of individual opinions corresponds to or diverges from the reality worlds of a population can significantly influence events in a way that cannot be anticipated merely on the distribution of individual opinions. Furthermore, because these misperceptions of what the social environment is like are part of individual reality worlds, they can function as social norms that constrain individual behavior without necessarily changing underlying attitudinal systems and associated individual opinions. Thus, when those who hold a minority opinion incorrectly think they are in the majority, their misperceptions can have substantial effects on public policy (Merton, 1968).

THIRD-PERSON EFFECTS, PLURALISTIC
IGNORANCE, AND MINORITY DOMINANCE

Third-Person Effects

The third-person effect "predicts that people will tend to overestimate the effect that mass communications have on the attitudes and behavior of others ... (and) to have a greater effect on others than on themselves" (Davison, 1983, p. 3). Rather than looking for the effects of mass communications only in changed attitudes and behaviors of audiences, we must also pay attention to "the behavior of those who anticipate, or think they perceive, some reaction on the part of others" (Davison, 1983, p. 8). Public discourse involves much more than transmitting messages to individuals for the purpose of influencing their opinions.

When individual opinions are not directly affected by a communications campaign, over time they may still be influenced by third-person effects on the opinion process. For example, perceptions of the climate of opinion—what others are thinking and why, plus the trend of the opinions of others—can be sensitive to third-person effects (Davison, 1983; Mutz, 1989). The self–other aspect of collective opinion may then lead to a change in the ways in which collective opinion is expressed as well as in individual opinion. In this context, it is noteworthy that support for censorship is positively correlated with the third-person effect (Rojas, Shah, & Fisher, 1996).

The third-person effect is especially robust, having been repeatedly observed in a variety of contexts (Brosius & Engel, 1996; Cohen, Mutz, Price, & Gunther, 1988; Lasorsa, 1989; Mutz, 1989; Perloff, 1993; Price & Tewkbury, 1996; Rucinski & Salmon, 1990; Willnat, 1996). It is the product of a number of influences. The expectation that you, yourself, are immune to mass communications while others are highly susceptible is relatively common among the better educated and informed. The self-conceptions of the well educated lead them to see their own opinions as well-founded as compared to others, because they think they are better qualified to assess message content. Also influential are beliefs concerning the quality of the message source, so that the magnitude of third-person effects is greater with respect to political advertising, especially negative advertising, than to straight news reports and broadcasting of political debates. The closeness of one's relationship to the other also affects the size of third-person effects.

Expectations of third-person effects can mislead experts such as media consultants regarding the effectiveness of their communications efforts, so that they overestimate their success (Lasorsa, 1989). Furthermore, communicators who are aware of the existence of third-person effects may seek to manipulate opposition experts by inducing the latter to react to expectations of how "others" will be influenced. In such cases, the real target of the communications is not the ostensible audience but others who in some way are concerned about that ostensible audience's reactions and whose activities may be altered by influencing expectations of those reactions (Davison, 1983).

Pluralistic Ignorance and Minority Dominance

The communist atmosphere in the working-class neighborhoods studied by Cantril, the difference between actual individual opinions and perceived majority opinion in the Detroit Area Study, and the discongruity in the O'Gorman study can be considered examples of "pluralistic ignorance," that is, the unwarranted assumptions made by individuals regarding the thoughts, feelings, and behaviors of others (F. Allport, 1924). Typically, pluralistic ignorance has been investigated in terms of individual dynamics that lead to inaccurate perception. On the other hand, there is evidence that believing one is in the minority does not in itself lead to change in individual opinion. Perceptions of what is minority and majority opinion are relatively independent of one's own position (Glynn & McLeod, 1984). It is, therefore, important to distinguish between the possible effects pluralistic ignorance can have on collective opinion as a social force versus its effects on individual opinions. For example, pluralistic ignorance on any given issue might be integrated into the collective opinion of the public, or part of it. How that might take place cannot be understood if our attention is limited to pluralistic ignorance as an individual phenomenon.

Closely related to the phenomenon of pluralistic ignorance is "minority dominance," that is, the fact that the views of numerical minorities often exert an influence disproportionate to their numbers. One case in point is the effectiveness of National Rifle Association (NRA) supporters in election campaigns. Beginning in 1938 (Gallup, 1972b), the Gallup Poll has consistently reported huge majorities of up to four-fifths favoring legislation to control gun ownership. Yet, for decades the NRA was able to marshall voter support for adherents of its position and defeat candidates for office who favored gun control. National gun-control legislation was not enacted until 1994, and since then there has been a strong movement for repeal. The effectiveness of campaign contributions from the NRA and its well-organized lobbying must not be overlooked in any analysis of this discordance, but neither should the effectiveness of the grass-roots support from a numerical minority that the NRA has been able to mobilize.

A similar contrast between numerical support and political effectiveness exists with respect to opinion as to what should be the legal status of abortion. Polls conducted by many survey organization across 20 years reported majorities endorsing the legality of abortions during the first three months of pregnancy. It has also been the case that the proportion endorsing legality varies appreciably under different scenarios, so that majority approval exists only for a limited number of scenarios (Adamek, 1995). Nonetheless, the majority has consistently opposed outlawing abortion under all conditions, the position taken by the most committed prolife activists. In the face of this opposition, the committed prolife view that all abortion should be outlawed has become a major force in American politics. With abortion, as with gun control, the workings of collective opinion as a social force cannot be inferred solely from a tally of individual opinions.

To some degree it is possible to ascribe minority dominance to the strength of commitment among individual adherents to the minority position. On the other hand, it would be a mistake to underestimate the commitment of gun-control protagonists aroused by political assassination, terrorism, mass killings using assault weapons, and general concern about violence in the streets. Neither does the commitment of "prochoice" adherents take second place to that of their "prolife" opponents. Something beyond individual commitment underlies minority dominance.

The collective significance of both pluralistic ignorance and minority dominance is a product of whether, and to what extent, individual opinions have been organized to create effective support groups and to mobilize those groups to action. An important aspect of that process is the readiness or disinclination of individuals to communicate with each other by voicing their opinions in public.

UNVOICED OPINIONS

Individuals sometimes are reluctant to express their opinions in public discourse. One explanation for this reluctance has to do with the interface between individual motivation and group process, namely, that ego-defensive motivations make public opinion a repressive force for ensuring conformity, thereby creating a "spiral of silence" (Noelle-Neumann, 1984). Fear of social isolation is said to make those in the minority on some public issue unwilling to voice their opinions publicly, whereas those in the majority are free of this pressure. The latter receive the most visible support and are encouraged by that fact to be outspoken whereas those in the minority become increasingly prone to remain quiet. The result is that in "a spiralling

process, the one view dominate(s) the public scene and the other disap-
pear(s) from public awareness as its adherents become mute" (Noelle-Neumann, 1984, p. 5). To the extent members of the minority correctly perceive
that they are in the minority, rather than incorrectly think they are in the
majority, their resultant silence creates an exaggerated perception of majority dominance (Noelle-Neumann, 1984). To this formulation, we should
add the observation that a spiral of silence may function differently within
segments of the public characterized by a dominant opinion that is in the
minority in the general public.

A contrasting but parallel explanation of silence substitutes the positive
motivations of ego enhancement and desire for group acceptance in place
of fear: A "positive attraction to desirable social groups may be a stronger
motivator than (is) conformity" (Katz & Baldassare, 1994, p. 10). However,
because both positive and negative motivational explanations of silence
focus on the social control consequences of collective opinion on individuals, neither tells us much about how collective judging is influenced by
silence.

"Rhetorical reticence," a tactic adopted to strengthen and not weaken one's
opinion in public discourse (Goldner, 1991), suggests a different reason for
silence. It calls attention to the possibility that, in order not to support the
opposition when faced with extremist versions of their own position, those who
hold moderate or qualified versions of a position may remain silent and not
express their reservations and qualifications. Also, it reminds us of the possibility
that who is associated with a given opinion may be a more important determinant of silence than the frequency with which it is held. Finally, we should note
that there is some evidence that fear of isolation is less of an influence on silence
than are social and demographic characteristics, the kind of issue that is at
stake, and the issue's salience (Price & Allen, 1993).

An unresolved problem is how silence affects each side's ability to
organize and activate effective support in the struggle to achieve opinion
dominance. As we have seen, those in the minority may nonetheless be
collectively effective. Their organizational effectiveness can be appreciably
influenced by the outspokeness of their adherents. That is why political
factions seek to avoid being weakened by silence among their supporters
and to encourage willingness to speak out. They assume that to protect their
position in the public arena, they must exert every effort to maximize their
visibility—through rallies, bumper stickers, e-mail, staging newsworthy
events, advertising, and so on. How effectively these communications media
are manipulated can be crucial to creating a favorable climate of opinion
that may, eventually, influence individual opinions—as part of the social
process of creating a strong collective opinion.

SHARED VERSUS OPPOSING
UNIVERSES OF DISCOURSE

It is axiomatic that for individuals to exchange and discuss their opinions, they must have a common understanding of the fundamental meaning of what is being said. That is, they must communicate within a common universe of discourse (Blumer, 1939). Without that, discussion and debate are impossible and a collective opinion cannot emerge. Moreover, conversing within a shared universe of discourse is a basis for mutual identification; using incompatible universes of discourse can be an alienating experience.

Sharing a universe of discourse is not merely a matter of speaking the same language—English, Spanish, Russian, Chinese, or what have you. Beyond dictionary definitions of individual words, there must be agreement regarding the underlying assumptions, expectations, implications, associations, and feelings those words have. To the extent such agreement does not exist, communication is hampered by an incomplete or distorted understanding of what each is saying. Some indication of the extent to which people speaking the same language may nonetheless be participating in different universes of discourses comes from a survey that compared collective memories in Great Britain and the United States. In each country, national samples were asked to name "the one or two ... *national or world events or changes* over the past 60 years that come to your mind as important" (Scott and Zac, 1993). A follow-up question asked for the reasons why an event was named.

Given the similarities and differences in national histories, it is not surprising that although there are a number of parallels in the results from the two surveys, there are also significant differences. One difference is that although World War II was named most frequently in both countries, the proportion that did so was far greater in Britain (45%) than in the United States (29%; Scott & Zac, 1993). Moreover, for many in the United States, the war was associated with postwar prosperity and patriotism, associations that did not come up frequently in Britain (Scott & Zac, 1993). This difference, of course, reflects the contrast in the real life experiences of many Americans and British during the war years. But, that contrast also indicates that when Americans and British talk with each other about World War II and its meaning, even though the words may appear to be the same, there is a strong likelihood that in important ways they connote something different to each.

A phenomenon of 1980s and 1990s American politics is the extent to which the term *liberal* became a negative political epithet. During the 1988 presidential election campaign, using the phrase "the L-word" became one of the Republican George Bush's most effective ploys, whereas in the 1995–1996 struggle over the federal budget, Congressional Republicans effectively used the label "liberal" in their attacks on President Clinton's budget. To understand why the negative use of the terms "L-word" and "liberal" became so effective whereas previously being considered "liberal" had been a political asset, it is necessary examine how the word's connotations had changed.

In a December 1945 survey, the Gallup Poll asked the question:

> Which of these three policies [listed on a card] would you like to see the government follow—(1) go more to the left by following more of the views of labor and other liberal groups, (2) go more to the right by following more of the views of business and conservative groups, or (3) follow a policy halfway between the two? (Gallup, 1972b, p. 558)

In this question, liberals were defined largely as being prolabor and conservatives as being probusiness—this at a time when memories of the 1930 Depression were still strong and New Deal legislation that created a government-administered economic safety net was widely approved. In that 1945 poll, almost as many identified themselves as liberals as conservatives: 18% endorsed the liberal position, 21% the conservative position, and 52% the middle-of-the-road position.

In the 1980s, the relative strength of liberal to conservative identifications was shifting. According to a 1988 *New York Times*/CBS News Poll (which asked a question worded differently from Gallup's so that absolute numerical comparison is not possible), at the time of the 1988 election 23% thought of themselves as political liberals, 34% felt they were conservative, and 37% saw themselves as in the middle of the road. Those numbers changed little by the 1992 presidential election when the Democratic candidate, Bill Clinton, was elected: 21% liberal, 33% conservative, and 39% moderate. By the 1994 Congressional election, in which the Republicans gained control of both houses of Congress, a further shift toward the conservative end of the political spectrum occurred: 18% liberal, 36% conservative, and 40% moderate (*New York Times*/CBS News Poll, Dec. 6–9, 1994).

This shift in ideological identification was only partly a change in sympathies between labor versus business. It also reflected success in redefining liberals as favoring "tax and spend big government," counterculture values, and permissiveness regarding drug use and criminals. This is not to say that there was no continuity in the meaning of liberal across the intervening 40 years. Still, the associated overtones had changed. The conservative victory in the 1994 Congressional elections was not simply a matter of converting liberals to conservatism but, more fundamentally, of redefining what it means to be a liberal or a conservative, that is, of redefining the universe of discourse.

By changing the terms of debate, redefining the universe of discourse can change collective opinion with little shift in individual opinions on specific issues. The alternation between class and status politics that has characterized so much of American politics (e.g., Bell, 1955, 1964) is a case in point. Getting the electorate to think in terms of social issues such as race, abortion, and family values rather than the class pocketbook issues that dominated the New Deal era has been an effective way for Republicans to attract votes from once dedicated Democratic constituencies—without necessarily having to change individual opinions on class issues.

The process of redefinition illustrates the fact that public debate consists of much more than efforts to change individual opinions, voter by voter. Intrinsic to the political struggle, and determinative of the direction of its trend, is the social conflict about what should be the terms of discourse. The conflict is social in that its resolution requires at least an implicit consensus regarding the words that should be used in political discourse and their meanings. In a similar vein, the effectiveness in political discourse of what have come to be called *code words* is contingent on their incorporation into the political universe of discourse.

An example of this principle comes from the December 1994 *New York Times*/CBS News Poll just cited. Survey results regarding welfare reform varied significantly depending on whether, and in what context the word "welfare" was used in question wordings. Fifty percent of those who were interviewed were asked which is more to blame when people are "poor"—lack of effort on their part or circumstances beyond their control—and the other 50% was asked which is more to blame when people are "on welfare." Lack of effort was blamed by 53% for being on welfare, but by only 44% for being poor. Similarly, when half of those interviewed were asked whether government spending on "programs for poor children should be increased or decreased or kept about the same," 47% said spending should be increased and 9% said it should be decreased. However, when the other half were asked about "government spending on welfare," 48% replied it should be decreased and 13% said it should be increased.

The large effect of seemingly small changes in question wording on expressed opinion, such as the previous discussion, is less a methodological issue than a matter of properly conceptualizing how collective opinion is a product of communicating within a common universe of discourse. "Welfare" and "poor" are words that conjure very different beliefs and feelings. For example, in the same Dec. 6–9, 1994 *New York Times*/CBS News Poll,

57% said that "most people who receive money from welfare could get along without it if they tried," 71% thought "there are jobs available for most welfare recipients who really want to work," and 87% favored government "work programs for people on welfare and require people to participate in the programs." It seems likely that racial stereotypes and biases also affect the meaning of the term "welfare": 46% incorrectly thought that most poor people are Black, whereas only 20% knew that most are White.

Replacing the word "poor" with "welfare" calls forth a system of thinking that, when shared by a large segment of the population, lays the foundation for a collective opinion committed to severe cuts in welfare expenditures. Thus, talking about welfare rather than about poor people facilitates expressing opinions critical of assumed welfare cheats even as it inhibits the expression of individual opinions sympathetic to the "deserving, working poor." In this way, using the word "welfare" rather than "the poor" can convey an implicit sense of solidarity with others who are critical of the welfare system and welfare recipients, even for someone sympathetic to the needs of poor people receiving welfare. Concurrently, using the term welfare tends to inhibit expressions of sympathy for "the poor," reinforcing the dominance of the more vocal members of the public and the silence or reticence of the less vocal. More generally, sharing the same universe of discourse contributes to a sense of participation and identification with others. The origin and strength of collective opinion as a social force in large part derives from the social bonds created by this process.

OPINION LEADERSHIP

The idea of opinion leadership—that some people's opinions are looked to with more respect than are the opinions of others and, therefore, are more influential—may appear self-evident and commonsensical. However, the question as to how, exactly, opinion leadership acts to create a collective opinion, and not only to influence individual opinions, is a complex one that to a surprising extent has been ignored. Even so, a sufficient base exists at this time for us to delineate in general the role of opinion leadership in the emergence of collective opinion as a social force.

To the extent that any group (or larger social entity) is organized, it is characterized by a pattern of super- and subordinate relationships, with communications within the group characterized by a correlative pattern. Up to this point, our discussion of mutual awareness has not taken into account the existence of these usually complex social distinctions and relationships. The mutual awareness out of which collective opinion emerges is normally not an awareness only among peers but also among leaders and followers. As Ross (1901) observed nearly a century ago, "the source of public opinion in a healthy community is not an amorphous crowd, but an organic combination of people," influencers and the influenced, with the former acting as the "rallying points of public opinion" (pp. 102–103).

Bryce made much the same point when he noted that the formation of opinion is in largest part the work of the small minority (1 in 20) who are concerned with public affairs. He went further by observing that the politically passive majority does not merely reflect leader opinion but modifies it so that the resultant collective opinion is the product of the mutual action and reaction between opinion leaders and the masses (Bryce, 1891). The patterning of leadership–followership relations that channel any communication within a group, or larger social structure, also shapes and structures the emergence of collective opinion within that group.

The ability of some to dominate communications within a group makes the emergent collective opinion a function of existing social relations and not only of the numerical strength of individual opinions within a group. Among other things, to the extent that conflict, or only partial agreement, exists, competing individual or factional opinions will vie to achieve acceptance as the group's collective opinion. In this competition, existing patterns of group leadership can significantly affect which opinions will be heard and which will not. Leaders can also influence the group's agenda of issue concerns by giving or denying saliency to specific issues. Additionally, the development of any consensus is conditioned by the credibility that leaders may lend to some beliefs, values, and interests, and deny to others. For all these reasons, to understand fully the emergence of a collective opinion, it is essential to take into account the process of opinion leadership.

Preliminary to doing that, we need to specify the understanding of leadership that provides the framework for our discussion of opinion leadership. Leadership in general, and opinion leadership in particular, is a relationship between leaders and followers in which the focus, control, and direction that leaders provide to communications is central. Thus, leadership is not restricted to influencing the behavior of other individuals, important as that is, but in responding to the desires and thoughts of those individual in ways that enhance a sense of common identity. As part of those responses, their opinions may be influenced by the opinions of their followers (Bryce, 1891). In any case, through their ability to influence the flow of communications and through serving as role models, leaders contribute to group identity and effectiveness.

Leaders also, perhaps primarily, provide cohesion, force, and direction to both organized group action and to more inchoate forms of collective behavior. They do this either by virtue of the office or position they hold in a group (formal leadership) or their personal qualities as expressed in intragoup activities (informal leadership). Because formal and informal leaders tend to influence different types of followers (Lowe & McCormick, 1957), we are concerned with both the formal and informal aspects of leadership, and the interactions between both aspects.

Complicating any attempt to analyze the role of opinion leaders is the fact that their empirical study derives primarily from a research tradition that focused on the effects of mass communications on individual opinions. Typical of research done in this tradition is the use of exposure rates, predispositions, type of medium, message content, and interpersonal relations as intervening variables to measure effects on individual opinion. (Katz & Lazarsfeld, 1955). As a result, opinion leadership has been studied by many solely in terms of personal influence exerted through informal, intimate, everyday contacts, excluding more formal and structured forms of influence (Katz & Lazarsfeld, 1955; Rogers, 1995). This has led to a neglect of the important role of opinion leadership in the emergence of mutual awareness and collective opinions, creating group consensus, and in linking primary groups to the larger society.

Despite the limitations of the opinion leader research tradition just noted, a valuable contribution was its rejection of the once prevalent "hypodermic needle" metaphor of mass communications. According to that metaphor, the presumably all-powerful mass media affected individual opinions by exerting an immediate, direct influence on a passively receptive mass audience (Rogers & Shoemaker, 1971). In its place, the opinion leadership concept led to the "two-step flow" model of communication, in which much of the content of mass communications reaches the general public through intermediary personal transmission from opinion leaders (E. Katz, 1957).

The two-step flow model proved to be inadequate and has since been replaced by multifaceted models that attempt to account for complex interactions among the mass media, opinion leaders, and opinion followers (Rogers & Shoemaker, 1971). Common to all those models is the realization that even in societies that rely on advanced technology to communicate to mass audiences, in order to explain the responses of individuals to communications campaigns we must analyze how interpersonal relationships and social milieus affect communications (Rogers & Shoemaker, 1971). A refinement is to emphasize the idea of discourse, which conceptualizes the mass media and their audiences as participants in an ongoing conversation, in place of communication models in which the mass media convey messages to citizens conceived of as political consumers (Delli Carpini & Williams, 1994). Such an interactional conceptualization of mass communications appears to be particularly suitable for any analysis of collective opinion as an emergent phenomenon. In any event, the validity of the insight that opinion leadership in modern societies is embedded in a network of interactions between mass and interpersonal communications is unchallenged.

Another aspect of opinion leadership that has attracted much attention is the personal qualities and attributes that differentiate informal opinion leaders from their followers. Research on this question has compiled considerable evidence that, as compared with opinion followers, informal opinion leaders tend to have greater exposure to the mass media, are more cosmopolitan, have more contacts with change agents, have greater social participation, tend to have higher social status, and tend to be more innovative (Rogers & Shoemaker, 1971; see also Weimannn 1991). However, research on the personal qualities of opinion leaders has not attempted to analyze how those qualities affect interpersonal communications in a way that leads to the development of mutual awareness. Research is sorely needed to remedy this deficiency.

Opinion leaders excel in their ability to utilize existing social mechanisms, such as networks of citizen organizations, to mobilize individual opinions into some form of organized expression (Wiebe, 1951, 1952). Formal leaders are particularly well placed for that purpose, given the control over communications that derives from the authority, prestige, and power inherent in their office. Theodore Roosevelt's depiction of the office of President of the United States as a "bully pulpit" fully captures this idea. Much of the effectiveness of Franklin D. Roosevelt, and later Ronald Reagan, as political leaders was based not only on their skill in manipulating political institutions, but also on their use of the presidential office to mobilize and direct the public opinion process. Roosevelt's radio "fireside chats" and Reagan's televised press conferences are outstanding examples of a president's ability to dominate public discourse, thereby stimulating the emergence of a forceful collective opinion in support of their policies. Similarly, the outcomes of election campaigns, although historically dependent on skill in directing organizational activities, are increasingly determined by an ability to use the office of candidate to motivate, mobilize, and activate collective opinion.

Nonetheless, it is equally clear that holding office in itself is not sufficient to be an effective opinion leader: The public was far less responsive to presidents like Gerald Ford and Jimmy Carter than to Franklin Roosevelt and Ronald Reagan. Personal qualities beyond the trappings of office come into play, making some formal leaders effective opinion leaders, while others fail. Furthermore, even powerful office holders are not guaranteed access to news media: In 1995, within a 10-day period, two of the three national television networks refused to carry either a live press conference held by President Bill Clinton or a speech of Speaker of the House Newt Gingrich (Kolbert, 1995). Conversely, personal qualities can enable some individuals to transform less publicized, although powerful, offices such as Speaker of the House into bully pulpits in their own right. Speaker Gingrich accomplished that after the Republican victory in the 1994 Congressional election. The role of formal leaders in the emergence of an effective collective opinion is always a problematic consequence of the interaction between personal qualities and formal roles within specific historical contexts.

In addition to formal offices, a source of effective opinion leadership is communication gatekeeping, that is, controlling what messages reach the public. Formal leaders are usually well-placed to exert considerable influence on what messages reach the public (or at least that part of the public included in the membership of their organizations) through their control over organizational channels of communications. But that is only part of the gatekeeping function. Gatekeeping also involves the important, but sometimes overlooked, efforts to control message dissemination amongst members of the public to each other. By denying access to existing channels of communication to some factions or segments of the public (creating an artificial spiral of silence, as it were), formal leaders may seek to manipulate the climate of opinion and the agenda of public concerns to their advantage. Persistent allegations of White House attempts (by both Democratic and Republican administrations) to influence news coverage by television networks is but one example of this phenomenon.

Because the owners of communications media can affect message content and volume, they are important actors in the gatekeeping process. For this reason, conflict and controversy have long surrounded the question of whether communications media are monopolized, dominated, or otherwise controlled by partisan and biased owners (see, e.g., Blumberg, 1954; Commission of Freedom of the Press, 1947; Gans, 1980). In addition, somewhat analogous to the significance of personal qualities among formal leaders, the personal qualities and skills of individuals strategically placed in the communications process may enable them to capitalize on their gatekeeper positions and become opinion leaders in their own right: Notable examples in United States history are newspaper columnists Walter Lippmann, James Reston, and David Broder; television news anchors Edward R. Murrow, Walter Cronkite, and Peter Jennings; and talk show personalities Larry King and Rush Limbaugh.

Informal leaders often play a decisive role in small familial, friendship, neighborhood, and work groups. The authority they wield or the esteem they command within the group enables them to dominate interpersonal communications, giving prominence to their opinions. Similarly, differences in their personal attributes—including personality traits, rate of media exposure, individual esteem, other group memberships, and demographic and socioeconomic characteristics (Weimann, 1991)—can strengthen the saliency and credibility of their opinions to group members. They are also a source of social pressure to conform to a group's way of thinking and a source of social support for an individual's opinions (E. Katz, 1957). It is not surprising, therefore, that the evidence strongly suggests that individual opinion is integrally related to the collective opinion of small, informal membership groups (Berelson, Lazarsfeld, & McPhee, 1954).

The effect of informal opinion leaders on the formation of individual opinions is embedded in a group process and cannot be reduced to one-on-one relations between leaders and followers.

> Interpersonal relationships seem to be *"anchorage" points for individual opinions, attitudes, habits and values.* Interacting individuals seem collectively and continuously *to generate* and *to maintain* common ideas and behavior patterns which they are reluctant to surrender or to modify unilaterally. (Furthermore), ... an individual's seeming personal opinions and attitudes may be by-products of interpersonal relations. ... individual expressions of opinions and attitudes is not strictly an individual affair. (Katz & Lazarsfeld 1955, p. 44, 65)

By influencing individual opinions within a group so that they are largely consonant with each other, informal opinion leaders further the development of mutual awareness.

Informal group leaders may also contribute to mutual awareness by acting as role models who legitimize innovative ideas that have been introduced to the group by others. Insight into this legitimization function is provided by marketing research on the adoption of new products. New products are often first adopted by individals who have a relative propensity to innovate and experiment. Innovaters, however, are not necessarily opinion leaders; in fact there is evidence that indicates that in some social contexts they are unlikely to be leaders (Rogers & Shoemaker, 1971). Although they serve as important conduits of information from the mass media to group members, their innovativeness is by itself insufficient to firmly establish new product use within a group. Whether that happens depends on acceptance by highly respected and esteemed group members (Menzel & Katz, 1956). That is to say, even when informal leaders do not transmit information from the mass media, they may validate that information for the group regardless of its source.

Applying this multistep model of new product adoption to the opinion process, we describe informal opinion leadership as a process through which highly esteemed group members influence the development of mutual awareness by validating some opinions at the expense of others. Those esteemed individuals serve as opinion leaders in that they not only directly influence individual opinions but, equally significantly, they also help establish normative standards for what opinions may be expressed within the group. The fact that, as previously noted, climates of opinion are not merely a reflection of the statistical distribution of individual opinions within a group is the outcome of networks of interpersonal communications whose nexus is informal leadership.

Informal opinion leaders are important in the emergence of collective opinion in ways that go beyond their influence on the opinions of individual group members and intragroup communications. They can also affect the functioning of primary groups within the larger society. However, the role of informal opinion leaders in relating primary groups to the public at large, especially in mass societies, is still uncertain. This uncertainty is in large part due to the polling methodology commonly used to study public opinion. Polls were developed to document the distribution of individual opinions in the larger society, and segments thereof, but not to explore the interactions between primary groups and the larger society (Katz & Lazarsfeld, 1955). New research methodologies may be needed to thoroughly investigate this area.

For any group's collective opinion to become a social force, it must reach beyond the group in a manner that links it to the larger society. Unless and until informal group leadership actively links primary group substrates to the larger, organized society, they will be truncated and unlikely to contribute to the development of a forceful collective opinion. However, if they not only speak for themselves, but represent the opinions of a group's members (opinions that in all likelihood they helped form) to formal organizations and in public forums, informal opinion leaders bring a weightiness to public discourse that otherwise might not exist. They do this by, for example, collecting petitions, hosting at-home gatherings where aspiring political candidates can meet voters face-to-face, speaking out in public meetings, officially transmitting the opinions expressed in some primary groups to which they belong to other groups, speaking to prominent acquaintances on behalf of friends and relatives, and contributing to the formation of spontaneous demonstrations.

These, of course, are all activities that may be initiated by organized groups. But, often they are spontaneous outcomes of internal primary group interactions, as in the case of mothers who blockade dangerous intersections on the routes their children take to school, or neighbors who arrange to attend a city council meeting with each other to protest a planned zoning change. Across time, a growing awareness of such informally led events can create a sense of a groundswell of public opinion led by politically obscure informal leaders, events that formal leaders may hesitate to ignore. This is how many "grass-root" movements—such as Mothers Against Drink Driving (MADD), tax protests such as the California Proposition 13 movement, led by Howard Jarvis in 1978, and the anti-Florio Hands Across New Jersey movement in 1992, led by Patricia Ralston and John Budzask—become politically important. Informal, nonpolitical leadership may also be involved in other forms of upward communications such as letters to the editor and public testimony by nonpolitical figures in legislative hearings.

These anecdotal examples illustrate that the role of informal opinion leaders in the emergence of a collective opinion includes their role in communications *from* as well as *to* primary groups. Systematic research is needed on this largely neglected aspect of informal opinion leadership.

COLLECTIVE OPINION AS A SOCIAL FORCE

Depending on situational circumstances, collective opinion can be either morally conservative or socially innovative. To avoid conceptual confusion on this point, we need to emphasize the distinction between the collective *judging process* in which it is decided what should be done, and the *act* of implementing the decision. That is, collective opinion is not in itself the implementing force but, rather, an influence on what is decided. It is in the specific sense that collective opinion usually supports actions that protect communal values that we can consider it to be a morally conservative force. Comparably, it is in the specific sense that collective opinion may in other circumstances support the introduction of new forms of acting that we can consider it to be an innovative force that, over time, may lead to profound social change.

As part of the process through which a society makes collective judgments about matters in dispute, it strives to protect the implicit consensus that is essential to its stability and orderly functioning. To that end, some judgments may support, or oppose, imposing a variety of informal and formal sanctions—ranging from social isolation (e. g., avoidance, shunning, ostracism, and excommunication), to fines, imprisonment, and execution. But a society may also need to resolve disputes that threaten its comity even though communal values are not at stake. To that end, other judgments may support, or oppose, establishing new laws, procedures, or organizations.

Also, many disputes involve issues that combine both kinds of concern. That is, the disputes to be judged vary in the extent to which they relate to value or to interest conflict.

Value Conflict.   In some situations, the problem to be solved is to how to react to deviant or dissident thought and behavior that challenge communal values, but without calling on the full force of formal institutional authority (Ross, 1969). By way of illustration, consider homogeneous, stable societies that by definition are characterized by a rarely challenged consensus on communal values. In the absence of any centers of opposition, collective opinion in such societies will normally support repressive sanctions intended to protect communal values against social deviance. Consequently, relying on collective opinion to support the imposition of sanctions that discourage and suppress deviant thought or behavior is particularly characteristic of culturally homogeneous and stable societies.

Interpersonal communications are particularly likely to be associated with value-threatening situations. Gossip is the archetype of how interpersonal communication rouses and marshals individual opinions into a socially forceful collective opinion when communal values are threatened. Much gossip is, of course, unpatterned and unfocused, moving in an unorganized manner from one item to another. However, when gossip focuses for any length of time on a particular event or person, this signals that important community norms and values are at stake and that group resources are being marshalled to maintain conformity. Expressions such as "people say" and "what will they think" call attention to a collective opinion that expresses "the spontaneous reaction of the community against conduct that displeases it" (Ross, 1969, p. 89), a displeasure that demands some kind of action be taken. In this way, gossip can create an agenda for communal action.

The capability of gossip to generate collective opinion is most obvious in small, self-contained communities. But it plays a role in large, complex societies, for example, in the salons of 18th-century French aristocracy and in 20th-century Washington, D. C. cocktail parties. Furthermore, the use of modern communications media by, for example, newspaper columnists and television talk shows, makes it possible for gossip to go beyond the confines imposed by interpersonal communication. This potentiality has been realized under the loosened standards of journalism that characterized the 1990s. Alleged extramarital affairs and heavy drinking that were once "hush-hush" topics within the Washington Beltway have become standard grist for the political mills of mass-media journalism.

In mass societies, as well as in smaller communities, when communal values are perceived as having been violated, public condemnation is a call for action to reaffirm and preserve those values. Thus, through the expression of a value-oriented collective opinion, the conservative dynamics of closed, homogeneous societies, characterized by a nonlogical adherence to traditional standards, can become operative within more rationally oriented modern societies. In multicultural societies, characterized by the coexistence of competing communal values, this can lead to bitter and even violent confrontations such as those regarding abortion and homosexuality. That is to say, the very qualities of collective opinion as a conservative social force that act to maintain a stable social order under conditions of homogeneity may instead generate highly destabilizing conflict in heterogeneous societies.

A very different problem arises in heterogeneous, rapidly changing societies when they seek to resolve competing and conflicting interests about which there is no established consensus but that, by the same token, are not value threatening. In those cases, the need is to forge agreements that will be accepted, even if not favored, by the society at large—accepted if only because they are not seen as violating fundamental values. One task of collective opinion in such circumstances is to constrain decisions so that they do not weaken the underlying communal consensus. In that context, collective opinion can be a force that supports more proactive, interest-oriented, creative judgments. Disagreement and attempts to change opinion may persist, in fact they often do, but so long as the underlying value consensus is not threatened, the formation and expression of collective opinion need not be destabilizing to the underlying community.

Interest Conflict. The exchange of utilitarian information through personal conversation plays a different role from gossip in the coalescing of individual opinions into a collective opinion. Although such communications often amount to no more than individuals exchanging useful bits of information, occasions do arise when individuals discover that they have mutual or conflicting interests. In the absence of differences, a perceived community of interest may arise, leading to an opinion consensus that may in time generate new norms of behavior. However, when interests conflict and debate develops over which goals of action and means of acheiving them should be adopted, those with common or similar interests may coalesce into opposing interest groups. Through this process, there emerges a public divided into conflicting interest groups, each characterized by a distinctive collective opinion espoused by its own opinion leaders. The resultant debate can at times become rancorous and highly divisive and can, unless constrained, make factional collective opinion a destabilizing social force. Constraints on divisive debate can be generated by a concerned general collective opinion, or a political order may exist that can impose effective sanctions against uncontrolled factional conflict.

In its pure form, interest oriented debate is characterized by a problem-solving rationality that is capable of accepting sociologically innovative solutions (although in its empirical form, this rationality is likely to be tempered by considerations based on value-laden norms). As a consequence, in contrast with gossip-generated collective opinion, when an interest-oriented collective opinion develops, it may favor policies and actions that are not necessarily sociologically conservative and may even be subversive of established norms and authority. The revolutionary activities of planters and merchants in 18th-century colonial British America is illustrative of such developments.

Although interest-oriented interpersonal communications can occur in a variety of settings, gatherings that take place for explicitly utilitarian purposes are particularly conducive to such discussions. For this reason, marketplaces such as the agora of ancient Athens, the Roman forum, and the medieval fair have served as historical settings where collective opinion emerges. In such settings, when interpersonal discourse focuses on how that issue should be handled, the existence of consensus or dissensus on what should be done is soon apparent. Accordingly, as is commonly the case with value-oriented collective opinion, an interest-oriented collective opinion may emerge directly out of face-to-face communications. But, advances in communications technology and how it is organized have significanly altered this process.

In technologically advanced media environments, much public debate is transformed into a competition between rival propagandists seeking to attract the attention of mass audiences and then persuading them to a particular viewpoint (see chap. 4 for a full discussion of the interaction between communications technology and communications process). Such efforts to mobilize politicized collective opinions typically do not rely solely on arguing the virtues of a particular set of interests. Instead, to varying degrees, efforts are made to associate interests with communal values. Furthermore, rather than taking place in spontaneous, unstructured interpersonal exchanges, discussion and debate under conditions created by sophisticated communications technology can be planned and directed by those who have access to and control that technology. Correlatively, instead of collective opinion being an unplanned product of public discussion and debate, it increasingly becomes a manufactured product. As a result, competition for control of communication media, and counterefforts to protect open access for all, converts the social process of public discourse into a political struggle in its own right. In this way the struggle to dominate communications—through media monopolization if possible and, if not, through the manipulation of messages—becomes a central drama of the public opinion process.

COLLECTIVE OPINION AS PROCESS

We have seen that the social force that emanates from mutual awareness is not simply a statistical aggregate of individual opinions. Neither does it represent some general will of a people— a unitary group decision. Collective opinion as a social force can be likened better to the output of a musical group than to a group decision. In a homogeneous society with little structural differentiation, the analogy would be with the output of an assemblage all of whom are playing a simple theme on the same instrument—the expression of a simple unity of opinion that grows out of and validates accepted communal values. In heterogeneous, structurally differentiated societies, a better analogy is with a "jam session" in which a group of jazz musicians improvises around some central theme, with their contrasting and complementary voices sometimes taking that theme along familar paths and at other times into unexplored and unanticipated areas.

Sometimes there is a blending of many interests and values into a single theme, as in times of consensus; in other circumstances, there is a clash of competing voices each striving to acheive dominance; in still other circumstances, opposing themes are carried by alliances of different sectors of the public. Still using the musical metaphor, as in jazz combos in which the group structure tends to be pliable, even when there is an acknowledged leader in public debate, the possibility always exists that at any given time someone else will assume a dominant role. What emerges is the image of a process of becoming, an unceasing ebb and flow that stems from the interplay of sometimes harmonious, sometimes competing, sometimes clashing voices, and that creates something new out of what had existed originally.

At the risk of overworking the musical metaphor, we should note that just as the technology of musical instruments affects the nature of the music that is played, change in communications technology can have profound effects on collective opinion as process. Consider, for example, the effects of the change from harpsichords to pianos or from the acoustic to the electric guitar. Many have expressed concern that technological developments in communications have led to new forms of communications that may displace conversation as the medium through which collective opinion emerges. Yet, new technologies like telephones and e-mail have also made for effective person-to-person communication over long distances.

At the most basic level, available technology determines the extent to which direct, interpersonal communications can be supplemented and even replaced by other means. Beyond that, available technology influences the geographic coverage of interpersonal and mass communications networks. It also shapes the forms that relationships between audiences and communicators can take. For this reason, the adoption of new technologies often leads to the evolution of existing social relationships into previously unknown patterns. As a consequence, the size, composition, and structure of publics will change with the introduction of technologies that transcend face-to-face communications. These developments cannot be understood soley in terms of the social processes that we have been considering so far. For this reason, before considering the political dimension of the public opinion process, our next task is to examine how the introduction of new technology can influence the communication process itself.

4

Effects of Communication Technology

The introduction of major new communications technologies like the Internet and the World Wide Web often tempts their enthusiasts to predict that they will produce revolutionary changes in the public opinion process. We must acknowledge that available technology channels the scope, breadth, depth, and structure of communication networks (see, e. g., Goldhamer, 1980). However, although the technical capabilities of communications technology are primarily determined by their engineering attributes, it is also the case that social processes will direct how that technology is used. The impact of technological developments on the public opinion process is not the consequence of technology alone, but of the interplay of technology and social process.

This interplay is evident in the effects new communication technologies have had on the public opinion process in Western societies across the past 500 years. The institutional structure that now characterizes communications in the United States came into being during this period, so it is of special interest to us. As we see in the following historical review, the introduction of printing in the 15th century, the adoption of telegraphic communications and advances in printing in the 19th century, and the rise of broadcast and other electronic communications in the 20th century have all significantly conditioned communications as a social process, but so have the historical circumstances surrounding their introduction.

PRINTING

The introduction of printing in western Europe occurred at a time characterized by a priestly monopoly of learning. This created a volatile mixture because printing helped make religious heresy and schism permanent, unlike the more transient effects of earlier medieval heresies (Eisenstein, 1987). The combination of the new technology and the Protestant Reformation then contributed to the emergence of the public opinion process as a significant force beyond the local community in western Europe (Speier, 1980). To understand how that happened, we must consider the interplay between then-existing communications media and printing as a technology.

In the preprinting era, libraries had been priestly monopolies of a scarce resource. Single copies of any given book (laboriously and often inaccurately copied by hand) were the treasured possessions of a limited number of libraries in monasteries and universities. Instead of many people reading important texts, only a few had any opportunity to even see them. Audiences were often assembled to listen to text readings and/or to oratorical disquisitions on them (Eisenstein, 1987).

Once the use of movable metal type was developed in the 1450s by printers in Mainz, Germany (a development that culminated in Johan Gutenberg's printing in 1456 of a Vulgate Bible), the new technology spread rapidly throughout western Europe: For example, in 1470, a printshop was set up in Paris, followed within a few years by printshops in the Lowlands, Switzerland, Castile, and Aragon (Trager, 1992) and in England in 1476 (Bridgwater & Kurtz, 1963). An outpouring of books, tracts, and periodicals throughout much of western Europe resulted.

Three immediate effects of this rapid diffusion of printing were: (a) a sharp increase in the sheer number of books that were produced, (b) a sharp increase in the number who read the now standardized versions of any given work, and (c) a sharp increase in the geographic diffusion of those works. Libraries now consisted of standardized copies of many books owned by, in addition to the clerical hierarchy, a sizable literate population of merchants and artisans. They were increasingly privately owned and clustered in cities all over Europe, making for a relatively dense penetration of books within widely scattered communities. In contrast with the clerical monopoly of the medieval period, there came into existence a wide social spectrum familiar with diversified collections of standardized texts. One revolutionary effect was that scattered clusters of literate, urban populations were at the same time both pulled apart, reading silently to themselves, and linked to each other through reading books with virtually identical texts and illustrations (Eisenstein, 1987).

The religious and political effects of this interplay between communications technology and social process were profound. Sixteenth century heresy and schism had permanent consequences, in contrast to earlier, medieval heresies that did not result in the establishment of permanent sectarian churches in opposition to Roman Catholicism. The introduction of printing made it possible for Protestants to overcome the priestly monopoly of learning and to propagandize the populace without relying on established institutional resources (Eisenstein, 1987). When, in 1517, Martin Luther posted his 95 theses on the castle church door in Wittenburg, they were intended for an academic, priestly audience and went unchallenged. But, once they were printed in the vernacular, they were quickly disseminated to a relatively large audience by book peddlers who traveled village to village, door to door. Luther was thereby able to address "the whole world — (throughout Germany) in a fortnight and throughout Europe in a month" (Eisenstein, 1987, pp. 150–151). This is an important reason why Wycliffe, who had had to depend on copyists to make his ideas available to a limited, largely priestly audience, achieved what were essentially localized transitory effects, whereas Luther's ideas had widespread, permanent effects (Eisenstein, 1987).

Although an immediate effect of printing was to strengthen the position of dissidents (an effect reminiscent of what happened in the early days of the Internet), it soon became apparent that the long-term effects would depend on nontechnological developments. The 1526 printing in Worms, Germany of the Tyndale Bible, an English translation, was successfully smuggled into England despite efforts to burn all copies (Trager, 1992). Soon afterwards, also in England, Thomas Cromwell used printed documents written in the vernacular to mobilize support for Henry VIII's 1534 schism from Rome (Eisenstein, 1987). Later, comparable effects of printing occurred in the purely secular world. In France, Louis XIV relied on the printed word to gain support for his military ventures. More generally, the intense conflict for ascendancy between centralized monarchies versus parlements and assemblies, whose roots were in more localized medieval institutions, was exacerbated by the propaganda wars made possible by printing (Eisenstein, 1987).

By the 17th century, geographically dispersed and sociologically diverse, but nonetheless linked, publics existed all over western Europe (and were evolving in colonial America). Although by modern standards these emergent publics constituted a small segment of the total European population, the public opinion process became less and less restricted to interpersonal communication within public groupings that could gather in a single location. Moreover, innovative social organizations, most notably national postal systems, were developed that ameliorated the technological limitations that still hampered long-distance communication among the members of these publics (Bridgwater & Kurtz, 1963).

Although intended primarily for commercial use, these postal systems facilitated the rise of collective opinion on a national scale. The Committees of Correspondence that formed in the 13 British colonies during the period leading to the American Revolution is an historically significant example. Supplementing the printed materials available to them, individual dissidents scattered throughout the colonies organized a network of correspondents who carried on a long-distance written debate on English tax and trading policies. Out of that debate there emerged an influential collective opinion opposed to those policies. After independence was declared, this network of correspondents became the core of a significant faction in the Continental Congress (Miller, 1943). Nonetheless, the demand for ever more reliable and speedier means of long-distance communication was still not satisfied.

LONG-DISTANCE COMMUNICATION, TELEGRAPHY, AND ADVANCES IN PRINTING

A dramatic transformation in how news is transmitted across long distances took place during the 19th century, a transformation made possible by developments in both technology and socioeconomic organization: In 1815, receipt of news in London of the outcome of the battle of Waterloo within four days, obtained through the use of carrier pigeons by financier Nathan Meyer Rothschild, enabled London's *Morning Chronicle* to scoop the competition (Trager, 1992). By the end of the century newspapers were using almost instantaneous telegraphic and telephonic transmission of news by national wire services over continental and transoceanic distances.

Introducing the telegraph, the telephone, and the transoceanic cable for long-distance communication involved much more than inventing them. A complex of private companies founded by individual entrepreneurs, and not the innate attributes of the new technologies, was responsible for developing communications networks capable of transmitting news at high speed over long distances. Constructing long-distance telegraph and telephone lines and laying underwater cables required considerable capital investment. Therefore, the existence of patent laws that made the new technologies personal property whose ownership could be commercially exploited by private enterprise was decisive. Additionally, entrepreneurial capital was often supplemented by government subsidies. A brief review of the early years of telegraphy is instructive.

In 1837, three of the leading inventors of the telegraph obtained patents: Charles Wheatstone and William Fothergill Cooke in England, and Samuel B. Morse in the United States. In 1842, the U.S. Congress appropriated money to enable Morse to build an experimental telegraph line connecting Washington and Baltimore, while businessmen Ezra Cornell and Hiram

Sibley provided further backing. Then, in 1855, Congress authorized the construction of a New York–San Francisco line. By 1856, Western Union was established as an amalgamation of a number of hitherto independent telegraph companies, and in 1859 the North American Telegraph Association was formed as a near monopoly. In England the Electric Telegraph was organized in 1845 and, in a parallel development, the Siemens and Hanske Telegraph Company was founded in Germany in 1847. (Trager, 1992).

These companies rapidly developed long-distance communications networks. In 1848, a telegraph line was completed between New York and Chicago while, by that same year, two regional systems were operating in England. A privately owned cable link between Dover and Calais was completed in 1851, and by 1855 there was a telegraph line that extended from London to the Crimea. Private transatlantic service was established during that same period, initiated in 1858 by an exchange of messages between President James Buchanan and Queen Victoria. Although that cable soon failed, it was replaced in 1866, and in 1869 another cable was completed between France and Massachusetts. On the other side of the globe, in 1871 cable service was established from Vladivostok to Shanghai, Hongkong, and Singapore—via Nagasaki. Although most of the world still lay outside this communication network, most major centers (and, in some countries, even secondary centers) were linked in an interconnected, corporately owned communications network.

A new institutional framework for the economical long-distance transmission of news sprang up almost in lock-step with the corporately developed and controlled telegraphic networks, namely, news-gathering organizations that exploited the newly available technology. The first national news agency, Agence Havas (today Agence France-Presse), was established in 1835. When the New York–Chicago telegraph line was constructed in 1848, a group of New York newspapers formed the New York News Agency that enabled each member to use the line at an affordable cost. In 1851, this became the Associated Press. At about the same time, Paul Julius Reuter, who in 1850 had used carrier pigeons to convey financial news, especially final stock prices, took advantage of the 1851 opening of the Dover–Calais cable to found the Reuters News Agency. This dual development fostered the emergence of collective opinion on a national scale in the more highly developed countries.

Advances in the long-distance transmission of news did not in themselves change the fact that the final stage of the transmission of news to a national audience remained dependent on local newspapers. The accessibility of news to the general public was, therefore, contingent on the existence of a literate population. In the history of the public opinion process in the United States, it was of critical importance that a high literacy rate was reached at an early date; by the 1840s, less than one-fourth of the adult population was illiterate (Bureau of Census, 1975). The existence of such a large literate population set the stage for the rise of a mass newspaper audience and not only an elite business readership.

On the other hand, printing technology at the end of the 18th century was insufficent to serve a mass newspaper audience. A sequence of incremental improvements in paper manufacturing and printing furthered a trend that culminated in the economic feasibility of low-cost, mass newspapers. In the United States, from 1797 to 1854, shortages in paper supply were alleviated by new production methods that lowered costs, improved the quality of paper, and made paper available in continuous rolls in any desired size (Trager, 1992). The invention of lithography in 1797, the Adams power-operated press in 1827, the rotary press in 1846, the cylindrical stereotype press in 1866, and the linotype in 1884 were important advances that furthered the economical and speedy printing of newspapers in increasingly large daily printing runs (Trager, 1992). Without these developments, penny newspapers directed to mass audiences, such the New York *Sun*, founded in 1833 and the New York *Herald*, founded in 1835 (Reynolds, 1995, p. 81), would not have been possible. The full impact of the trend to low-cost newspapers, however, was not felt until the end of the century, when the *New York Times* reduced its price to one penny in 1898 (Trager, 1992).

A highly significant end-of-the-century complement to technological change was the creation of the first newspaper chains. Until then, newspapers had been exclusively local. However, in 1882 Joseph Pulitzer, owner of the St. Louis *Post-Dispatch*, acquired the New York *World* while William Randolph Hearst, owner of the San Francisco *Examiner*, bought the New York *Morning Journal* (later renamed the New York *American*). Similarly, the Ridder chain can be traced to 1892 and the Knight chain to 1903 (Trager, 1992). Although local city identification still remained important, if only because of the importance of local retail advertising, news and editorial policies could now be coordinated on a broader scope, strengthening the emergence of collective opinion as a significant national force.

Also critical to the rise of the mass newspaper were developments in newspapers as an advertising medium. Advertising had long been a major source of American newspaper revenues, with the front pages of most papers given over completely to advertising. In the 1840s, a typical newspaper was "a four-page, multi-columned paper with editorials and news on the second page, the other three pages being filled with advertisements, real estate listings, and political announcements" (Reynolds, 1995, p. 115). Advertising was at that time more business than consumer oriented, so that a newspaper's financial stability was not dependent on circulation to a mass audience. Of particular significance, advertising copy was set in solid columns of small agate type with illustrations and company logos virtually unknown, so it had little visual appeal to a mass audience. It was not until after the Civil War that display advertising became commonplace, a development primarily due to department stores seeking large consumer markets (Boorstin, 1974). Although still stodgy by late 20th-century standards, by the late 19th century the appearance and content of American newspapers were increasingly influenced by the efforts to reach large consumer markets.

The post-Civil War period also witnessed the rise of advertising agencies as important actors in the newspaper world. Still prominent in the 1990s, N. W. Ayer was founded in 1868, initially to service religious publications, whereas, in 1878, J. Walter Thompson took over the 14-year-old Carlton and Smith agency. As advertising agencies strengthened their position, their financial relations with newspapers changed. Increasingly, newspaper publishers had to share control with them in a formal and rationalized manner. In 1869, George P. Rowell published the first accurate open list of newspapers; in 1875, N. W. Ayer, acting as an agent for the advertiser rather than for the newspaper, offered open contracts, which, for the first time, gave advertisers the true rates charged by newspapers; and in 1893, the American Newspaper Association (ANPA) adopted a resolution agreeing to pay commissions in the form of discounts to recognized advertising agencies and not to give discounts on space sold directly to advertisers (Trager, 1992). These last developments did not directly affect the public opinion process. However, they clearly wedded the communication of news to commercial interests that were largely independent of, and potentially in conflict with, the public's interest in learning the news.

The technological and institutional developments that have been sketched out did more than create the mass newspaper. They established a business model that in the years to come strongly affected the role of radio and television as news media. Two salient, and continuing, characteristics of this model that concern us are:

1. News has become a commercial commodity whose monetary value depends not only on its ability to inform the public, but also on its ability to attract a mass audience for advertising.

2. The commercial control of how news is transmitted, in interaction with the technical attributes of the technology used, largely determines the size and structure of the news audience.

Neither of these two characteristics can be ascribed directly to the transformation of communications technology that occurred in the 19th century.

BROADCAST MEDIA

Radio's capacity to bring news almost instantaneously to a vast, dispersed audience was evident almost from its birth. In 1912, only a quarter century after Hertz's discovery of electric waves, and less than two decades after Marconi's installation of the first permanent transmitter (in 1896), David Sarnoff became the focus of worldwide attention as he sat for 72 hours in a New York department store window operating a wireless transmitter—first relaying the SOS from the sinking Titanic and then the news of who had survived (Trager, 1992; Barnouw, 1975). There was no question that broadcast technology would transform how news is transmitted. What was not certain was what the nature of that transformation would be.

As was the case with printing in the 19th century, radio and television technology evolved through an accretion of scientific discoveries and technological developments. However, instead of individual inventors and entrepreneurs deciding how to develop the new technology, investment decisions were increasingly made by corporate mangements, often in negotiation with each other (as well as with the federal government). Corporate considerations also overrode the desires of individual engineers and scientists with respect to how the broadcast media would function. When the first paid commercials were aired by radio station WEAF in 1922, thereby establishing advertising as the financial foundation for private control of the airwaves in the United States, Lee DeForest, who had played a pioneering role in developing radio technology, complained, "What have you done with my child?" By 1930, $60,000,000 was spent annually on radio advertising (Trager, 1992).

In the United States, technological advances in radio were a product of intense competition among AT&T, Westinghouse, General Electric, United Fruit, and later RCA—plus the intense involvement of the Navy Department. Not only did these corporations have access to the large sums of capital needed to develop broadcast technology, they each had established business interests to promote and defend. At stake was who would control the manufacture of transmitting and receiving equipment, the actual transmission between transmitting sites, and the content of what was to be transmitted (Barnouw, 1975).

By 1928, the system that was to dominate broadcast media in the United States for at least the next half-century was in place. Its key elements were:

competing broadcast networks using longwave rather than shortwave communication, funding primarily from advertising revenues, with separate but linked equipment manufacturers, with long-distance transmission over telephone networks—all subject to oversight regulation by the federal government intended to protect the public interest (Barnouw, 1975).

As a result, the broadcast of political communications via both radio and television evolved within an environment dominated from its earliest years by commercial interests seeking large audiences for advertising purposes. This commercial domination explains why, unlike developments in some other nations, despite the exceptional capability of the broadcast media to transmit news, in the United States this capability has been subordinated to entertainment (Bogart, 1956; Comstock, Chafee, Katzman, McCombs, & Roberts, 1978). Two circumstances in which this pattern is broken—when extraordinary news events capture national attention (as in national crises, overwhelming disasters, etc.) or when there is competition for advertising revenue (e. g., during election campaigns)—underline the extent to which nontechnological developments have influenced how the broadcast media affect the generation of collective opinion.

Despite the rapid commercialization of radio (and television), politicians recognized early on that the broadcast media gave them a powerful new channel for communicating to the public. In 1918, Woodrow Wilson's "Fourteen Points" were broadcast to Europe from New Brunswick, New Jersey. In 1923, the opening session of the U. S. Congress was broadcast for the first time. In 1924, Calvin Coolidge's election-eve campaign speech was broadcast on a 26-station coast-to-coast hookup. And in 1933, by which time more that 50% of U.S. households owned radios, newly elected President Franklin D. Roosevelt gave his first "fireside chat," bypassing newspapers to explain directly to the public his plan to deal with the banking crisis that faced the nation. Similarly, with respect to television, in 1927, then Secretary of Commerce Herbert Hoover appeared on an experimental telecast for AT&T (Barnouw, 1975). And in 1948, at a time when only 1,000,000 households had a television set, both the Democratic and Republican national conventions were televised. Thus, even though radio and television were primarily entertainment media, from their beginnings they played a crucial role in the revolutionary transformation of political communications that matured in the 1970s.

To a considerable degree, the revolutionary impact of radio and television on the development of mutual awareness is based on two technological factors. During the 19th century, telegraph and cable had made it possible to transmit messages almost instantaneously over transcontinental and transoceanic distances, but only between physically linked points. Also, advances in print technology had made mass communications, such as newspapers, economically feasible, but at the cost of any semblance of direct, personal contact between writers and their audiences. The broadcast media differ sharply in these two respects, compensating for both types of limitations.

Because the broadcast media do not require any physical linkage between transmitters and receivers, they introduced a flexibility in communications combined with centralized control over both short and long distances that had far-reaching implications. Geographically dispersed, even national, audiences became directly reachable at the same instant in time, facilitating central control of communications to those audiences and the coordination of multiphase campaigns. As Lang and Lang noted, centralized control of the microphone and camera provided an opportunity to focus and monopolize audience attention, reducing the likelihood that nonprogrammed or unwanted stimuli might introduce unwanted message content (Bogart, 1956). Furthermore, scattered individuals, families, and other small groups could be reached at locations suited to their varying convenience and comfort needs, and in ways that could nonetheless foster a sense of participating in a common, transcendant event. In this way, the emergence of mutual awareness on a scale not hitherto imaginable became possible. On the other hand, the lack of any feedback in broadcast technology was an inherent weakness. Across the years, public opinion polling became a major, although imperfect, substitute for this technological limitation.

Of a consequence at least equal in importance to eliminating the need for physical linkage, transmitting voice and (later) visual images helped break down two social barriers to the rise of mass publics that print media cannot overcome. First, literacy was no longer a precondition to communicating to mass audiences. As illiterates and nonliterates become effective members of mass audiences, they become participants, albeit passive, in the communications process essential to the emergence of mutual awareness. For the first time, the entire population of national societies became potential, and often actual, members of "The Public."

Second, much of the feeling of personal contact—conveyed by the tone and modulation of the speaker's voice, later enhanced by facial expression, gesture, and body language—that adds to the effectiveness of interpersonal communication was in large part restored to political discourse. In particular, the charisma of extraordinary individuals could now reach out to mass audiences (including nonliterate populations). At the same time, seemingly individual-to-individual, this communication also called individuals in the mass audience to membership in a national effort. The effectiveness of Franklin D. Roosevelt's radio "fireside chats" in rallying public support for the New Deal in the early 1930s is legendary, as is the morale-sustaining effect of Winston Churchill's radio addresses during Great Britain's darkest days in World War II.

But the value of mastering radio (and later television) was not limited to those in high office, or even to those in office. During the early 1930s, Francis Townsend, Father Charles Coughlin, and Senator Huey Long stood out as leaders of politically significant mass movements based largely, if not completely, on their use of radio. Although noncharismatic personalities suffered in this new environment, the need to overcome deficiencies and nurture qualities that could be effectively broadcast was rapidly recognized. In a precursor to the extensive and elaborate training in how to perform on television that became standard for politicians in the 1980s, in 1936 the Republican party hired a voice coach for Alfred Landon whose flat, dull voice hindered his unsuccessful presidential campaign. The Republican National Committee also organized a radio division that year (Brinkley, 1994).

NEW NONBROADCAST MEDIA

Along with the growth of the broadcast media was the development of nonbroadcast technologies including movies, audio- and videotapes, closed circuit television, and fax machines. Unlike the typical pattern for broadcast media, all these technologies make it possible to transmit standardized messages to geographically dispersed but centrally controlled and organized audiences. In common with the broadcast media, except for fax, they are suitable for communicating to both literate and illiterate audiences. When coordinated with broadcast media, often in organized group contexts ranging from mass rallies and demonstrations to local meetings linked electronically to a central source, these nonbroadcast media make it possible to integrate mass and group modes of communication. In such a communications environment, public debate becomes an intricate process of mass and targeted communications that, on occasion, may be integrated with interpersonal communications.

The role of movies in the public opinion process is most obvious when they are controlled by governments. Leni Riefenstahl's 1934 paean to the Nazi party, *Triumph of the Will*, is an outstanding example of the political use of movies by a government. But even when they are ostensibly merely entertainment, movies can play an important role in building a common universe of discourse and dedication to a collective purpose. World War II movies such as *Mrs. Miniver* and *Destination Tokyo* are examples of entertainment movies made and distributed by private, profit-seeking corporations that also served a government's propagandistic purposes. Additionally, numerous movies about politically significant events and conditions—ranging from *Birth of a Nation* and *Gone with the Wind*, to *Grapes of Wrath*, *Dead End*, and *Boyz N the Hood*, to *Platoon*, *JFK*, and *Hoop Dreams*—have affected public debate about those events and conditions. In all these cases, movies made it possible to reach mass audiences with partisan interpretations of controversial events and circumstances.

Audiotapes, and to a lesser degree videotapes, are relatively inexpensive media that, like movies, do not depend on literacy and benefit from the effectiveness of voice and gesture. Because they are free from many of the production and distribution problems to which movies are subject, they make it practical for disadvantaged political factions to communicate to geographically dispersed, minimally organized, and often illiterate audiences.

A politically significant example of the capability of audio tapes to reach subrosa mass audiences is their use in the 1970s in Iran by adherents of the then-exiled Ayatollah Khomenei. Those tapes circumvented government control of broadcast media and brought the Ayatollah's voice to groups of his supporters scattered throughout the country. By using audiotapes, a tightly controlled central source was able to transmit its messages to a mass audience and foster the rise of a revolutionary collective opinion.

Subversive, subrosa groups are not the only users of audio and videotapes. The low-cost flexibility of tapes makes them suitable for use by a variety of political factions, including local political party organizations, single-issue movements, and dissident groupings. In the United States in the 1990s, the relatively low production cost of videotapes in combination with widespread ownership of VCRs made it feasible to distribute them during election campaigns to preselected lists of likely adherents. Moreover, the effectiveness of videotapes need not be based only on the transmitted messages. When shown to small gatherings, their audiences experience being part of small groups that are, in turn, part of larger networks, all of which can be centrally organized and controlled. Similar considerations apply to the use of closed circuit television.

Fax and telemarketing technologies have not created a new approach to the conduct of political campaigns but they do enhance the reach and efficiency of those campaigns. They make it economical for a single source to target standardized messages to individual members of very large, geographically dispersed audiences, and within a very short span of time. This capability overcomes much of the inefficiency in reaching narrowly targeted audiences typical of mass media, both broadcast and nonbroadcast. Furthermore, as a byproduct of the personalized addressing of fax messages or direct voice contact, audience identification with the sponsoring organization may be reinforced.

Fax communication differs technologically from the nonbroadcast media in ways that have been used to create a hitherto unusual combination of interpersonal and mass communications. Especially noteworthy technological attributes include the following: Communication is between points that are electronically linked through an already existing wired network; access to that network is achieved by installing supplementary equipment at a relatively modest cost; automatic fax machines receive messages without the recipient's consent, even though the recipient's "address" must be known; although pictures and graphics can be transmitted by fax, it is particularly well-suited for sending written messages; the time needed to transmit a message over long distances and to many dispersed points is greatly reduced compared to mail. This combination of technological attributes makes fax communications an efficient alternative to mail and to most forms of mass communications for reaching dispersed, but targeted audiences with short, standardized written messages, and within short time frames.

A variant use of existing telephone systems, comparable to telemarketing in the commercial world, is substituting direct voice communications for fax messages. The key to this use is acquiring computerized telephone listings of targeted audiences. Such lists are typically developed by political action groups or political parties as part of their fund-raising activities. They may also be bought from commercial organizations. When telephone calls are made by volunteers in local areas, costs become minimal. Taped messages can also be used, though their effectiveness may be limited.

A limitation of most mass media noted earlier is the paucity of feedback channels of communication. The availability of fax and telemarketing technology facilitates centrally controlled feedback from mass audiences, again within very short time periods. Appeals for mass response through mail or telegram have long characterized political campaigns, and they continue. But, normally, response to such appeals takes time and relatively small proportions of mass audiences respond. Fax and telemarketing technology shorten the response time by getting appeals out much faster. Very importantly, by targeting those known to be committed, a high rate of response from these audience can be expected. In any event, the use of these technologies in political communications cannot be attributed to technology as such but to their applicability in long-established activities.

Communications environments dominated by a complex of broadcast and nonbroadcast mass media like those just discussed contrast sharply with those characterized primarily by conversation and other forms of interpersonal exchange. Most important, rather than discussion and debate emerging out of spontaeous interpersonal interchanges, they can now be planned and directed by groups that have access to and control these media. Correlatively, rather than mutual awareness and collective opinion being spontaneous products of public discussion and debate, they increasingly become manufactured products. One major aspect of this development is the decline of traditional political parties with grass roots in local precincts. Parallel to this decline is the rise of centrally controlled single-issue movements that seek to mobilize opinion through cultivating personal involvement. A consequence of these developments is that competition for control of communication media, and efforts to protect freedom of access to them, convert the social process of discourse into a political struggle in its own right.

COMMUNICATIONS IN CYBERSPACE

The rise of the Internet, a decentralized computer communications medium, has been welcomed by many as a powerful stimulant to the unrestricted exchange of individual opinions. Since its formative years, regardless of distance and political boundary, anyone on the Internet has been able contact anyone else on it free from central control, on topics determined by personal interest and at times set by individual preference and convenience. And the World Wide Web has made it possible for corporations, political organizations, private groups, and individuals alike to create specialized bulletin boards and town halls to pursue their varied interests. A specific application of the World Wide Web relevant to the public opinion process is the extent to which sites set up by news organizations, private corporations, government agencies, and even individuals are referred to in times of crisis (*New York Times*, August 6, 1996). By facilitating individual participation in public debate, the Internet technology might, therefore, stimulate the reemergence of mutual awareness as a spontaneous outcome of interpersonal and group communications rather than as a manufactured product.

Although the Internet may indeed have the potential for such a development, we must remember that its liberating attributes are not technologically innate. They are the result of a particular historical context and as such are subject to change. By the mid-1990s, Internet communications became increasingly subject to restrictive influences that may in time limit its countervailing effects vis-á-vis mass communications.

The evolution of the Internet as a decentralized communications system was determined by military and political interests. The Advanced Research Projects Agency (ARPA) had responsibility for developing technology in areas of relevance to national security. In the late 1960s and 1970s, the Department of Defense was concerned that reliable high-bandwidth computer communications among four university-based research centers depended on the national telephone system. Because the telephone system was centrally organized, anything that disabled part of the system (e. g., a nuclear attack) could disable all communications among the four centers (nodes). The solution was to take advantage of developments already underway that made it feasible to establish direct links among the four research centers that were independent of the centralized telephone network. Initially, leased telephone lines were used. Later, these were supplemented by other links such as satellites, which made the Internet accessible to areas with poor telephone facilities. To facilitate internodal communications, all four research centers agreed to adhere to the same procedures. Thus, even if one node were knocked out the others could still communicate directly with each other. (Elmer-Dewitt, 1994; Hahn & Stout, 1994).

As the original system was expanded to include other nodes, a decentralized international network evolved in which each node could communicate directly with each of the others independently of the functional status of any one node—without having first to go through some central point that coordinated linkages among all nodes. As participation expanded over time, communications capabilities were improved and expanded by programs that were contributed by participants, who also developed informal procedural rules and conventions to their mutual satisfaction. The outcome has been described as "one giant, seamless global computing machine" (Elmer-Dewitt, 1994, p. 52), a machine with no-one in charge, that functions without laws or police, and without any single organization paying the cost (Hahn & Stout, 1994). The Internet as a large cooperative of interconnected computer users who voluntarily agree to follow common rules of interaction is, therefore, the product of a specific historical context and not simply intrinsic technological attributes.

Under other circumstances, computer technology could have been used to develop a very different kind of network, for example, a centralized corporately owned facility. A case in point is the French Minitel system that was developed by the French telephone system as an economically efficient, centrally controlled facility that would replace hard-copy telephone directories. Telephone subscribers were provided with small, nonstandard display terminals and display boards that could be used to look up any other subscriber in the nation. Although this development facilitated nationwide interpersonal and intergroup communications, we should not forget that it gave only limited access to a centralized phone company facility for the latter's advantage and was not a product of the subscribers themselves.

The principle of open access has led to controversy over such issues as the use of Internet for advertising, access of minors to pornography, and use of abusive language. Concern about the pornographic use of Internet led to a Department of Justice investigation of the content of Internet messages that resulted in the arrest of alleged violators of existing pornography laws and a demand for the passage of additional laws (Elmer-Dewitt, 1994; Johnston, 1995). It also led a German government agency to threaten sanctions that suddenly raise the prospect of government controls that far exceed traditional limits on national sovereignty. And major services like America Online, AT&T Worldnet, and Compuserve now impose severe restrictions on what many consider to be offensive vocabulary and topics (Johnston, 1996).

We must also take into account the fact that "not all the new [communications] technologies have been snatched up by the American public. ... The way a nation communicates is dependent not only on what is technologically possible but also on what the average person is willing and able to pay for" (Mayer, 1994, p. 125). With respect to the Internet, it evolved under circumstances that obscure two restrictive factors—cost and literacy. The importance of these factors is evident in the 1995 incidence of households with personal computers. This incidence differed sharply by the combination of education and income—ranging from a high of 73% among college graduates with household incomes of $50,000 or more and 62% among those with some college and incomes of $50,000 or more down to 29% among those with high school or less and incomes of $30,000–$49,999 and 14% among those with high school or less and incomes under $30,000 (*Times Mirror*, 1995).

Even though the computer hardware and programming necessary to participate in the Internet can be costly, at its inception the Internet was accessible to the staff of participating institutions at no perceived cost to the individual user. Staff members who had access through their places of employment were able to use the system for their private purposes, a practice that spread rapidly and contributed to making the Internet a national and even worldwide medium for exchanging opinions at no personal cost.

But, over the years, the Internet was transformed from a network dominated by academic and government research institutions into a primarily commercial network used by large corporations and, through commercial gateways, by small companies and individuals. The desire for access to the Internet among individuals and corporations outside the system has created a market for commercial nodes such as America OnLine, Compuserve, and Prodigy, as well as specialized gateway centers. These services are available at monthly subscription charges (between $10–$35 in the mid-1990s), plus telephone line charges. In 1995, an initial $100 registration fee plus a $50 annual fee was imposed to compensate the National Science Foundation for costs it had been incurring in maintaining a central register of domain addresses (Lewis, 1995). The Internet is no longer cost-free to individual users.

We also need to consider that the typical financial status of individual users at the early research institutions was comfortable, that they had multiple personal uses for computers, and that hardware prices fell. Consequently, many of them felt justified in purchasing the personal computer hardware and needed software, and in addition to paying access fees to commercial gateways. Similar considerations led to a growing population of middle and upper income computer-owning households independent of participating institutions and corporations. As a result, awareness of, and participation in the Internet expanded far beyond its initial boundaries.

Literacy, both with respect to ability to read print and ability to use a computer, may also limit further growth in Internet participation. Because the Internet began in a highly educated and computer-literate environment, exchanging opinions through written messages, especially through computer communications, was not a strange behavior to adopt. Neither were the necessary skills particularly difficult to learn for those who had access. At this writing, whether the need to be literate to participate in the Internet will in the future be a serious barrier to increased participation is a moot point.

When considering the possibility that lack of interest and skill, compounded by cost considerations, will limit the public's use of computerized communications, it is instructive to compare the speed with which other communications innovations have been adopted. In the 6-year period from May 1949 to May 1955, ownership of television sets increased phenomenally from 6% to 74% of U.S. households. In comparison, home ownership of computers increased from 3% to 14% during the 6-year period of December 1982 to December 1988. Across the next six years, during which the cost of a personal computer had dropped, the average annual rate of increase was slightly higher, so that by 1995, 36% of U.S. households had a personal computer of some type. However, only 20% had a modem that enables them to connect with other computers through telephone lines. Furthermore, knowledge of how to use a computer, often learned on a job, grew slowly from 22% of adults in 1983 to 36% in 1989, whereas in 1995 32% used a computer at home (Mayer, 1993, 1994; *Times Mirror* Center for the People and the Press, 1995). What is still uncertain is the extent to which cost considerations and computer literacy will continue to limit participation in the Internet primarily to those in the middle and upper socioeconomic strata.

Finally, we must remember that many personal-computer owners do not use them in ways related to the public opinion process. In 1995, 14% of U.S. adults were online users of some type, but mostly for reasons that have nothing to do with the public opinion process. Only 6 in 20 of those users (or about 4% of all adults) went online at least once a week to get news, and less than 1 in 20 (or less than 1% of all adults) to discuss politics. (*Times Mirror* Center for the People and the Press, 1955). Ten years after the the introduction of personal computers into the general consumer market, their role in the public opinion process was confined to furthering communications within a tiny socioeconomic elite.

It is possible, perhaps even probable, that the Internet's potential to counteract the effects of mass media on mutual awareness and collective opinion will be limited to an educated, economic elite. If that were to happen, the rise of computer communications may intensify existing opposition between mass and elite collective opinions (see chap. 6). In addition, the commercialization of the Internet, plus the demand to control offensive message content, has changed the "information highway" from an open road to a patrolled toll road. At this writing, it is uncertain what long-term effects the Internet will have on the public opinion process.

THE IMPACT OF NEW TECHNOLOGIES

There is no doubt that the way in which mutual awareness emerges and collective opinion forms can be significantly altered by change in communications technology. Just as clearly, the institutional frameworks within which technological capabilities are organized and directed can be equally significant. What is decisive is the interaction between technological and institutional factors in particular historical contexts. It is as a result of those interactions that over the centuries, (a) the size and heterogeneity of populations that participate in the public opinion process have increased, (b) opportunities and capabilities to engage in public debate have in some ways been extended and broadened and in others narrowed and centralized, (c) the cohesiveness of groups participating in public debate has, in a number of ways, become more dependent on formal organization and formal leadership and less on personal leadership, (d) access to public channels of communication has become increasingly dependent on financial resources, and (e) the susceptibility of the public opinion process to centralized control and manipulation has been strengthened.

These changes in the functioning of collective opinion, important as they are, have not in themselves determined the ways in which collective opinion is integrated into the political process. In particular, they have not caused any change in the political channels through which collective opinion is allowed to be expressed and so influence the governance of a people. To deal with the political role of collective opinion, we must turn our attention to the question of how that role is affected by the premises on which a people's political organization is based.

5

Public Opinion in Nondemocratic Societies

The mere existence of an aroused collective opinion tells us little about how it will affect a people's political life. That depends on how much *legitimacy* is accorded to the political expression of collective opinion—that is, whether, and under what conditions, the expression of collective opinion is accepted as a basis for governing. To analyze the political functioning of collective opinion, we must examine the legitimization process and its consequences within different political systems.

Throughout history, political thinkers have argued about the legitimacy of collective opinion, differing as to what kind of political role, if any, it ought to have. Some have endorsed it, welcoming its forcefulness, whereas others have been dismayed by an alleged mindless and riotous quality. Controversy has also raged about how to tell whether there has been an authentic or true expression of public thought concerning some issue. In our review of these controversies, we focus on whether a political system provides some kind of role for the public opinion process in governance, and if it does, how. This enables us to to examine the ways in which the political role of collective opinion is shaped by the degree of legitimacy the public opinion process has within a political system.

THE LEGITIMIZATION PROCESS

To some, the sheer existence of a universally forceful collective opinion signifies that it always incorporates some element of legitimacy. Bryce's assertion that "opinion has really been the chief and ultimate power in nearly all nations at nearly all times" (Bryce, 1891) must be understood in these terms. He recognized that throughout history many regimes began in military conquest and that despotic monarchies and oligarchies have been able to rule against the will of the people through military tyranny. But, he also pointed to the force of unspoken, even unconscious opinions, asserting that even if affection and active approval are lacking, governmental authority rests on the reverence, awe, and silent acquiescence of the numerical majority. Bryce concluded that public opinion has been primarily an acquiescent, passive force in history and that not unless and until a nation reaches an advanced stage of development can it play an active role in governance.

The perceived contrast between an active versus a passive role for collective opinion in large part derives from an opposition between two views—the assumption that governments rule through the active consent and will of those governed versus the position that all that is required is a people's acquiescence. In both cases, however, the continuing existence of any political system is believed to depend on an element of voluntary obedience that testifies to the right of those in power to rule. Furthermore, voluntary obedience is assumed to reflect adherence to a system of beliefs as to who has the right to govern and why they have that right. Those beliefs also define the powers that can properly be wielded by those in authority and under what conditions (Weber, 1968). That is why:

> every ... system attempts to establish and cultivate the belief in its legitimacy. But according to the kind of legitimacy which is claimed, the type of obedience, the kind of administrative staff developed to guarantee it, and the mode of exercising authority, will all differ fundamentally. Equally fundamental is the variation in effect. (Weber, 1968, p. 213)

When relating the legitimacy of collective opinion to variations in political systems, we must take into account the fact that historical political systems have differed profoundly in the roles they assign to the public opinion process in ways that cannot be predicted solely from their other distinguishing characteristics. Consider, for example, Weber's typology that differentiates systems whose claims to legitimacy are based on legal-bureaucratic, traditional, or charismatic grounds, that is, systems in which authority (a) is exercised in accord with rules of legal competence, regardless of how those in authority originally came to office; (b) is exercised in accord with what are considered to be age-old rules and powers; or (c) flows from individuals perceived to have exceptional powers or qualities (Weber, 1968). Historically, legitimacy has been denied to the public opinion process in all three types, whereas there is no apparent reason why legitimacy could not be granted in any one of them. Therefore, instead of trying to correlate the legitimacy of collective opinion to some comprehensive political typology, we ask which of three conditions describe its status in a polity:

1. Whether collective opinion is accepted as a legitimate basis for governing.
2. Whether collective opinion is tolerated only for so long as it acquiesces to a system based on a different governing principle.
3. Whether collective opinion is rejected as an illegitimate challenge to any existing system.

Applying these criteria, we can specify and compare three empirical types of political systems—authoritarian, totalitarian, and democratic—differentiated in terms of the legitimacy that the public opinion process has in each. Although totalitarianism is often treated as a subtype of authoritarianism, for reasons later discussed related to differences in the functioning of the public opinion process, it is meaningful and important for our purposes to distinguish the two as separate types. By defining these three types in terms of the legitimacy of the public opinion process, an attribute that typically receives passing if any attention in the construction of political typologies, we give legitimacy a needed saliency in our analysis.

The differentiation into authoritarian, totalitarian, and democratic political systems is not intended to serve as a comprehensive typology of political systems, something that would go far beyond our needs. Moreover, our treatment of authoritarianism, totalitarianism, and democracy does not preclude relating each to a more general typology at some later time.

AUTHORITARIAN POLITICAL SYSTEMS

As we use the term, *authoritarianism* is a heterogeneous concept, applicable to many different historical types of political systems, including traditional legitimate regimes such as monarchies and aristocratic regimes, as well as the variety of nontotalitarian military and political dictatorships that characterized much of the 20th-century (Linz, 1970, 1975, 1993). These various authoritarian systems differ with respect to such matters as their tolerance for some degree of political pluralism, their efforts to mobilize the populace politically, their bureaucratic structure, the sociodemographic origins and composition of the ruling elite, the primacy of charismatic leadership, and their roots in history and tradition (Linz, 1993). Authoritarian regimes also differ with respect to the extent to which their political thinking is intellectually organized and elaborated (ideology) as compared with more emotional, noncodified ways of reacting (mentality). Additionally, some are revolutionary whereas others seek to preserve established political, economic, and social institutions (Linz, 1975).

Typologies of authoritarian regimes have been developed to deal analytically with all these differences (see Linz, 1975). Although these differences can and do have major consequences, in all authoritarian systems collective opinion at most has a limited political role. For this reason, we do not attempt to delineate how this role may vary across all types of authoritarian regimes. Instead, we examine in detail only one historical example, medieval Europe—plus some obervations on a 20th-century military dictatorship. One advantage of focusing on medieval Europe is that the political principles on which its governments were based differ markedly from contemporary authoritarian regimes. This lack of familiarity graphically highlights the very different role collective opinion played in that system. First, however, we need to define the authoritarian view of the public opinion process.

Advocates of authoritarian systems maintain that it is the right and duty of established elites to rule, and that the well being of the society as a whole will suffer if that right and duty is undermined. They espouse entrenched hierarchical orders whose power and privilege is justified by some transcendant principle such as "the divine right of kings," right of conquest, tradition, or lineage that protects a society. In medieval Europe, "Prelates and kings were (believed to be) … blessed with divine grace and presented as those who voiced the Vox Dei (voice of God) in actual reality" (Menache, 1990, p. 213). Thus, in the authoritarian's view, substituting the common man for the principles that sustain the existing order can only lead to immorality, disorder, and violence (Ortega y Gasset, 1950). Clearly, anyone who seeks to overthrow authoritarian government as such, and not only a particular ruler or dynasty, first faces the task of undermining its legitimizing transcendent principle. The anticlericalism of 18th-century philosophers played that role antecedent to the French Revolution (de Tocqueville, 1955).

Under authoritarian systems, the only tolerable collective opinion among the general populace is a prepolitical one, relevant to social control at the communal level, for example, local enforcement of communal values within villages. Matters of state are considered to be the prerogative of the authorities and should be of no concern to a ruler's subjects. Symptomatic of this position is the desire expressed by Frederick the Great that his subjects not concern themselves with the wars he was waging (Speier, 1951). Under such conditions, any politicized collective opinion that might exist must be clandestine (Speier, 1980). To maintain political and social order in times of unrest, stirrings of public discussion must be discovered as soon as possible so that any nascent rebellious collective opinion can be squashed before it becomes a political force. The hangman's noose, Maistre's symbol of a well-ordered society, is the authoritarian's ultimate answer to collective opinion.

PUBLIC OPINION IN NONDEMOCRATIC SOCIETIES

Of course, politically significant differences of opinion do arise within and between authoritarian elites—for example, between contending aristocratic or courtly factions— stemming from conflicting personal and group aspirations and interests. In the normal course of events, such differences can be expected to lead to the emergence of a collective court opinion limited to members of the elite. That emergence will, of course, be subject to the dynamics of such processes as mutual awareness and opinion leadership discussed in chapter 3. Only in the restricted sense of "court opinion" is it possible to speak of legitimate collective opinion in authoritarian states. Similarly, many 20th-century military dictatorships have tolerated limited political pluralism. Even in fascist Italy, in its early years, existing centers of power such as the king, the army, the Church, and big business were able to maintain considerable independence and did not depend on Mussolini's will (Lytelton, 1976). But this restricted sense contrasts sharply with the legitimacy of a collective opinion that encompasses the population at large. This contrast is evident in the difference between propaganda wars as waged before the French Revolution and in the 20th century:

> One may properly speak of diplomatic propaganda during the *ancien regime*, intended to influence the decisions of foreign courts, but there was nothing of modern propaganda devised to arouse war enthusiasm in civilians. (Speier, 1951, p. 5).

Therefore, we differentiate between court opinion, which can be politically legitimate in authoritarian regimes, and collective opinion, which cannot.

Perhaps the most influential argument in western philosophy against giving any legitimacy to collective opinion is in Book VII of Plato's *The Republic*. Plato's position has been described as denying any value at all to collective opinion (Palmer, 1950). As developed in Plato's analogy of prisoners in a cave who can see only shadows and hear only echos, the truth that is known to those prisoners is nothing more than the "shadows of images." True knowledge is denied even to those who are released, blinded as they are by the glare of the sun and believing as they do that "the shadows which he formerly saw are truer than the objects which are now shown him" (Plato, pp. 253–255). Only through habit and exercise can the " power and capacity of learning (which) exists in the soul already" (Plato, pp. 258–259) be developed to the point that the soul turns to the world of being—the world of what Plato considered to be valid knowledge.

Therefore, Plato continued, the best minds of the state should be developed and then compelled to return to the prisoners in the cave to lead and rule them. The perfect state will exist only if a people's rulers are those who have been educated to rule and not left to the mistaken opinions of the people. This concept of the perfect state as one ruled by philosopher-kings clearly denies to collective opinion any legitimate role in governance. It further leads to the image of the ideal ruler as a benevolent despot, a despot who follows not the passions of an ignorant, untutored people, but his own understanding of what is good and true as derived from a lifetime of study. This image, even if it has never been realized in history, nonetheless epitomizes a set of beliefs that has been used to justify rule by presumably qualified aristocrats or monarchs.

Although authoritarians deny collective opinion the right to participate in governance, they have had to recognize its existence and potential political significance. For example, in 1809, Prince von Metternich, the Austrian Empire's ambassador to Napoleonic France, advised his government that collective opinion needed a "peculiar cultivation" because "it penetrates like religion the most hidden recesses where administrative measures have no influence" (Speier, 1951, p. 4–5). Clearly, to comprehend the political role of the public opinion process in authoritarian regimes, we must examine the ways in which authoritarians resolve the discordance between their belief that collective opinion is illegitimate and their recognition that it nonetheless persists.

The medieval European concept *Vox populi, vox Dei*, and the Chinese concept "mandate from heaven" each in its way exemplifies a standard authoritarian resolution, namely, that the legitimate role of collective opinion is passive acquiesence. The idea that the voice of the people is the voice of God stems from the inference that the forcefulness of the people's voice is a manifestation of a presumed sacred origin. An aroused collective opinion, it follows, is a dangerous aberration and should be placated rather than ignored. In the same vein, so long as a regime retains its mandate from heaven, the populace at large can be expected to accept that regime's right to rule and will not support hostile forces. But, if a regime deviates from righteous rule, its mandate will be lost. Natural catastrophes, unrest, and disobedience will become rampant, and the previously stable regime will topple.

But even when authoritarians accept that an aroused collective opinion cannot be safely ignored, they reject the idea that the voice of the people should have an active role in governance—in establishing policy, in deciding how to deal with issues, in promulgating laws. In their view, those functions should be reserved only to established authority, with the scope of the public's judgment limited to rejecting that authority's legitimacy only when its underlying morality has been violated. Even if a passive, acquiescent role for collective opinion is given some legitimacy in authoritarian regimes, it is limited to judging whether a specific ruling authority's legitimacy has been compromised. It has no legitimacy to govern in its own right.

Many authoritarians deny even that limited role to collective opinion. Alcuin, the 8th century medieval scholar, condemned the maxim, *Vox populi, vox Dei*, arguing that the "opinions of the populace are always close to insanity" (Menache, 1990, p. 3). This contempt for collective opinion from a leading theologian was of particular importance at a time when a major goal of ecclesiastical thinkers was to defend the principle that the unquestionable source of all political legitimacy is the voice of God, and that that voice can be heard only through the Church. Alcuin's position was that the vox populi is to be led, and led by the Church, rather than followed.

SOME HISTORICAL MANIFESTATIONS OF AUTHORITARIANISM

The role of collective opinion in authoritarian regimes is exemplified in two of the most important political episodes in medieval European history—the investiture controversy and the First Crusade. Because the investiture controversy was the core of one of the most dramatic and decisive political conflicts in medieval European history, it is instructive to consider what role collective opinion played in it. With respect to the First Crusade, the enthusiastic popular support that it sparked makes it a crucial test case. As descibed later, in both instances, the significant actions were taken by theocratic or monarchical authorities with little regard for the collective opinion of the day.

The investiture controversy, which originated in the struggle of the medieval Catholic Church to establish itself and the Roman Pope as the true and sole source of political legitimacy, sounds strange to modern ears. The Church maintained that through the unbroken line of Bishops of Rome back to Peter, and so to Jesus and God, it represented the true Vox Dei. It further asserted that the legitimacy of kings was established by the sacred rite of anointment, thereby subordinating them to the Church. In opposition were two secular principles of political legitimacy—the feudal principle of personal loyalty to a military or other secular leader and the dynastic principle of inheritance of office (Menache, 1990).

The conflict, therefore, was between two authoritarian principles for establishing political legitimacy —theocracy versus monarchy— with no reference whatsoever to the opinions and wishes of a king's subjects or the Church's parishioners. The former offered a Christ-centered concept of a monarch—someone who reigns by the grace of God, whose legitimate occupation of office is enhanced and supported by a personal charisma that, in turn, is testified to by adherence to standards of social justice promulgated by the Church. In contrast, according to the monarchical principle, a king's legitimacy derives, initially, from his having earned the personal loyalty of his followers. By the same token, his legitimacy is lost by failure to live up to his office or to command personal loyalty. Loyalty is then handed down to his descendants by appeal to the dynastic principle. Furthermore, the dynastic principle can act to maintain a dynasty even when a "bad" king reigns, that is, when a king violates his people's standards of justice and morality, does not conform to its laws, or is incompetent (Menache, 1990).

The investiture controversy came to a head in the 11th century when, in opposition to the Holy Roman Emperor Henry IV, Pope Gregory VII attempted to establish "the complete freedom of the church from control by the state, the negation of the sacramental character of kingship, and the domination of the papacy over secular rulers" (Cantor, 1993, p. 245). In that struggle, Gregory threatened Henry with excommunication, which among other things, would have resulted in Henry losing most of his army, because more than two thirds of it came from ecclesiastical lands (Cantor, 1993). In the winter of 1077, an apparently repentant Henry was received by Gregory at the Italian village of Canossa, temporarily ending the conflict.

Some have contended that Gregory agreed to receive Henry because to do otherwise "would have sufficed to turn public opinion against him" (Cantor, 1993, p. 270). But this was the " public opinion" of crowned heads, Church statesmen, and other European rulers, what we have called court opinion, and not the collective opinion of the general populace. Moreover, the significance of this court opinion lay in the direct control of military strength wielded by those involved. Nowhere in this process can we find signs of a general collective opinion playing a role in resolving which principle of legitimacy should be adopted, or whether some compromise should be developed.

Whereas the investiture controversy was clearly a struggle between medieval elites for political supremacy with limited, if any interest, to commoners, the Crusades touched on the deeply felt convictions of commoners as well as elites. The Crusades had an avowed religious goal—restoring Christian rule to the Holy Land—that, at least at first, appeared to transcend usual military, economic, and territorial interests. Church functionaries worked hard at arousing popular support for participating in the First Crusade through their sermons and letters (Menache, 1990). As spread by such popular leaders as Walter the Penniless and Peter the Hermit, this goal captured the imagination and commitment of French and German peasants, and of urban masses from the Rhineland. They then set out on their own "people's crusade" for the Holy Land before the army that conducted the First Crusade could be organized (Bridgwater & Kurtz, 1963; Cantor, 1993). At first glance, it would appear that, in this case at least, collective opinion had played an independently significant role in medieval history. In fact, the various "people's Crusades" were no more than tragic footnotes to history. When their participants reached the eastern Mediterranean, they were mostly slaughtered or sold into slavery.

The First Crusade was conceived and carried out by the established authorities of medieval Europe. The idea of the Crusade came from Pope Urban II who carefully planned his proclamation long before he announced it at the Council of Clermont in 1095. He summoned French bishops and abbots to the Council, urging them to bring with them the prominent lords of their provinces (Cantor, 1993). That is to say, Urban's audience at Clermont consisted, according to plan, of representatives of the feudal elite and their immediate followers.

The enthusiastic response of Urban's audience, echoing back to him his call "God wills it!", the speed with which knights all over western Europe "took the cross," and the response of commoners just noted all testify that his appeal touched a wellspring of popular feeling. However, the spontaneous grass-roots response of commoners was not wanted by the Church, which sought rather to enlist the aristocracy and their knights (Menache, 1990). People's crusades, even when inspired by legitimate authority, were irrelevant to medieval elites who went about their business in their accustomed ways. "The papacy ... dismissed the momentary social earthquake of the people's crusade with a bewildered shrug and set about organizing the French feudal princes and knights into a crusading army" (Cantor, 1993, p. 294).

The First Crusade was finally launched, a year after Urban's call, as a joint enterprise of the papacy and the feudal aristocracy with minimal participation by commoners. As subjects, the latter had no legitimate political role to play. The collective opinion of commoners not only did not play any role in decision making, it was not even allowed to play much of a supporting role.

The authoritarian disdain for the public opinion process is also evident in the Salazar dictatorship that governed Portugal for half of the 20th century. Seeking a return to the stable, ordered, and class-structured society of 19th century Portugal, Antonio de Oliveira Salazar's conservative authoritarian regime based its legitimacy on Catholic and corporatist doctrines. It did not tolerate more than a modicum of popular participation in government: "independent from society, the regime was not obliged to innovate or evolve, and conflicts were not structured into the decision-making apparatus" (Bruneau, 1981, pp. 2–3; see also Schmitter, 1978).

In line with this orientation, only individuals trusted by the government and selected by official organizations were allowed to register to vote (Bacalhau, 1990). The effectiveness of this policy is clear in the results of the 1969 election in which 62.5% of the voting age population were not registered and an additional 14.4% did not vote even though they were registered. And of the 23.1% who did vote, 20.3% supported the ruling party. The governing authorities simply felt that the public opinion process was irrelevant to their concerns.

TOTALITARIANISM

Although totalitarian and authoritarian regimes are similar in that they both restrict legitimate political leadership to elites only, repress dissent, and use violence to overcome political opposition, there is a sharp contrast between them with respect to the legitimacy of collective opinion. Authoritarian regimes are prone to ignore collective opinion unless forced to do so in a crisis and assume anyone not in opposition to be a passive supporter. In contrast, totalitarian governments actively seek to control even apparently trivial stirrings and consider nonparticipation to be an act of opposition.

Totalitarian governments seek to monopolize power and authority throughout a nation, including its economic and social spheres, erasing the boundaries between state and society. Rule is by a single party that claims to speak for the entire nation and tolerates no rival party. Not even the limited political pluralism that might be tolerated by an authoritarian military dictatorship is allowed. Moreover, totalitarian parties not only monopolize political power and authority, they seek to " govern the entire associational life of a society" and to control the economy either through direct state administration or through tight government control and regulation of the privately owned economy (Meyer, 1993, pp. 916–917). The resultant political coordination of an entire people, what the Nazis called *Gleichschaltung*, leads to what can be called the "coercive unanimity" of an entire people (Linz, 1979).

By politicizing everyone and everything, totalitarians seek to establish their claim that they express the valid voice of the people they rule and, therefore, represent a true democracy. This is why the continuous political mobilization of the entire populace under the direction and control of a single party is a fundamental activity of any totalitarian regime. Under Italian Fascism, for example:

> There cannot be any single economic interests which are above the general economic interests of the State, no individual, economic initiatives which do

not fall under the supervision and regulation of the State, no relationships of the various classes of the nation which are not the concern of the State." (Palmieri, 1972, p. 353)

Totalitarian parties are mass movements whose leaders claim to speak for an allegedly authentic collectivity. The successful organization of a nation's masses is a central aim of totalitarian movements: "totalitarian regimes, as long as they are in power, and totalitarian leaders, as long as they are alive, command and rest upon mass support up to the end" (Arendt, 1973, pp. 306, 308). In this spirit, fascist spokesmen claimed that:

> The Fascist State ... is a people's state, and, as such, the democratic State *par excellance*. ... Hence the enormous task which Fascism sets itself in trying to bring the whole mass of the people, beginning with the little children, inside the fold of the Party. (Gentile, 1972, p. 342)

Similarly, the right to rule of totalitarian leaders derives from the belief that they are the only true manifestation of the people's will, whether that be the will of a people, nation, or class. Thus, Hitler's legitimacy was justified by his asserted leadership of the "Aryan race," whereas Stalin's claim to legitimacy rested on his leadership role in the "dictatorship of the proletariat." Other contenders for power are rejected as false representatives, traitors, and candidates for extermination.

In order to validate their positions of power, even though they distrust and suppress an independent citizenry, totalitarian elites insist on the vocal, even if pseudo-participation, of the governed in the nation's political life. To combat political passivity and apathy, Hitler and Stalin held plebiscitarian "elections" in which all were compelled to vote, and staged mass rites of public adulation such as the annual Nazi party congresses at Nuremburg and the annual Soviet May Day parades. These elections and celebrations exemplify the distorted role that the public opinion process plays in totalitarian governments.

In totalitarian regimes, voting is a duty and not a right or privilege. It is an opportunity to acclaim the ruling party's leadership, "to express publicly, visibly and preferably joyously the identification with the regime," and not to help select that leadership (Linz, 1978, pp. 43–48; Linz, 1975). Enforcement of this concept of voting helps explain the near unanimity of totalitarian plebiscites: 99.7% approval of Germany's *Anschluss* with Austria and reelection of Stalin by votes of 99.4% and 99.6% (Gallup & Rae, 1968). Similarly, reported voter turnout rates in communist states in eastern Europe during the period of Soviet domination offer dramatic testimony to the effort made in those countries to document presumed public support.

During the 1960s, in Albania the lowest reported turnout was 100% and in Czechoslovakia 99.4%, and Poland, Hungary, and Romania reported turnouts ranging between 96% and 98% (Pravda, 1978).

Because acceptance of a totalist ideology is a central defining characteristic of totalitarianism (Friedrich, 1969; Linz, 1978), competing public opinion is, by definition, treason. Spontaneous public discussion and the spontaneous collective opinion it generates are feared and extirpated as threats to the presumed legitimate exercise of power by the entrenched elite. "The only theoretically possible identification (in the Soviet Union) was ... to be communist or anti-communist—the second position being punishable by law" (Popov, 1992, p. 323). In support of the Soviet regime's legitimacy, an official cultural myth was that "the 'moral and political unity of the Soviet people' rallied around communist ideology and Party." This explains why a primary goal of the state's repressive apparatus was to create "the impression of a total and unshakable faith of the people in official dogma." (Popov, 1992, p. 323).

To protect their claimed legitimacy, totalitarian rulers allow only collective opinions that they manufacture in conformity with official ideology and that are administered by the parties they lead. Thus, in the Soviet Union,

> In the general atmosphere of totalitarianism, an important element was the suppression of any independence of thought, initiative, or self expression. People felt pressured to repeat official communist ideology, encompassing all spheres of education, science, and culture. ... Under such conditions, it is hard to speak of the existence of a public opinion that differed in any way from official ideology and the system of directed norms and values implanted in mass consciousness. (Popov, 1992, p. 322).

Under such conditions, public opinion can be no more than a demonstration of the extent to which the populace accepts official ideology and party policy. Only in periods during which totalitarian controls are relaxed, as occurred under Khruschev and Gorbachev, is the idea tolerated that there may be an unofficial public opinion that can have independent political significance (Shlapentokh, 1986).

In a totalitarian state, deviations from accepted community norms are always subject to political interpretation, thereby making them subject to political as well as communal sanctions (Friedgut, 1979). Consequently, no expression of opinion, individual or collective opinion, even on what are otherwise considered nonpolitical or trivial issues, can be tolerated except under conditions established and controlled by those in power. Those conditions convert self-generated collective opinion into an administrative tool for controlling the public, and not a right of citizens to participate in and contribute to governmental decision making.

In the U.S.S.R., the merging of state and society into a single framework led to the intrusion of government into all areas of life, creating unusual problems of control—especially at the local level. Local governments managed mundane operations like running restaurants, repairing roofs, or resoling boots that in other systems are, at most, subject to licensing or other forms of general supervision. Establishing contacts between local government authorities and citizens for dealing with the everyday strains and dissatisfactions that inevitably arise in such operations became a political matter.

The reality was that "every expression of dissent or discontent at the local level is considered dysfunctional for the system and is therefore repressed." At the same time, the government recognized that "expressions of citizen discontent serve as signals to the central authorities, informing them of local authorities' faults and failures." These signals were considered so valuable to governing that "throughout the Soviet system special patterns of activity and channels of communication (were) constructed to facilitate the legitimate expression of such discontent" (Friedgut, 1979, pp. 6–9). For example, executive committee agendas of local Soviets typically contained items dealing with matters such as the efficiency of roof repairmen whereas deputies and neighborhood representatives were exhorted to find out how local services were evaluated by their customers (Friedgut, 1979).

More generally, it is essential for totalitarian regimes to encourage the rise of communication channels between government agencies and citizens—but only under the government's administrative control. Thus, a defining characteristic of totalitarian regimes is their monopolization of communications media as part of their efforts to politicize all social life in accord with official policy (Friedrich, 1969). The ubiquitous streetcorner loudspeakers in Soviet Moscow symbolized the intrusion of totalitarian communication into daily life.

Politicizing a populace in the expectation that a single, official collective opinion can be successfully managed is risky. Even with forced participation and monopolization of communications media, as it does in all societies, informal interpersonal communication exists in totalitarian societies. Therefore, if an entire population is politicized, there is always a potential for subrosa discussion of issues that are not satisfactorily resolved by those in power, thereby creating a subrosa collective opinion (see, e. g., Shlapentokh, 1986). In the Soviet Union, the rise of a subrosa collective opinion opposed to the Afghan War (even in the absence of the extensive television coverage the Vietnam War received in the United States) is a case in point. The early success of Mikhail Gorbachev in the 1980s derived in part from such a subrosa collective opinion. Afghanistan was experienced as "a watershed for our generation" (Smith, 1990, p. 26).

Subrosa collective opinion within totalitarian states can function in a manner analogous to court opinion in authoritarian states, that is, become part of the struggle for power between elite factions. This is evident in the tactics used by Gorbachev as he sought support for the economic reforms he was pursuing to overcome his opposition. Needing fresh thinking in place of the old party line, he sought ways of coping with the frustrations that beset the Soviet Union by tapping into the subrosa collective opinion of intellectual elites. In particular, he loosened restraints on the intelligentsia's use of communication media (Smith, 1990). By the time he had consolidated his position, the movement for reform could draw upon these hidden constituencies. Without that support, " the flame of reform would have flickered out and died" (Smith, 1990). However, rather than remaining a power struggle among elites, the reform movement led to a questioning of the legitimacy of the system itself. Seemingly overnight, that culminated in the fall of the Soviet Union.

In light of the subversive quality of any independent collective opinion, constant surveillance is necessary to identify and eliminate any questioning of the regime's legitimacy. This makes secret police an essential aspect of totalitarian regimes (Friedrich, 1969) and accounts for their ubiquitous presence. In the Soviet Union, "in a crowd, Big Brother was always assumed to be present" (Smith, 1990, p. xxvii). This is also why, to sustain themselves, totalitarian governments ultimately depend on the twin strategies of incessant propaganda and terror to control public opinion (Arendt, 1973). Because the public opinion process has no legitimacy in its own right under totalitarian regimes but only as it is manufactured and guided by the ruling party, the relaxation of propaganda and terror can be fatal to the regime.

THE POLITICAL REJECTION OF COLLECTIVE OPINION IN NONDEMOCRACIES

Under authoritarian and totalitarian regimes, no provision is made for collective opinion to be expressed in ways that are incorporated into the legitimate functioning of government. In the former, there simply are no institutional forms through which collective opinion can be linked to the setting and implementation of public policy. Collective opinion is either ignored, if at all feasible, or if it cannot be ignored, it is monitored to identify and squash potentially disruptive rumblings. In the latter, institutional forms exist, but they are allowed to function only under the tightest, most rigid controls. Collective opinion as a natural emergent of communication is not given access to those forms, which are open only to a pseudocollective opinion that is manufactured by the ruling elite.

For legitimacy to be granted to a politicized collective opinion, two prerequisites must be satisfied: (a) acceptance of the principle that collective opinion is morally and practically a sound foundation on which to base government institutions, and (b) the creation of effective linkages between collective opinion and government agencies. We next turn our attention to an examination of these prerequisites.

6

Public Opinion in Democracies

Although democracy and public opinion are intimately related ideas, they are not synonomous. The idea of democracy has to do more with how people are politically organized whereas public opinion has to do more with what people desire. In a democracy, the free expression of collective opinion is the accepted source of *legitimately* organized political authority. What is required is not unanimity, nor even a majority, but that everyone, including those in the minority, accept the principle that government action should be guided by public opinion (Lowell, 1926).

Even among those who favor democracy, controversy has long existed regarding three aspects of the public opinion process:

How much confidence can and should be placed in the leadership capabilities of a collectivity? In dispute is the moral quality of the public's thinking, whether that thinking has relevant factual content, and how well the public understands those facts.

How should the public's desires be linked to government? In dispute is the extent to which there should be direct or represenative linkages between citizens and their governments, and which of various alternative voting procedures should be used, and under what circumstances.

What should be the public's day-by-day role in government? In dispute is whether collective opinion should have a proactive political role or whether it should have no more than a reactive or passive influence.

Our task is to understand how, in light of these three controversies, the public opinion process functions in a democracy.

THE DEMOCRATIC FAITH IN PUBLIC OPINION

The belief that public opinion should legitimize governance can be traced back at least to ancient Greece and Rome. Aristotle, in opposition to Plato, felt that there is an element of truth in the principle that there is more wisdom in a multitude than in an individual because a superior wisdom is created by joining the correct though incomplete bits of knowledge from everyone in the multitude (see Palmer, 1950). The Roman principle, "What touches all should be approved by all concerned" (Menache, 1990, p. 5) adds the idea that those who have a concern in a public issue have a natural right to participate in its resolution. In combination, confidence in the public's competence and belief in the public's natural right to participate endow public opinion with a transcendant political quality.

A major influence on modern democratic philosophy has been Rousseau's argument that the will of the people is the only legitimate basis of government. Rousseau asserted that all nondemocratic forms of government rely on the use of physical force to usurp mankind's natural rights, buttressed by some artificial justification to create the facade of voluntary obedience to that force (Rousseau, 1952). He further maintained that relying on the will of the people is legitimate because it does not require abdication of inherent individual rights to any other individual or set of individuals, such as a king or an aristocracy. Instead, an association is created through a voluntarily entered social contract in which "each member is an indivisible part of the whole" (Rousseau, 1952, p. 392). Thus, the will of the people is a corporate phenomenon, residing in the collectivity as such. Similarly, sovereignty, the right to govern, resides in that corporate body, the people. In other words, in a democracy the people are sovereign and public opinion is the way in which that sovereignty is expressed.

All new nations and postrevolutionary governments face the problem of gaining acceptance of a new set of shared beliefs that can replace those that justified the authority of the displaced regime (Lipset, 1963). If a democracy is to be established, the new government's legitimacy must be based on the people's sovereignty and on the expression of its collective will. In U.S. history, this is evident in the newly independent nation's written claims to legitimacy. The opening paragraph of the Declaration of Independence states that it was written out of a "decent respect for the opinions of mankind" and goes on to say that governments derive "their just powers from the consent of the governed" (The World Book Encyclopedia, Vol. 5, p. 68). Similarly, the Preamble to the Constitution states that "We the people ... ordain and establish this Constitution." These phrases underline de Toqueville's (1954) observation that the American Revolution rested on the overt acceptance of the people's sovereignty as expressed through voting.

The American principle was echoed a few years later, at the time of the French Revolution, in the "Declaration of the Rights of Man and Citizen," which begins with the phrase, "The representatives of the French people, organized in National Assembly" and continues by stating that, "Law is the expression of the general will: all citizens have the right to concur personally, or through their representatives, in its formation" (cited in Eisenstadt, 1971, p. 341). It is further noteworthy that both the American Declaration of Independence and the French Declaration of the Rights of Man refer to natural rights stemming directly from nature's God, Creator, or Supreme Being—without any intervening authority, be it a religious institution, kinship system, tradition, or an individual's charisma.

Two hundred years later, with the end of the Soviet Union in December 1991, the new government faced the problem of establishing its legitimacy. At least initially, this was accomplished by having the old legislature enact the transition to the new governmental form. For the intellectual dissidents who helped bring about the fall of the Soviet Union, it was also essential to establish the new government's legitimacy as a democracy. They emphasized the interconnectedness of democratic government and having an active public opinion. The following comment by a Russian dissident (who also happens to be a pollster) makes this point succinctly:

> Democratic form of government and public opinion are genetically insepara-
> ble. If democracy stimulates public opinion as a means of expressing the
> interests of the majority, public opinion in its turn becomes an indispensable
> instrument to make democracy function and spread. Democracy and public
> opinion are thus drawn so closely together that they become interrelated,
> reciprocal, and interpenetrated (Bashkirova, 1988).

ELITIST VERSUS POPULIST CONCEPTIONS OF DEMOCRACY

Acceptance of the democratic principle that a government's legitimacy flows from the people's sovereignty does not determine what will be the division of labor, as it were, between elites and experts on one hand, and the citizenry-at-large on the other. Democratic philosophers like Rousseau assumed universal citizen participation in the public opinion process, so that the general will would be expressive of all citizens rather than of just a few. But, political reality is far removed from that ideal. A century ago, Bryce

observed that except for a politically active and informed 5% of the population, opinion is mostly a matter of prejudice and aversion, an unreasoned
adherence to political party or faction, or unanalyzed acceptance of phrases
or catch-words that embody an argument—sound-bites in the jargon of the
1990s (Bryce, 1891).

Elitists and populists disagree as to whose opinions about a controversy
are most "prudent" to heed (Key, 1961, p. 14), prudent in the sense of getting
oneself elected as well as dealing adequately with the controversy. This
disagreement leads to conflict over alternative ways of institutionalizing the
linkage between the public and government. It must be emphasized that
this conflict is distinct from political differences between liberals and conservatives because it is independent of questions about how to resolve
specific controversies. At various times, both liberals and conservatives have
been populists, as well as elitists.

Although the terms *elitist* and *populist* have both acquired pejorative
connotations in political rhetoric, they refer to objectively definable phenomena. Elitism refers to reliance on elected representatives, especially
those who are indirectly elected, who, despite any vested interests they may
have, are expected to be guided by the needs of the larger community. Elitists
assign a decision-making and tutelary responsibilty to those representatives
that is reminiscent of Plato's philosopher-kings: they relegate the general
public to a limited and passive role. Populism refers to reliance on the direct
participation of an active and presumably qualified citizenry in government
decision making. Populists espouse the general public's maximum, active
involvement in government: they define leadership responsibility in terms
of being the people's servant.

There are, of course, many gradations between the opposing polar
positions, gradations that seek to balance considerations of how account-
able, responsive, and responsible political leaders should be to collective
opinion. That requires reconciling conflicting beliefs as to how experts
compare with the general public with respect to such matters as: Knowledgeability, reason versus susceptibility to emotional appeals, proclivity to
promote personal interests versus disinterestedness and commitment to the
general welfare, and involvement in the political process. As is discussed
later, how to achieve a balance that will further the common welfare through
democracy can become a political issue in its own right.

Whether an elitist or populist judgment of the electorate's competence
dominates a nation's political life is much more than a matter of philosophical dispute. It can be decisive in setting the tone with which candidates and
other political leaders conduct themselves in political campaigns and in
performing their duties as elected officials (Key, 1996). One view can lead

to a politics that, having little confidence in the electorate's collective judgment and wisdom, caters to a presumed irrationality by relying on manipulating candidate images and styles; the other view can lead to an issue-oriented politics that seeks to engage an often uninformed electorate's involvement in public policy. In the former case, elections may become little more than a form of public entertainment, with substantive decision making left to elite factions to hammer out. The latter view creates the expectation that, for better or worse, elections will establish mandates that governments are obligated to pursue.

The Elitist View

Elitists believe that democracy requires government to be responsive to collective opinion but that collective opinion should not be actively involved in policy and decision making. The classic elitist position, that the development of policies and programs should be left to the people's informed and responsible representatives was eloquently stated in the 18th century by Edmund Burke: "(T)he people are the masters" who express their wants and describe their problems, whereas the leaders are the "expert artists" who are qualified to design solutions and prescribe remedies (cited in Macpherson, 1980, p. 29). But, although the people are the masters, their opinions should not be faithfully followed since "your representative owes you, not his industry only, but his judgment; and he betrays you, instead of serving you, if he sacrifices it to your opinion" (cited in Macpherson, 1980, p. 25). Burke went on to say that legislatures should function as deliberative bodies that debate and reason together to achieve the common interest, and not as gatherings of envoys from hostile interests instructed to work out agreements that protect the separate interests they represent. The proper link of collective opinion to government, therefore, is elections that do no more than select qualified representatives and set agendas.

One of the most convinced, articulate, and influential 20th-century proponents of the elitist perspective in the United States was Walter Lippmann. As he saw it, democracy involves a system in which the executive asks and proposes, the legislature consents, and the citizenry does little more than elect the executive and legislature. He did concede that executive proposals should be responsive to public concerns. However, for a variety of reasons, he argued that collective opinion cannot and should not be relied on to represent the true interests of the community as an organic whole, the interests of what he called "*The People* as an historic community" (Lippmann, 1955, pp. 29–33, 185, italics added).

Lippmann felt that repeatedly asking the public for its opinion does not compensate for its lack of information, time, or interest (Lippmann, 1925). It was his contention that no one individual could possibly have an opinion on all issues of the day, or be alert and informed about them. He also contended that because the real questions never quite fit broad principles, it was no solution to ascertain the public's position on those principles. He concluded that appealing to the public makes for bad decision making and that those appeals were an imposition rather than a compliment to the public.

He further maintained that the burden of decision making should be placed on experts within the government who are qualified to compile and analyze relevant information, and on elected representatives who are qualified to debate the conclusions that can be drawn validly from expert reports. In his view, the public's competency is limited to judging results or consequences after the fact and to judging whether proper procedures are followed when policies and programs are implemented. The role of collective opinion, he concluded, should be limited to insisting that problems of concern be dealt with, that proper procedures be adhered to when seeking solutions to those problems, and judging how well those solutions worked (Lippmann, 1946).

A variant of the elitist assessment of public opinion combines a lack of confidence in a predominantly uninformed and politically uninvolved public with distrust of powerful government. Proponents of this view express concern that the 20th century has witnessed the rise of strong, activist states in reaction to the demands of collective opinion for services that can only be provided by such states. The fear is that such a state inevitably seeks to harness power for itself, and in that process, even while it responds to collective opinion, seeks to regulate it (Ginsberg, 1986). Note that the description of a strong state regulating a collective opinion to which it is nonetheless sensitive in some ways approximates what exists under totalitarian regimes. An additional concern is that the growing role of public opinion polls gives inordinate prominence to the alleged un-thinking moderation of the uninvolved and uninformed in comparison with the strong issue positions of the informed and politically active segments of the public (Ginsberg, 1986). Elitists who take this position ultimately tend to think that unlimited governmental responsiveness to an uninformed and uninvolved collective opinion can lead to the real, if unintended, loss of freedom.

The Populist View

There is no populist theory of public opinion separate from a commitment to democratic philosophy per se. The unbounded faith of populists in the practical and moral strength of collective opinion leads them to favor its ever-expanding legitimacy. Increasing democracy is the populist answer to the problems of relying on collective opinion that concern elitists.

Populists are suspicious of elites and experts and seek political leaders who, in their responsiveness to collective opinion, rise above politics. Populist sentiment is also manifest in support for counter-organizations that empower otherwise voiceless segments of a community. Similarly, populist sentiment is evident in hostility to government experts and functionaries, sometimes expressed in such derogatory terms as "striped pants cookie pushers" and "the best and the brightest" and sometimes in criticism of "unelected bureaucrats." Such sentiment is as likely to be expressed by a self-described "silent" middle class as by an economic underclass. What gives such disparate groupings a common populist coloration is opposition to a perceived entrenched power structure.

In light of the significant role George Gallup played in the development of public opinion polling as a major feature of the political landscape, it is instructive to review his populist approach to polling. The contrast between him and Lippmann could not be sharper. Gallup's position was that the people's wisdom, in which he put so much trust, does not derive simply by amassing individual opinions. Instead, he maintained that the people's wisdom emerges out of public communications. Thus, in a 1940 defense of polling, Gallup & Rae (1968) argued that "[Public opinion] is not the product of an omniscient group mind, but rather, a dynamic process resulting from the communication and interaction of individuals in an ever moving society" (p. 15). Additionally, even as Gallup conceded that maximum democratic effectiveness requires an informed electorate, he also stressed that equally necessary is "the communication of the views of the people to elected officials. Unless the public actively participates in the democratic process, nothing much is gained by being well-informed" (Gallup, 1972a, p. 11).

In accord with this populist view, Gallup made testing public support for various proposals a major task of his polling activities. In this endeavor, on occasion he went far beyond headline issues of the day. A 1936 poll that asked about setting up a "Government bureau that would distribute information concerning venereal diseases" (Gallup, 1972b, p. 44) and a 1938 poll that measured the opinion of women as to whether doctors should be required "to give every expectant mother a blood test for syphilis" (Gallup, 1972b, p. 86) challenged the conventions of the day, thereby bringing into open debate a topic that was then usually treated in a "hush-hush" manner. And decades before imposing term limits on members of Congress became a major national issue, in 1947 he polled on imposing such limits on U.S.

Senators (Gallup, 1972b). By defining the scope of polling in such broad terms, Gallup implemented his populist belief that rather than restricting public opinion's legitimacy "democracy assumes that our economic, political and cultural institutions must be geared to the fundamental right of every person to give free expression to the worth that is in him" (Gallup & Rae, 1968, p. 11).

THE ELITIST-POPULIST STRUGGLE
IN THE UNITED STATES

Throughout United States history, elitists and populists have clashed on how collective opinion should be linked to governance. Two questions that have dominated this clash are: (a) Who should vote—should the franchise be expanded beyond the limited base that existed at the time of the nation's founding?; and (b) to what extent should indirect election of high office be maintained or replaced by direct election?

The American Revolution was largely led by, and the American Constitution largely written by, men who had an elitist view of democracy rooted in the semi-aristocratic colonial period. Most did not expect nor want universal suffrage and when they talked about public opinion they meant the opinions of rational, intellectually cultivated gentlemen like themselves (Wood, 1992). Moreover, at the onset of the American Revolution, property, especially landed property, not only represented economic interest but was considered to be the foundation of legitimate authority. Some argued that the franchise need not be extended to small backwoods farmers because educated and cosmopolitan landowners virtually, if not explicitly, represented everyone (Wood, 1992). In fact, at the time of independence most states limited the franchise to property owners. As late as 1825, Rhode Island, Virginia, and Louisiana still denied the vote to those who did not own property.

Expanding the franchise involved more than eliminating property requirements imposed by the individual states. It took constitutional amendments to extend the franchise to African Americans after the Civil War and to women after World War I. Poll taxes, literacy tests, and residency requirements are three specific devices that were used to deny the vote to those presumed to be incapable of making reasonable, intelligent choices and that persisted well into the 20th century. At the end of the 20th century, measures that would simplify and facilitate universal voter registration (such as eliminating local residency requirements, registration by mail, and registering when receiving drivers licenses) were still politically controversial.

At the local level, Dahl's (1961) description of political change in New Haven, Connecticut during the early 19th century exemplifies the elitist–populist struggle:

> The elite seems to have possessed that most indispensable of all characteristics in a dominant group—the sense, shared not only by themselves but by the populace, that their claim to govern was legitimate. ... [U]ntil the winds of Jacksonianism blew in from the West, a man of non-patrician origin must have regarded it as an act of unusual boldness, if not downright arrogance, to stand for public office. Given the perspectives of the times, who after all were more entitled to rule than those who had founded and governed town and colony, city and state for nearly two centuries. ... Yet the elect did meet with opposition, and once their legitimacy as rulers began to be doubted, they were too few in number to maintain control over public office in a political order where office could be contested in elections. (pp. 17-18)

The nature of the Jacksonian wind that blew in from the West is captured in Curti's (1959) description of pioneer Trempealeau County, Wisconsin. Integral to that community's political life was a belief in the value of the long ballot, with most political officials elected to office rather than appointed, appointment being a practice that enables factions to preserve their privileged position; short terms of office, another means of preventing monopolization of office by entrenched factions; and holding town meetings to educate voters on political issues of the day and so make officeholders more responsible to the electorate than they would be otherwise.

For many reasons, elite dominance in local communities has not disappeared, even though the composition of those elites may have changed. Hunter (1890) described mid-20th-century Atlanta as a power structure controlled by a self-selected leadership representing corporate interests:

> Community-wide policy is determined by a handful of men in the large private corporate group, who prod a smaller handful of public and private bureaucrats from time to time and who are in accord, generally, on what is wanted or needed by the ccrporate powers. (p. 40)

Correlatively, radical populism at the local level persists in the efforts of underprivileged strata to achieve empowerment. An outstanding example is Alinsky's (1969) program of neighborhood self-organization of the poor independent of official government agencies. Dating back to pre-World War II days, the principle of self-organization continued to manifest itself in "war on poverty" movements in the 1960s that sought to empower disadvantaged populations. Programs like these have been praised by some for counteracting the political alienation of the poor by encouraging their social participation, and criticized by others as being no more than a means for the poor to express their alienation that encourages violence (Bailey, 1974). A middle-class manifestation of local populism in the 1990s is the demand for the devolution of federal power to state and local governments, and that mandates from higher levels of government on local governments be funded at the higher level.

Indirect representation, especially for high office, was a technique used at the founding of the Republic to protect it against the alleged excesses of an unreliable collective opinion. The Constitution specified that U.S. Senators were to be elected by the legislatures of each state, and it was not until the 17th Amendment went into effect in 1913 that Senators were elected directly by popular vote. The Electoral College method of electing presidents is another example of indirect voting that is still used.

Populist–elitist disagreement persists with respect to a host of other controversies, including: which offices should be elective and which appointive; whether practices such as initiatives, recalls, and referenda should be adopted; whether there should be term limits on elective offices; and whether primaries should be substituted for party caucuses and conventions when nominating candidates for political office.

SURVEY RESEARCH AND THE ELITIST–POPULIST CONTROVERSY

There is a large body of survey data bearing on the elitist–populist controversy regarding the competency of individual and collective opinion. Although these data provide an equivocal answer to the controversy as usually formulated, they do help us evaluate the relation of ideology to empirical reality (see also the discussion of the quality of individual opinion in chap. 2). On one hand, survey data consistently demonstrate that, at the individual level, only a minority of the adult U.S. population—about the 1 in 20 estimated by Bryce—is politically well-informed and involved. On the other hand, there is evidence that the emergence of collective opinion creates a degree of competency that the individual-level data do not suggest exists. Also, before reviewing what has been learned from survey data, we should take note of Bryce's 100-year-old observation that most of the socioeconomic elite is no better informed than the "humbler" classes, so that their opinions, in the main, are of equal quality (Bryce, 1891, pp. 243–244).

The Gallup Poll

From their first years, Gallup Polls documented widespread political ignorance. Nonetheless, Gallup asserted, in direct opposition to Lippmann's views just noted, that his polls demonstrated the public's collective judgment to be consistently wiser than that of many of the nation's political leaders. He felt that the collective thought of the public is wise and should be listened to. In light of the apparent contradiction in Gallup's position, it is useful to consider it in some detail.

The Gallup Poll did not attempt to investigate in any systematic manner the dimensions of the public's political ignorance. Yet, replies to information questions soon made it clear that a large segment of the public had little information about the nation's political system and how it functions. A few illustrative examples make the point (Cantril & Strunk, 1951; Gallup, 1972b):

52% had not been following the Congressional debate on whether the Neutrality Act should be changed, this at a time when keeping the United States out of the impending war in Europe was a major topic of national debate (1939; Cantril & Strunk, 1951, p. 967).

50% did not know their Congressman's name (1942; Gallup, 1972b, p. 329).

62% did not know for how many years members of the House of Representatives serve (1944; Gallup, 1972b, p. 485).

52% would not even hazard a guess as to the salary of Congressmen (1944; Gallup, 1972b, p. 611).

51% had not heard of or read about the Marshall Plan, this at a time when it was a major topic of Congressional debate (1947; Gallup, 1972b, p. 661).

67% could not locate Greece on a map at a time when a virtual civil war in that country was a major factor in United States–Soviet conflict (1947; Gallup, 1972b, p. 661).

Even more disturbing from the elitist perspective is the extent of public willingness to voice opinions on matters about which they admittedly were uninformed:

In 1940, 50% could not estimate how many war planes the United States was producing a month. Of those who did make an estimate, half were on the high side. Despite this poor information base, 58% felt that war plane production was not going ahead fast enough and another 28% felt it was, for a total of 86% who voiced an opinion (1940; Gallup, 1972b).

In a 1946 poll, only 47% knew that members of the House of Representatives serve for two years. Still, 40% favored lengthening the term of
office from two to four years and 51% disapproved, for a total of 91% who
voiced an opinion (1946; Gallup, 1972b).

Poll results such as these did not weaken Gallup's populist belief that in
a democracy the nation's political leaders should heed collective opinion.
Instead, in direct opposition to Lippmann's position, he argued strongly that
his findings prove that collective opinion provides a sound basis for governmental decision making, even in international affairs (Gallup, 1972a).

As an outstanding example of this alleged superiority of the people's
collective judgment, specifically regarding foreign policy, Gallup often cited
poll results on what should be done in response to Hitler's and Mussolini's
aggressive actions at the onset of World War II. He liked to point out, in
personal conversations as well as in his writings, contrasts such as the
following between his poll results and what he considered the lack of
Congressional leadership:

In 1938, a time when Congress was resisting any build-up of military
budgets, large majorities of 69% to 80% favored building a bigger army, navy,
and air force (Gallup, 1972b, p. 84).

In 1940, 71% favored using the draft to increase the Army's size, yet a
year later, just months before the attack on Pearl Harbor, the House of
Representatives voted to extend the draft by only one vote (Gallup, 1972b,
p. 238).

In the face of the strong isolationist bloc in Congress, repeated polls in
1941 registered consistent majority support for helping Great Britain and
opposing Germany and Italy: Although only 20% would vote to go to war
against Germany and Italy, 66% would do so "if it appeared certain that
there was no other way of defeating them"; 61% thought it was more
important to help England versus 39% that it was more important to stay
out of war; an increasing majority favored using the U.S. Navy to guard or
convoy ships carrying war materiel to Great Britain, by a margin of
52%–40% in May and 56%-35% in June (Gallup, 1972b).

These findings did not reflect a desire to go to war but, rather, what Gallup
considered to be the public's informed and realistic belief that there was
little alternative: A majority of 62% felt that if they defeated Great Britain,
Germany and Italy would start a war against the United States within 10
years (Gallup, 1972b).

Similarly, during the Vietnam War period, commenting on what he considered to be the dangers of relying on expert leadership, Gallup (1972a) wrote:

> The Pentagon Papers have revealed how easy it is for leaders to make wrong judgments when surrounded by intimates who think the same way, and when the public is not aware of the nature of the problem, and has no opportunity to question or to debate policies under consideration. (p.6)

Gallup's populist conclusion is that "we must listen to what the people have to say, for public opinion can only be of service to democracy if it can be heard" (Gallup & Rae, 1968, p. 15).

Academic Studies

Turning to systematic analyses of survey data by academic survey researchers, pioneer studies on voting behavior quickly established that non-rational interpersonal dynamics were a major influence on voting decisions, and were apparently of greater significance than rational issue-oriented communications and thought. Although one study of the 1940 presidential election had been designed expressly to investigate the role of newspaper and radio communications, the results led to a "sharp recognition of the importance of the voters' personal influence on one another and pointed up the unsolved problem of the role of political issues in the campaign" (Berelson, Lazarsfeld, & McPhee, 1954, p. ix; Lazarsfeld, Berelson, & Gaudet, 1948).

A follow-up study of the 1944 election concluded that most voters were not highly informed about the details of the campaign and fell far short of the democratic ideal in terms of interest and involvement, knowing what are the issues, relevant facts, alternatives under consideration and their implications, and party positions. In fact, voting decisions were explainable "less as principle than as traditional social allegiance" to the groups to which voters belong (Berelson et al., 1954, pp. 307–311). This unflattering portrait of the electorate in action conforms far more closely to elitist criticism of unfettered public opinion than to the populist vision of the public's competency.

Paradoxically, the most volatile members of the electorate, those most prone to have changed their voting preference during the course of the campaign were disproportionately the politically apathetic, inconsistent, and uninformed. It was they who accounted for most of the campaign movement and not the most highly involved and presumably attentive segment of the electorate (Berelson et al., 1954). Apparently strength of conviction and commitment among the politically involved and attentive was so great that their minds were made up early in election campaigns and resistant to persuasion (compare with the discussion in chap. 2 of the stability of opinions based on integrated, internally consistent belief systems).

The imperviousness of the politically involved and informed to political debate does not fit elitist expectations. As Berelson and his colleagues (1954) pointed out, "if the decision were left only to the deeply concerned, well-integrated, consistently principled ideal citizens ... the political system might easily prove too rigid to adapt to changing domestic and international conditions" (p. 316). Thus, even though elitist doubts as to the limited extent to which the general public is involved in and informed about public issues are borne out by these survey results, the systemic implications of those same results are not clear.

Subsequent independent studies that have measured differences in the "ideational worlds" of the public have gone far beyond recording the proportion of the public that is uninvolved or uninformed on particular issues or events. Converse's path-breaking analyses of the public's political involvement and knowledgeability identified "belief strata" who differ in the extent to which their political thinking is subject to internal logical constraints. His analyses provide strong support for the elitist position.

When the belief strata are placed on a scale of differentiation, they display predictable differences in their belief systems, defined as "configurations of ideas and attitudes bound together by functional interdependence" (Converse, 1964, p. 206). At one end of the scale, thinking is ideological, that is, highly constrained logically, whereas at the other end, there is no identifiable logical structure or issue content. Intermediate to these polarities, in descending order, are (a) near-ideological thinking in which dissimilarities occur despite a seeming logical constraint, (b) group interest thinking in which idea elements go together because of social rather than logical constraints, and finally (c) nature-of-the-times thinking, which reacts to discrete issues as they arise. In other words, thinking changes from a contextual grasp of abstract political beliefs buttressed by a wealth of information at one end to disconnected, concrete–nonabstract thoughts with little factual content at the other (Converse, 1964).

Applying this model to national survey data, Converse found a tiny minority of the total U.S. population at the ideological end of the scale, whereas the bulk of the population is to be found at the other end. Only one tenth were ideologues (2.5%) or near-ideologues (9%) who can be expected to have clearly thought out, factually grounded opinions. The views of the largest single segment, constituting 42% of the population, exhibit group interest thinking; that is, they are more likely to reflect social constraints than consideration of the merits of an issue. The remaining two segments, which account for just under half the population (24% nature-of-the-times thinking and 22.5% no-issue content), are unlikely to hold opinions that represent anything much more than off-the-cuff observations without any sense of conviction (Converse, 1964).

Using a somewhat different analytical model, Neuman (1986) defined three strata, or publics, into which the total U.S. population can be divided. Although the details of his model differ from Converse's, in broad outline the picture it paints is congruent: Most people are largely uninterested in political debate and decision making. Political activists, characterized by a high level of ideational and cognitive sophistication and political involvement, at a maximum comprise Bryce's 5% of the public. According to Neumann, public opinion, as it is commonly understood, relates primarily to the views of those in this stratum. At the other extreme, about 20% of the population is unabashedly apolitical. Not only are those in this stratum uninformed and uninvolved, they reject the idea that being so represents a failure on their part. The intermediate 75% consitute the mass public that is "marginally attentive to politics and mildly cynical about the behavior of politicians, but they accept the duty to vote, and they do so with fair regularity" (Neuman, 1986, pp. 170–171; see also Bryce, 1891). This picture is a far cry from populist expectations.

The pessimistic assessments of the general public's political incompetence that we reviewed rest in large part on the assumption that the quality of public thinking is measured by the sum of individual competencies. But if, as we saw chapter 3, collective opinion is more than the sum of individual opinions, we need to examine that assumption. In doing so, we must keep in mind that even though collective opinion is more than the sum of individual opinions, we cannot assume there is a correlative increase in quality. That has to be determined in its own right.

Stimson's (1991) analysis of the political implications of the "mood" of collective opinion is pertinent (see also chap. 3). If the task of collective opinion is to demand what is to be done and how to do it, the independence of changes in mood from individual issues suggests that collective opinion can be unstable and willfully errant. That assessment must be changed, however, if the task of collective opinion is restricted to defining goals and acquiescing in, or rejecting, actions taken to achieve those goals. Stimson argued there is no "smart public opinion" with respect to the limited task because the public's wants come from their values and not from the quality of their thinking (Stimson, 1991, pp. 124–125). That is to say, there is a kind of "value-oriented rationality" (compare with Weber's, 1961, *wertra-tional*) in the public's thinking that can justify the restricted role for collec-tive opinion that elitists favor.

Despite all of what was just discussed, there is empirical support for the populist position that, however poor the quality of individual opinions may be, the process of combining them can result in a qualitatively superior collective opinion. Analyses of voting behavior and time series compiled from opinion poll results do not reveal the erratic, uninterpretable patterns that would be expected if mass opinion were merely the random or uncon-sidered response of the uninformed and uninvolved.

In his analysis of the relation of voting behavior to policy preferences, instead of analyzing the psychological structure of beliefs, feelings and opinion, Key (1966) sought to answer the questions, "Why do some people remain loyal to one party's candidates from election to election while others switch?" and "Why does the number of standpatters and switchers change from election to election?" (pp. 7–8). For this purpose, he analyzed the policy positions endorsed by standpatters and switchers in presidential elections from 1936 to 1960. He found that being a shifter (disloyal to one's party) correlated highly with policy disagreement. Conversely, among party stal-warts, there was a mutually reinforcing pattern of agreement on policy grounds and satisfaction with performance (Key, 1966). Key concluded that, as evident in the congruence between voting behavior, policy preference, and satisfaction with peformance, and regardless of the use of nonrational campaign appeals and tactics, "voters are not fools" (pp. 144, 150).

After analyzing the 30-year trend in responses to the question as to what is the country's most important problem, Smith (1980) concluded that fluctuations in response are strongly associated with the flow and intensity of historical events, both at the aggregate level and at the level of intergroup differentiation. More than 10 years later, further analysis of national trends confirmed the conclusion that opinion change is not chaotic but slow, steady, and largely explicable (Smith, 1994; see also the discussion in chap. 2 on the quality of individual opinion.)

Similarly, in their analyses of public opinion poll results, Page and Shapiro (1992) found that opinion trends formed patterns related to specific events, to social and economic trends, and to the acquisition of new information. In foreign policy, as the international situation improved, opinions shifted from militant activism to more peaceful reactions. Collectively, policy preferences were generally stable and when they changed they did so in understandable, predictable ways.

It is noteworthy that Page and Shapiro found expected inadequacies at the level of individual opinions. At that level, the data they reviewed consistently documented that most of the public has low interest, lack knowledge, and hold opinion characterized by weak ideological structure. They also concurred that voting behavior studies demonstrate the importance of group affiliations in voting decisions. In other words, even though they found weaknesses of individual opinions, when analyzed at the collective level they also found that opinions "make sense: ... they draw fine distinctions among different policies; and they form meaningful patterns consistent with a set of underlying beliefs and values" (Page & Shapiro, 1992, p. 385). As recorded in polls, collective policy preferences are real, knowable, differentiated, patterned, and coherent.

The qualitative contrast between individual and collective opinion identified by the studies just discussed is reminiscent of Aristotle's argument in favor of democracy, namely, that the joining together of individual knowledge and beliefs in some way raises quality:

> Collective public opinion reflects a considerably higher level of information and sophistication than is apparent at the individual level resulting from, among other things "information pooling" and from collective deliberation so that collective opinion, ... which is both an aggregation of many individual opinions and the result of a process in which many individuals interact ... far outshines the opinions of the average individual. (Page & Shapiro, 1992, p. 388)

Page and Shapiro (1992) found no reason to revise majoritarian democratic theory in favor of some form of pluralistic or polyarchical system in which organized interest groups play an important part and in which participation by, and responsiveness to, the general public is limited. Rather, they concluded that the general public is not incapable of knowing its own interests or the public good and that it generally reacts to new situations and new information in sensible, reasonable ways: "the twentieth-century U.S. public is more capable and competent than critics of majoritarian democracy would have us believe" (Page & Shapiro, 1992, pp. 384–389).

INTERACTIONS BETWEEN ELITE AND NON-ELITE OPINIONS

Many models of communications and of opinion leadership (see chap. 3) lead us to expect the quality of mass opinion to trail elite opinion. However, there are grounds for believing that non-elite opinions may sometimes develop to a considerable degree independent of elite opinions. To the extent that this is so, we need to understand how they become coordinated into a coherent political effort. Much remains to be learned about this.

Converse (1964) argued that even when the less-informed strata express support for the views of elite ideologues, their motivations and reasoning have little to do with the thinking of those elites whose "referents are remote from the immediate experience of their clientele" (p. 249). Similarly, the existence of a knowledge gap between elite ideologues and uninformed masses has led some to question the idea that, by serving as opinion leaders, elites contribute to the quality of opinions held by opinion followers. For example, persons of high socioeconomic status learn more from the mass media than those of low status, so that over time the size of the knowledge gap between them on particular issues tends to increase (Tichenor, Donohue, & Olien, 1970, p. 170). Testifying further to the independence of mass opinion is the fact that, as a result of differences in interest and involvement in specific issue domains, the size of the knowledge gap may in some cases remain unchanged or even decrease (Ettema, Brown, & Luepker, 1983; Moore, 1987).

"The mystery, for those who accept ... conventional wisdom, is how people manage to have opinions about as many matters about which they lack the most elementary understanding" (Gamson, 1992, p. 5). Some account for this mystery by noting that many opinions as measured in polls are artifacts of the survey method and do not represent meaningful judgments (see chap. 3 on the quality of individual opinion). However, this observation does not explain the coherence and patterning of allegedly meaningless individual opinions when they are analyzed at the collective level.

Two very different studies that investigated the extent to which individual (and collective) opinions are self-generated by the general public rather than derived from a dominant elite demonstrate the complexities that are involved. One study took it for granted that mass opinion is dominated by elite opinion in the sense that informational and leadership cues provided by elites guide the movement of mass opinion. In that study elite dominance was defined as a process in which elites induce "citizens to hold opinions that they would not hold if aware of the best available information and analysis" (Zaller, 1992, p. 311). The results of the study indicate that ordinary citizens respond selectively to elite opinions, accepting the presumably carefully thought out views only of those experts whose values and aims are most congruent with their own. Thus, instead of being uncritically dominated by elite opinion, the general public reacts creatively to it—and on its own terms. In this way, despite widespread individual apathy and ignorance, mass opinion turns out to be a selective distillation of expert consideration of the merits of public issues (Zaller, 1992).

It is intriguing that although, in this study, the opinions of individual members of the mass public were not independently generated, they represent more than passive acquiescence to elites. This is reminiscent of communications between informal opinion leaders and their less well-informed peers out of which mutual awareness develops. It may be that the apparent quality of aggregated opinion poll measurements demonstrates that there exists a functioning communications network that links elites and non-elites in some still indeterminate way.

A very different study provided evidence that ordinary citizens have the capability of forming meaningful opinions on their own, and without recourse to prior expert thinking. Small group conversations, or focus groups, were held on four very different issue areas—affirmative action, nuclear power, economically troubled industries, and the Arab–Israel conflict—that differ considerably in terms of personal immediacy or technical complexity. Awareness of media coverage of each of these issue areas varied across and within the groups (Gamson, 1992).

Despite the limited information held by the participants, and even with limited involvement, in each group participants conversed extensively and sensibly about the issues. There was a deliberative quality in the way they went about constructing a meaningful way of dealing with the issues, so that considerable coherence was achieved in all the groups (Gamson, 1992). However artificial the group discussion setting may be, it became evident that it was not necessary to have an expert or ideological base for a reasoned, rational discussion to take place, a discussion that could lead to a sensible group judgment. Whether that is apt to occur under likely real-world conditions, and what those conditions must be, is another matter. The personal experience of this observer who has moderated many focus group discussions is that how skillfully the moderator handles a group decisively influences the quality of its discussion.

A reasonable conclusion is that if favorable conditions of interpersonal communications are created, there may be considerable potential for the emergence of a competent collective opinion. In that case, mass opinion would provide a sounder input into democratic decision making than the elite perspective acknowledges. However, what constitutes "favorable conditions" is a separate question that still remains to be answered.

LINKING COLLECTIVE OPINION
TO DEMOCRATIC GOVERNANCE: VOTING

Except possibly in simple, preliterate societies, the public opinion process in itself does not provide the means for governing a people. Because it is not an acting agency, collective opinion cannot enact laws, issue regulations, or in some other way officially promulgate its desires. As an expression of public judgment, collective opinion can do no more than influence government decision making. Institutionalized procedures must be in place if the state of a people's collective judgment is to be translated into a government decision. Collective opinion cannot implement those decisions by administering laws and regulations. For that, administrative procedures must be established and administrative personnel must be on hand.

As we have seen, authoritarian and totalitarian governments utilize decision making and administrative mechanisms and procedures that largely ignore or manipulate collective opinion. In democracies, however, institutional forms and procedures must exist that effectively link the expression of collective opinions to political participation in a mutually supporting system (Luttbeg, 1974). Forging strong links that can perform this function is a fundamental task in any democracy, a task that again raises the issue of the public's competency.

The idea that in a democracy the people govern by actually taking over the conduct of public affairs has led many to assume that democratic governments depend on publics whose individual members, because they think about politics the way political leaders do, can determine government actions. However, as Schattschneider (1975) noted, it is unrealistic to expect everyone, or even most people, to know enough to run a government. Furthermore, because no one individual can be expected to know enough to run a government, he felt it was equally absurd to restrict political participation to those who do know. He concluded that the challenge is not to create a public whose members can all qualify as Platonic philosopher-kings. Rather, the challenge in a democracy is how to organize a political community in which "competitive leaders and organizations define the alternatives of public policy in such a way that the public can participate in the decision-making process" (Schattschneider, 1975, p. 138).

Meeting that challenge requires, above all, selecting political leaders in accord with accepted democratic procedures. Equally important is generating confidence that day-to-day political decision making is not only preceded by public debate but is responsible and responsive to the public. The legitimacy of collective opinion in a democracy relies as much on confidence in the forms and procedures through which its expression is linked to governance, as to acceptance of the underlying principles of democracy (Price, 1992). This is why voting has long been considered the defining institution of democracy. Across the centuries, diverse voting methods have evolved, many of which have been the objects of sharp criticism. This criticism has made the legitimacy of existing voting systems an issue in its own right.

Rule by consensus is a mechanism for linking collective opinion to decision making that has been used far more frequently than may be realized. Perhaps the earliest method for linking collective opinion to government is rule by consensus. In all likelihood rule by consensus evolved directly out of prepolitical institutional forms in preliterate societies. When disputes arise in the absence of a permanent political authority, acheiving unanimity of judgment through the functioning of other existing institutions, especially kinship systems, can be an accepted method for mediating them (Manglapas, 1987; M. Mead, 1937). This was the case in traditional Burmese tribes, second-century Indian castes, and traditional Naga Societies (Horam, 1975; Stevenson, nd; Tripathi, 1942). Even in ancient urban societies such as Mesopotomia, communal affairs were directed in assembly under a presiding judge, with some measure of consensus as the determining principle (Oppenheim, 1964).

Nonpolitical examples of rule by consensus in contemporary western societies include the unanimity often required of juries in criminal trials, and "sense of the meeting" decision making in voluntary associations. Politically, in the United States the frequent practice at presidential nominating conventions of entertaining a motion for a unanimous nomination once a candidate has achieved a majority also comes to mind. Similarly, in local party organizations, consensus candidates are often selected and factional coalitions often arise through informal agreements arrived at in ways reminiscent of the processes involved in consensus building, and not through formal votes.

Small groups are involved in many of the foregoing examples, so it is not surprising that achieving consensus in many ways is reminiscent of the informal communications through which collective opinion emerges. To the degree that the two are in fact congruent, rule by consensus can be considered a democratically acceptable linking mechanism. Consequently, the informal role that consensus building between political factions might play in linking collective opinion to governance should never be overlooked. On the other hand, neither should the possible susceptibility of consensus building to manipulation by established authorities and even to naked power be ignored. Also, difference of opinion that may initially exist in a small group may subside only as a result of the actions of a vocally dominant or powerful faction. For these reasons, rule by consensus is not always perceived to be democratic.

On the face of it, relying on voting, with decisions determined by majority vote, would appear to be a simple and straightforward way of linking collective opinion to governance. In actuality, creating and preserving effective linkage through voting can be quite difficult and contentious. Many different voting systems have been used in the United States as well as by other democracies throughout the world, with varying degrees of success in producing results that are accepted as valid expressions of collective opinion. Failure to establish accepted linkages is an ever-present danger that may undermine the political effectiveness of collective opinion.

When there is a failure of linkage, Merton's (1949) analysis of ritualization and innovation as types of anomie is applicable. Ineffective linkage has the potential of leading to ritualist adherence to the forms of democracy (e. g., voting with no expectation of it making any difference) or to the unrestrained innovation of new forms (e. g., seeking more new ways of linking collective opinion to governance). From this perspective, high voter turnout only among those who see voting as a civic duty even when they dislike all the available choices with low turnout among all others, and public enthusiasm for innovations such as term limits, recall, and referenda as ways of strengthening the responsiveness of government to the public can both be considered symptomatic of political anomie.

These observations provide a framework for discussing the perceived legitimacy of voting mechanisms used in the United States at the end of the 20th century. We must deal in particular with long-standing concerns about low voting participation and allegations about unfair voting procedures. We are also concerned with the widespread lack of confidence in U.S. governmental institutions and functionaries during much of the late 20th century. Common to all these concerns is the question of whether the United States is experiencing a crisis in maintaining effective linkages between collective opinion and governance.

Voting Participation

One underlying premise of any democratic voting system is that it will provide an opportunity for a population to express its desires in a way that truly represents everyone's views. However, if substantial numbers of a population do not vote, that in itself can undermine the perceived legitimacy of election results because the number of votes cast for a winning candidate may constitute a minority of the total eligible electorate. Jimmy Carter was elected President in 1976 by the votes of 27.2% of the total potential electorate (Burnham, 1978). Comparably, in the 1994 Congressional elections—which overthrew Democratic control of both the Senate and the House of Representatives and replaced it with sizable Republican majorities—only about one in six of all eligible voters cast their ballots for a Republican. On this basis, in 1995, critics of the Republican legislative program argued that although the election was "perfectly democratic … it is not a mandate" (Konner, 1995, p. A33).

These are not two isolated examples, but are typical of low voting participation in the United States. In fact, to a considerable degree low voter turnout in the United States seems to be related to influences unique to it. Every western democracy except for the United States provides for the automatic enrollment of voters (Burnham, 1978). In contrast, many jurisdictions in the United States have imposed requirements and procedures that make voter registration difficult. It has been estimated that, if adopted by all states, just four modifications in registration procedures would increase turnout by about 9.1 percentage points (Wolfinger & Rosenstone, 1980). Nonetheless, efforts to make registration easy have become a partisan issue, with some charging that restrictive registration requirements are intended to reduce voter turnout in disadvantaged segments of the electorate, and others claiming that measures intended to eliminate registration barriers would lead to fraud.

Also indicative of the uniqueness of the United States is that its voting turnout is consistently lower than in western Europe. Moreover, the long-term trend in the United States during the last half of the 20th century has been for turnout to drop, a trend that intensified in the 1970s, without any comparable movement in western Europe (Burnham, 1978; Pear, 1992; Wolfinger & Rosenstone, 1980).

Demographically, education is by far the single most important correlate of voting (Wolfinger & Rosenstone, 1980). Nonetheless, turnout in presidential elections declined from a high of 63% in 1960 to a low of 50% in 1988—precisely during a time in which the proportion of college-educated adults was steadily increasing and the proportion with only a grade school education was declining (Crespi, 1978). This suggests that the decline in voter turnout was an across-the-board phenomenon, reflecting some general influence on the nation.

Within this context, it is noteworthy that an influential, primarily elitist, segment of the public does not perceive barriers to registration nor low turnout as a potential threat to the perceived legitimacy of elections. They argue that there is no great loss if those not sufficiently motivated to make the effort to register do not vote and that a reduced turnout would add to the quality of government. George Will (1995) argued against the secret ballot, asserting:

> Abolish secret voting, have every voter call out his or her choice in an unquavering voice and have the choice recorded for public inspection. You

probably will have a smaller electorate, but also a hardier, better one. (Will, 1995, p. A-17)

The question to be answered is whether low voting participation represents a true threat to the continued health of democracy in the United States or whether all that is involved is continued ideological conflict between populists and elitists. A review of recent controversy over voting procedures, plus the trend in public confidence in the government, casts some light on that question.

Voting Procedures

The legitimacy of any democratic government is weakened to the extent that its voting procedures are challenged as not linking collective opinion to government in a way that is fair to and representative of all segments of the electorate. Establishing voting procedures that are generally accepted as fair and representative turns out to be a complicated and controversial issue.

Rousseau argued that forming the initial Social Contract requires unanimity, whereas no more than a simple majority is needed when deciding matters of limited importance or when speed is of the essence. He also considered the possibility of relying on supermajorities rather than simple majorities when what he characterized as important issues are at stake or when sufficient time is available (Rousseau, 1952).

By suggesting that various-sized majorities might be appropriate under varying conditions and for different purposes, in effect Rousseau raised the issue of protecting a voting system's perceived fairness and representativeness. Four questions are central to this issue:

1. Who shall vote? How, if at all, shall the right to vote be based on place of birth, ethnicity, citizenship, occupation, property ownership, length of residence, literacy, gender, age, payment of taxes, religion, and the like? (Most of these criteria have been used in the United States at some time or other and some are currently used.)

2. How shall votes be counted? When shall a simple majority suffice, under what conditions shall a plurality suffice and when shall run-offs be necessary, under what conditions shall a supermajority be required? Shall votes be cast for individuals or for party slates? Shall votes be counted in a way that assures representation to any group that receives a minimum number of votes—and what shall that minimum be, and so on?

3. How should constituencies be defined? Shall the basic voting unit be geographically defined communities or should some other criterion such as occupation or ethnicity be used? What criteria shall be used when drawing geographic boundaries—historical identity, compactness, economic inter-dependence, ethnic, economic or other homogeneity, and so on?

4. How shall candidates be selected? By lot, closed or open primaries, party caucus or convention, by any group that can demonstrate at least a minimum support, and so on?

As worded, these questions refer to elections for government office; but, especially with respect to how votes shall be counted, many also apply to the voting procedures used by legislatures.

The United States Constitution, the constitutions of individual states, and procedural rules of legislative bodies from the Congress down to local councils answer most of these questions. However, over the years, some of those answers, and how they are to be interpreted, have been criticized as creating undemocratic linkages.

One controversial procedure is the use of supermajorities when issues of presumably transcendant importance are at stake. This practice has been defended as protecting the rights of minorities regarding fundamental issues, thereby maintaining confidence in government. However, when superma-jorities are required, this can block action in a way that may also undermine confidence in the linkage between government and collective opinion. The use of filibusters in the U.S. Senate as a tactic for blocking legislative action is an outstanding example of what may happen when supermajorities are required. During 1993, the first year of President Clinton's administration, the Senate was controlled by the Democratic Party, but by less than the supermajority of 60 votes needed to limit debating time. As a result, the Republicans were able repeatedly to block action on key proposals of the new administration that otherwise would have passed with comfortable majorities (Clymer, 1993). Similarly, during the Civil Rights struggles of the 1950s and early 1960s, the filibuster was a powerful tactic for blocking consideration of antisegragation legislation that would otherwise have been easily enacted.

A particularly contentious issue in the United States has been the perception of being disfranchised even when technically not denied the right to vote. Integral to this perception is what has been called the "tyranny of the majority," the fear that the majority will consistently ignore the interests of a minority population whose legislative representation is so small that it cannot affect the passage of laws (Lewis, 1993, p. 18). At-large and winner-take-all voting procedures, separately but especially in combination, have been criticized as diluting the voting strength of minority ethnic groups, effectively disfranchising them. A number of ameliorative methods that have been proposed have been variously criticized by defenders of at-large and winner-take-all voting as "un-American," "Balkanizing" politics, as creating artificial voting blocs, and as giving disproportionate influence to small voting blocs.

Proportional representation is an alternative to winner-take-all voting intended to assure that the full complexity of collective opinion is linked to government. To acheive this, each political party or bloc is represented in a legislature in approximate proportion to the number of votes cast for it (McLean, 1989). Also, proportional representation virtually assures that votes will not be wasted on a weak party's candidates in districts that are dominated by another party (Burnham, 1978). A variety of proportional representation formulas have been developed, differing with respect to such matters as the minimum number of votes a party must receive before being guaranteed seats in the legislature. Although proportional representation can assure representation to all political blocs, when no one party wins a majority of seats, it can also give disproportional power to small parties needed to form a coalition. In countries in which proportional representation is used, cabinet crises have resulted as a consequence of this effect (e.g., Haberman, 1993).

Proportional representation is common in many democracies, including West Germany, the Netherlands, and Israel. In the United States it has encountered considerable resistance and has been used only to a limited degree in local elections. A possible reason for this opposition is that proportional representation is usually proposed as a way of giving voice to small, unpopular voting blocs.

A highly controversial alternative voting procedure is weighted voting. This procedure enables voter blocs otherwise too small to elect representatives to concentrate their voting strength in a way that increases the likelihood that they will gain some representation. In one form of weighted voting—cumulative voting—when a district elects several representatives, voters are allowed to cast all their votes for one candidate instead of having to vote once for each of the seats to be filled. Versions of weighted voting have been used by just a few constituencies in the United States, including Chilton County, Alabama (where some have claimed it reduced racial polarization) and in Pennsylvania. In 1993, opposition to weighted voting caused President Bill Clinton to withdraw his nomination of Lani Guinier to be Attorney General because she had suggested that it be used as a way of redressing black underrepresentation (Applebome, 1993; Margolick, 1993).

The "balanced ticket" is a once widely used strategy for strengthening the political voice of underrepresented ethnic groups. Such tickets enable ethnically oriented precinct party organizations to form coalitions large enough to win elections. Irish, Eastern and Southern European immigrants in the 19th and early 20th centuries relied largely on coalitions of ethnically homogeneous precincts and balanced tickets as they sought to be integrated into the political process (see, e.g., Glazer & Moynihan, 1963). The effectiveness of this strategy, of course, depends on the existence of a sufficient number of ethnic groups willing to work with each other to form a majority coalition. This willingness does not always exist, which explains why the balanced ticket strategy had limited effectiveness for African Americans in the latter half of the 20th century. In its place, they sought legislative relief. Their demands led to the Civil Rights Act of 1964, legislation that in turn became the stimulus for continued political conflict. That conflict highlights the problems attendant to preserving the perceived legitimacy of voting as a democratic expression of collective opinion.

Two actions specifically adopted to implement the 1964 Civil Rights Act were substituting geographically small and relatively homogeneous voting jurisdictions for at-large voting and carving out strangely shaped voting districts to assure victory to otherwise underrepresented populations. Remapping Congressional Districts to create predominantly African American or Hispanic constituencies proved to be effective in increasing Black and Hispanic representation in Congress. At the same time, it sometimes changed the party composition of legislatures as well. For example, after being remapped in 1992, the Georgia Congressional delegation changed from one Black and eight White Democrats, plus one White Republican, to three Black Democrats and eight White Republicans.

On June 29, 1995, the Supreme Court declared racially based districting to be unconstitutional, rejecting the argument that communities need not be geographically compact. In doing so, the Court overrode a lower court's decision that had upheld the constitutionality of oddly shaped, meandering, racially homogeneous Congressional Districts. One immediate reaction to the Supreme Court's decision was the claim that it would lead to the resegregation of politics. In any event, when the Georgia legislature attempted to create a new, constitutionally acceptable map that would also be acceptable to Blacks, Republicans, and Democrats alike, a political impasse resulted. (Greenhouse, 1995; Sack, 1995).

The creation of ethnically and racially homogeneous voting districts has been criticized on nonconstitutional grounds as well. Some have voiced the concern that if Black candidates for office come only from Black districts, this will disadvantage them when they run for higher office and must appeal to both White and Black voters. Another criticism is that this strategy depends on the preservation of residential segregation and that as progress is made in desgregating housing its effectiveness will decrease (Swain, 1993). As this criticism illustrates, the underlying issue is not so much the number of African Americans (or other ethnic group) elected to office, but how to create confidence in all sectors of the electorate that their views and interests are fairly and properly represented—that is, confidence in the legitimate linkage of collective opinion to governance.

CONFIDENCE IN POLITICAL INSTITUTIONS

Although elitists and populists differ as to whether the actions of representatives should closely follow the opinions of their constituencies rather than exercise their own judgment, they do agree that over time there should be a general correspondence in the views of an electorate and its representatives. Even a passive, acquiescent public is expected to vote out of office representatives whose voting records are disliked. Similarly, both elitists and populists agree that over time the general public should in general be satisfied with the performance of nonelected officials. Accordingly, when governments are in close tune with collective opinion, public confidence in and satisfaction with government tends to be high. Therefore, examining how satisfied the public is with how political institutions are functioning is a good way of assessing the linkage of collective opinion to government. To do that, we need to unravel complex interactions among the ways in which government is organized, issues, and partisanship, and how adequately existing linkage mechanisms are working.

One study found that even when elected legislators individually represent their constituencies, the way Congress is organized may itself be a significant barrier to linking collective opinion to governance. Although the sample sizes for individual Congressional Districts are small so that the results of the analysis must be treated cautiously, there is a good correspondence between the views of voters from each district studied and their separate representatives. On each of eight questions, the opinions of each representative were close to the mean of constituent opinions. The analysis also indicated that if the opinions of constituents were to change, in all likelihood so would the opinions of their elected representatives (Herrera, 1992).

However, a different relationship was found when the aggregated opinions of all representatives were compared with the opinions of all voters. There was a significant difference between the aggregated opinions of the representatives compared with the opinions of the total sample of voters on five of the eight questions. When Democratic representatives are compared with Democratic voters, and Republican representatives with Republicans, the degree of difference diminshes, but the difference between the aggregate and Congressional District levels of analysis persists. Thus, "individual members of Congress do a better job of representing their constituents than the House of Representatives as a whole does representing the nation" (Herrera et al., 1992, p. 191). Apparently, something about the institutional organization of Congress was acting to distort the national representative efficiency of the House of Representatives (Herrera, Herrera, & Smith, 1992). This finding may explain the fact that polls have consistently measured higher voter satisfaction with one's own representative than with Congress as a whole. For example, in a 1994 Gallup Poll, 51% said that most members of Congress and most congressional leaders are corrupt, compared with 29% who felt that way about their own respresentative (*The Gallup Poll Monthly*, June, 1994).

The 1994 Congressional elections, which ended decades of Democratic domination of both houses of Congress, were hailed by many as an expression of a collective opinion aroused by intense dissatisfaction with Democratic policies and practices. Poll data suggest that apart from the specific issues involved— especially taxes and reliance on government programs to deal with the nation's problems—public dissatifaction with the way the political system was functioning was also involved.

The years 1976–1990 were marked by widespread public distrust of the honesty and ethics of high-elected government officials. In a series of seven Gallup polls conducted over this period, nationally small minorities rated the honesty and ethical standards of Senators, Congressmen, and state officeholders as "very high" or "high." The percentage who did so for Senators ranged between a low of 16% and a high of 24%. For Congressmen the low was 14% and the high was 20%, and for state officeholders a low of 11% and a high of 17% (*The Gallup Poll Monthly*, February, 1990). This persistence and pervasiveness in low esteem suggests there may be a serious problem in the linkage between the public and government.

In a parallel development, during the period of 1976 to 1995, encompassing 6 years of Democratic and 12 years of Republican administrations, the proportion who felt that the government in Washington can be trusted to do what is right "always" or "most of the time" ranged between a low of 18% and a high of 51%. Only in 3 of those years did the proportion who trusted the government register at about half, whereas in 8 years it fell below 3 in 10 (*New York Times*/CBS News Poll, September 8, 1995). Responses to another question about satisfaction with "the way things are going in the United States at this time", asked by the Gallup Poll during the period of

February 1979 to March 1995, follow a similar pattern, although in this instance higher levels of public satisfaction were registered (*The Gallup Poll Monthly*, No. 355, p. 25; see also Lipset & Schneider, 1987).

In large part, these poll results reflect shifts in partisan strength during the period in question. In the *New York Times*/CBS Poll, the proportion expressing trust in the government never fell below 40% during Ronald Reagan's two terms of office whereas in only one of the six years of Democratic control of the White House did it reach as high as 40%. On the other hand, trust in government did fall below 30% during two years of the Bush Administration. Similarly, in the Gallup trend line, the highest levels of satisfaction all occurred during the Reagan and Bush administrations whereas satisfaction was depressed in the last years of Carter's incumbency and the first years of Clinton's administration. Also, the Democrats controlled Congress during the entire period, which might help explain why only once did a majority express trust in the government—and then only by the thinnest of margins.

However, further examination of the trend lines suggests that more than partisan sympathies were involved in expressions of public dissatisfaction. Concern over the state of the economy and international affairs is clearly involved. Thus, the high points in both the *New York Times*/CBS and Gallup trends were reached during a period of economic recovery (1986) and in the wake of the Gulf War victory (1991). Also, we should note that there was less variation in response to *New York Times*/CBS News question, which asked about trust in the government, than to the Gallup question, which related more to specific situational conditions. This last point, in combination with the tendency toward low levels of satisfaction in both trend lines, suggests that satisfaction was also being depressed by still another, persistent factor.

Initial public assessment of the new, Republican-controlled Congress indicates that there there existed, regardless of which party was in power, a continuous, deep suspicion of Congress and how government was functioning. In a poll conducted by the *New York Times*/CBS News Poll in July 1995, six months after the new Congress was installed, only 26% said the Republicans in Congress had been doing a good job in handling what they considered to be the country's most important problem, and 54% said they were doing a poor job. This is almost identical with the 26% who said President Clinton was doing a good job in handling that problem and 56%, a poor job. Furthermore, when asked whether Ross Perot (whose candidacy for President as an Independent in 1992 had been surprisingly strong) could do a better job than either the Republicans or Clinton, 20% replied "Yes" and 58%, "No."

In answer to two other questions in that same poll, 56% disapproved of the way Congress was handling its job and 47% were "mostly disappointed with the things the Republicans in Congress have done." Yet, 48% also said they felt that "on the whole" the things the "Republicans have done since they took control of Congress has been for the good of the country" (*New York Times*/CBS News Poll, September 8, 1995, pp. 4–9). And a Gallup poll found that 64% felt that what the Republicans were doing in Congress was merely politics as usual and 60% thought that they had not accomplished most of what they intended to do in the first three months of controlling Congress (*The Gallup Poll Monthly*, No. 355, April, 1995). To place this in context, at the beginning of 1995, by a margin of 44% to 11%, the weight of opinion was that the new Congress would get more done than the old one had (*The Gallup Opinion Monthly*, January, 1955, No. 352).

A belief that political corruption was endemic in Congress also dominated public thinking in the mid-1990s. In a Gallup Poll conducted half a year before the 1994 Congressional elections, 49% said that Congress was more corrupt that it had been 20 years previous, compared with 7% who said it was less corrupt (*The Gallup Poll Monthly*, June 1994, No. 345). After the Republican victory that fall, expectations for improvement were only moderately optimistic. A 56% majority still did not expect any improvement, although by a ratio of 28% to 12%, the weight of opinion was that the new Congress would be less corrupt than the old one. (*The Gallup Opinion Monthly*, January, 1995, No, 352). More generally, in the summer 1995 *New York Times*/CBS News mentioned above, 59% could not name one currently elected public official whom they admired.

Perhaps of even greater significance, even though the percentage who felt that having elections makes the government pay attention to what the people think rose to 41% up from a low of 34% who felt that way in 1992, that was still far below the 65% who gave that answer in a 1964 University of Michigan poll. Similarly, a majority of 58% felt that what people like themselves think "does not have much say about what the government does". It is, therefore, significant that polls conducted after the Democratic defeat in the 1994 Congressional elections provide evidence that that the crisis in public confidence had not been resolved and that more than the Republican victory would be needed to restore majority confidence. In a Gallup Poll conducted immediately after the 1994 Republican victory, a plurality of 48% said they expected the new Congress will be more responsive to what the public wants, but 36% said there would be no difference (*The Gallup Poll Monthly*, January, 1995, No. 352).

A *New York Times*/CBS News Poll conducted in the spring of 1996 reinforces the conclusion that more than partisan sympathies was involved.

In that poll, 45% felt that "having two parties gives voters enough options" whereas 48% said that "having only two parties can't provide voters with enough options." In answer to another question, a 53% majority felt that the country needs a third political party. Nonetheless, majorities said that a having a third party would not make much difference with giving "people like you more say in government" (57%) or "produce better candidates" (53%). What a third party was expected to accomplish was "raise issues that the current parties do not address" (*New York Times*/CBS News Poll, March 31–April 2, 1996). Apparently loss of confidence was not so much in the mechanics of voting, but in the responsiveness of who was elected.

There clearly are grounds for concern that, over time, repeated failure to maintain confidence in the responsiveness of successive administrations to collective opinion may weaken the continued legitimacy of democratic government itself among the citizenry at large. On the other hand, commitment to democratic government appears to have a resiliency that should not be underestimated. In April 1995, despite widespread dissatisfaction with both the Democratic and Republican parties and their leaders, by a margin of 64% to 27% the overwhelming majority of U.S. adults were very or somewhat satisfied with "the way democracy works in this country" (*The Gallup Poll Monthly*, June 1995, No. 357).

Public dissatisfaction with the functioning of linkage between collective opinion and political institutions may lead to a restructuring of party systems rather than a rejection of democracy itself. What restructuring might entail, and how it might over time affect the legitimacy of democratic government, is another matter about which we do not have any data. What we can state with confidence is that the continued legitimacy of the public opinion process in a democracy rests as much on how well collective opinion is linked to governing institutions as upon an ideological belief in democracy.

MAINTAINING DEMOCRATIC LINKAGES
BETWEEN COLLECTIVE OPINION
AND GOVERNANCE

There can be little doubt that for institutional linkages to function properly in a democracy, the quality of collective opinion must meet minimal criteria of knowledge and involvement. However, as we have seen, there are good reasons for concluding that whatever limitations may exist in this respect at the individual level, they may to a surprising degree be overcome at the collective level. Furthermore, although elitist–populist opposition is unlikely ever to be fully resolved at the ideological level, that in itself does not necessarily pose a threat to democratic governance.

More worrisome is the question of institutional organization. Because the emergence of democracy is not the product of a one-way evolutionary process, the continued legitimacy of governments based on the linkage of collective opinion to governance is not and should not be assumed to be inevitable. The possibility always exists that faith in the public opinion process as the basis for governing may at some time weaken to the point that some other form of government will be preferred by many. Also, we should not forget that contemporary faith in the legitimacy of collective opinion as a basis for governing contrasts with the age-old fear that democracy encourages demagoguery and ultimately degenerates into tyranny.

The United States Constitution established a political framework that created channels through which collective opinion can be expressed without unleashing any destabilizing potential in the public opinion process. Recent expressions of loss of confidence in the responsiveness of government, voting systems, and political leaders have led some to suggest that the overall framework may be in need of reform. Proposals for reforms have in large part been based on very different diagnoses of what is at fault.

Many populists contend that the public's direct involvement in government needs to be strengthened through such procedures as increased reliance on direct primaries, initiatives, and referenda. In opposition are those who think the need is to strengthen political parties and other institutional controls that limit the influence of an incompetent and undisciplined public. Both diagnoses share a concern that the United States is experiencing a breakdown in how collective opinion is linked with and integrated into the political process. To a considerable degree, these conflicting diagnoses can be interpreted as no more than manifestations of continuing ideological differences between elitists and populists. To do so is to focus attempts at reform on the question of just how competent and involved individual members of the public really are, neglecting the question of how adequately existing institutional linkages between collective opinion and governance are functioning.

A significant aspect of this last question is communication between the electorate and government officials. As we have seen, in the mid-1990s, much of the public perceives government as not being responsive to their needs in a responsible way. Apparently, elections are not functioning adequately as a channel for making collective opinion known to government functionaries and agencies in a way that has to be heeded. One likely reason for this is that election results often do a better job in reflecting what the public does not want than what it does. As a result, they seldom define clear public mandates. Difficulties in maintaining communications *between* elections exacerbate the situation. Even when there are decisive victories, there are myriad specific continuing issues, not to mention new ones, on which election results do not cast much light with respect to collective judgments.

If continuing dissatisfaction with government responsiveness and performance is to be reduced, existing linkages between collective opinion and government have to be strengthened. Although how to achieve that is a topic outside the scope of this work, the process model of public opinion is relevant to the problem: The legitimacy of public opinion in democracies has created a psychological environment that encourages people to have opinions and to feel free to express them. Even for the uninformed and uninvolved, freedom of speech is a value that creates the expectation that government should pay attention to their wishes, an expectation that must be met if confidence is to be restored. Concurrently, in a complex, heterogeneous society, collective opinion will normally not be dominated by a single point of view but by opinion competition and conflict. The problem, therefore, is not to develop solutions that will only give voice to majority opinion, but to develop a *modus vivendi* among often clashing factions.

7

Polls and the Public Opinion Process

According to their first practitioners, opinion polls were developed in the 1930s as a contribution to democratic governance. Their self-proclaimed goal was to make government more responsive to all the people and not only to powerful interest groups, to reverse the control of entrenched elites over the formation and expression of collective opinion made possible by new communications technology, to give continuous voice to the people's desires and not only at election time, to make the public aware of its own thinking and so add to its political strength, and to counter the threat to democracy posed by fascist and communist dictators (Bruner, 1944; Crespi, 1989; Gallup & Rae, 1940). The high level of dissatisfaction with government discussed in chapter 6 indicates that the proliferation of opinion polls has not led to the realization of this goal. To the contrary, polls have been repeatedly and sharply criticized as a methodologicically unsound threat to democracy (Ginsberg, 1986; Rogers,1949).

After polling was developed in western democracies, it was introduced into both authoritarian and totalitarian states. Given the limited legitimacy of public opinion in the latter, this seems strange. A review of the actual role of polls in democratic and nondemocratic states—why they are conducted, by whom, under what conditions, and how they are used—explains this seeming anomaly.

OPINION POLLS IN NONDEMOCRATIC STATES

Political authorities in nondemocratic states do not plan or expect opinion research to be used to make them responsive to their subjects. Their use of polls is not a sign that they have accepted the political legitimacy of public opinion. At most, in both authoritarian and totalitarian states polls might be used for administrative purposes, analogous to the use of marketing research to enhance a company's business planning. It is also the case that opinion research plays different roles in authoritarian and totalitarian states, and in a way that corresponds to the differences between the two with respect to the legitimacy of public opinion.

Franco's Spain

Spain under the military dictatorship of Francisco Franco is an outstanding example of an authoritarian regime in which surveys in general, and opinion polls in particular, were conducted under conditions of unexpected freedom. It would be a serious mistake to underestimate the repressive, dictatorial nature of the Franco regime. Yet, it would be equally wrong to assume that because collective opinion had no legitimate role in governance, any and all expressions of public thinking would inevitalby be extirpated. Opinion research was, to a considerable degree, tolerated as an intellectual activity that might even have practical use for administrators, but only if it did not become part of the nation's political life. Social scientists had considerable latitude in conducting surveys, but they had no opportunity to disseminate that information for general public discussion and debate. On the other hand, if the information they produced had administrative value, that enhanced their ability to study opinion. But, as is evident from the following description, conducting polls and other surveys did not have a democratizing effect.

The following summary description of survey research in Spain under Franco is based primarily on information that has been provided by Juan Linz, an American-trained sociologist who was involved in a number of major studies conducted during the final decades of the Franco dictatorship (Linz, personal communication, 1995).

From the early 1960s on through Franco's death in 1975 and the subsequent establishment of a democratic government, numerous surveys were conducted by academic groups and private commercial research companies. Although researchers were always sensitive to the realities of operating under a repressive dictatorship, they had considerable freedom in the design and implementation of their studies. They were also able to maintain frequent and continuing contact with social scientists, international agencies, and private businesses in other countries.

A variety of surveys were conducted for governmental and nongovernmental sponsors, including government organizations such as the Official Youth Organization, the Escuela de Organizacion Industrial (a management school of the Ministry of Industry), and the National Planning Office; private Spanish entrepreneurs, the Fundacion Fomental de Estudios Socialis y de Sociologia Aplicade (FOESSA; whose funding sources included the Ministry of Education and Science), and international sources (e.g., Organization for Economic Cooperation and Development [OECD], and the Volkswagen Foundation). Much of this research was conducted under the direction of leading academic sociologists like Amando de Miguel and Linz.

A number of commercial survey companies were founded in the early 1960s, including Data (Linz's firm affiliated with International Research Associates whose headquarters were in New York City) and ICSA (affiliated with Gallup International). Consequently, the principals of these two firms were in regular contact with survey researchers in western Europe, North America, and elsewhere. As private for-profit businesses, they were regulated by the government, but only by corporate law. Interviewers for both academic and commercial studies were on occasion subjected to local police harassment, but when that happened the researchers could usually turn to higher authorities for assistance.

These firms conducted standard marketing research surveys, but they also conducted government-sponsored surveys that were typically commissioned for practical administrative purposes. Among the topics covered were: local elites in rural communities; community power systems; Spanish social structure; consumption and saving; youth; industrial sociology; and social value systems. These firms also provided field and tabulation services to academic researchers and sometimes subsidized academic research. Marketing and administrative surveys were sometimes expanded by the researchers into broad sociological investigations (for example, interest group politics, pressure group activity, and the Common Market). This opened up the possibility of asking political questions, even some that related to the Spanish Civil War that had brought Franco to power.

When designing these studies, the researchers were able to draw on their knowledge of the theoretical and methodological literature in the United States and western Europe. They were typically free to design the questionnaires and analysis plans, and to write up the reports, with sponsors having little or no say in these matters. On the other hand, not many direct questions on then-current public issues were ever asked. Circumspection and self-imposed censorship enabled researchers to deal with sensitive topics. In one case, Linz put some of the more potentially politically disturbing findings in the middle of a book published by the Instituto de Estudios Politicos, a government institution not subject to censorship.

Despite the limited restrictions to which surveys were subjected, the results did not get wide distribution, especially not to the general public. Most surveys were performed under contract and solely intended for the client's information, or else were distributed only within government circles (some even to Franco). Lack of interest, inertia, and personnel turnover resulted in many government-funded surveys never being fully analyzed nor printed even for limited distribution. Also, although many surveys investigated public opinion and political topics, none were sponsored by news media for publication. On the other hand, there were few restrictions on publication for academic audiences. Censorship was usually not a serious problem; in at least one case a chapter that had been removed from a report on a FOESSA-sponsored survey nonetheless had considerable circulation within the academic community.

In the 1960s, the Minister of Information and Tourism founded an official Instituto Espanol de la Opinion Publica (IEOP) whose directors were largely academics who worked with considerable independence even though the government used the data they issued. IEOP initiated a publication—*Revista de Estudios de Opinion Publica*—that eventually became a leading social science journal. Among other things, this journal published raw data from many surveys.

Soviet Union

The position of survey and opinion researchers in the Soviet Union was sharply different. The discipline itself was ideologically suspect. Not only were researchers always subject to close political control, they were prohibited for extended periods of time from doing any empirical research. What little survey research was conducted was intended primarily for administrative use under tight security. Even so, the results were typically suppressed, either for ideological reasons or because of bureaucratic insecurity. Getting research published, even for academic audiences, was always difficult. Party controls attempted to bolster the impression that official policy and practice was in tune with and expressive of the populace's thinking. For as long as the Soviet Union remained a totalitarian state, the accepted role of what little opinion research was conducted was to maintain and further the fiction that the government was responsive to collective opinion even as its free expression was repressed.

Marxist-Leninist theory rejected opinion research because it was considered to be part of sociology, which in turn was rejected as a bourgeois pseudoscience. The orthodox view was that dialectic materialism renders sociology unnecessary; also that sociology is theoretically unsound because it assumes that social conflict (class conflict in particular) is characteristic of all societies, including communist ones. As a result, sociology was not taught as a separate discipline until the mid-1980s (Doktorov, personal communication, 1995; Smith, 1990).

Additionally, both party and administrative bureaucrats feared that survey results about their territory that contradicted official policy or revealed inadequate personal performance would be sent to their superiors and used against them. Under some conditions, surveys that produced results critical of the performance of specific individuals and their departments were permitted because of their value to central administration and not as input to public discussion. In 1979, at a time when barriers against survey research were being relaxed, Eduard Shevardnadze, later to become one of Mikhail Gorbachev's closest collaborators, organized a public opinion research center under the auspices of the Georgian Party Central Committee. The polls it conducted were used to monitor the quality of state services; officials whose departments got bad reports were fired (Doktorov, personal communication, 1995; Smith, 1990).

The Party sought to control all phases of the research process. There were only two types of sponsors, the political apparatus itself, namely, central, regional, and local Party organizations; and the economic apparatus, such as ministries, territorial commands, directors of factories, and so on, all subject to Party oversight and supervision. The Party itself did not provide financial support for the studies it requested be conducted. Instead, it used its power to order researchers to work on projects as part of their duties at their regular jobs. The researchers worked either for academic institutions, whose staffs were subject to KGB (secret police) review, or for industrial and other such organizations whose activities were subject to centralized administration (Doktorov, personal communication, 1995).

Opposition to sociological study was relaxed in the immediate post-Stalin period, especially under Khrushchev. This enabled a few small teams in Moscow and Leningrad that had managed to achieve political tolerance to conduct empirical studies using the survey research method. A leading pioneer in these activities was Boris Grushin, who conducted a few surveys for the newspaper *Komsomolskaya Pravda* in the late 1950s and early 1960s. However, after initial publication of results that revealed public opposition to some aspects of official government policies, the department that sponsored those surveys was closed and the work stopped. Another pioneer in conducting opinion polls for newspapers, Vladimir Shlapentokh, later migrated to the United States (Shlapentokh, personal communication, 1996; Zaslavskaya, personal communication, 1995).

Grushin moved to the Institute of Special Sociological Invesigations (ISSI) where he led the "Seven Fridays" project, an investigation that produced a complex picture of the social life of the city Tagonrog. That project was supported by the propaganda department of the Central Committee of the Communist Party of the Soviet Union, where some progressives as well as conservatives were represented. It "was dedicated to the study of public opinion" along with socioeconomic, legal, and demographic issues. He found that workers had a level of involvement in ideological activity that was much lower than of the intelligentsia (Shlapentokh, 1986). These results, which "were contradictory to many Soviet ideological myths," (Shlapentokh, 1986, p. 109) were discussed at a small meeting convened at the Academy of Sociological Sciences under the Central Committee of the Communist party. Only 30 people were invited to attend this meeting and most of the report was never published, although some minor parts were published many years later (Zaslavskaya, personal communication, 1995).

From 1972 to 1988, as part of a general negative turn against sociology, almost no empirical investigations of public opinion were conducted. Grushin was forced to transfer to the Institute of Philosophy of the Academy of Science, where he confined his work to theoretical problems of public opinion (Zaslavskaya, 1995). Indicative of the change in Grushin's status, and that of opinion research in general, around 1970 he was officially sent by his authorities to spend three months in Paris with the Institut Francais de l'Opinion Publique (IFOP, the French Gallup affiliate) to study research methodology, with the expectation that he would develop a similar research center in the Soviet Union. However, there was no follow-up, and the French, who came to understand that he was encountering personal difficulties, found it impossible to contact him (Riffault, personal communication, 1995).

The control system sought to use what little opinion research was conducted in its efforts to maintain the legitimacy of the Communist Party as the people's voice. But, over time, evidence was being accumulated that something was basically wrong. Researchers like Grushin, Zaslavskaya, and Levada, who used this evidence to urge basic reform, played important roles in the Gorbachev reforms of the late 1980s. A notable contribution came from work done by some sociologists and economists in remote or provincial locations, especially in Academic City outside Novosibirsk, some 2,000 miles from Moscow. They managed to take advantage of their geographic remoteness to integrate some opinion research into economic studies that were of administrative use—and without the knowledge of or interference from party functionaries.

One study, known as *The Novosibirsk Report*, which was issued in 1983, investigated the "opinions of non-urban people concerning their problems, structures, values, motivations, etc." (Doktorov, personal communication, 1995) within the context of a larger investigation of the socioeconomic problems of small villages. Two topics that were investigated were why young people left rural areas and why workers were poorly motivated. Studies like this led economists and sociologists like Abel Abalbegyan, Tatiana Zaslavskaya, and Yuri Levada to challenge official economic statistics and to conclude that extensive reform was needed to solve the serious problems that were being ignored by the Soviet bureaucracy. (Doktorov, personal communication, 1995; Smith, 1990; Zaslavskaya, 1995). *The Novosibirsk Report* was presented in April, 1983 to an invited audience of some 150 scholars at Academic City. A limited, numbered edition of the report was printed but was never publicly released. When *The Washington Post* published a story based on the report, high government officials denied there was any serious talk of reform and the KGB used the numbered copies to track down the source of the leak (Smith, 1990).

Numbering reports and KGB involvement in this incident were typical of the tight control exercised by the Communist Party over the distribution of survey resuts. Before Gorbachev, opinion research reports were confidential, typed in limited quantity, and distributed directly to clients such as official government bodies or directors of organizations. Newspaper publication was limited to favorable findings and "soft" critiques. Contributions to the scientific literature were limited to methodology, illustrations of theoretical concepts and, if a study's sponsor agreed, use in restricted dissertations. Disseminating research reports so that they could get into the general sociological literature, internally as well as outside the Soviet Union, was dangerous (Doktorov, personal communication, 1995).

During the 1960s, a period of relative liberalization, a number of surveys were conducted of readers of *Trud, Pravda, Izvestia,* and *Literaturnaia Gazeta* that investigated acceptance of and agreement with officially condoned beliefs and values. The results of these surveys contradicted official policy; they were quickly suppressed, and the surveys discontinued (Shlapentokh, 1986).

Despite the fact that some highly professional sociologists in protected positions were able to conduct research with some degree of freedom, they still had to protect themselves against Party discipline. Any negative implications of their research had to be restricted to discrete aspects of specific organizations and could not relate to the basics of the Soviet system and its values. Self-censorship, to avoid official intervention, was an effective supplement to direct control. A typical tactic was to word questions so that only positive findings could be obtained. For example, in one 1971 study of reactions to recent social changes, a question asked what measures in the new constitution will have a positive influence on various aspects of life. The response categories were "undoubtedly," "probably," and "difficult to say" (Doktorov, personal communication, 1995). With questions like these, researchers could hope that the results of their research would not be attacked as anti-Soviet.

Communist Eastern Europe

Opinion research was conducted in a number of communist states in eastern Europe, including East Germany, Poland, Czechoslovakia, Hungary, and Yugoslavia. The circumstances under which opinion research first developed in those countries differed in a number of significant ways from those in the Soviet Union. Many of the earliest practitioners had intellectual and personal contact with western sociologists and survey researchers. It was not unknown for them to have studied in the United States or western Europe, attended international professional conferences, and contributed to western publications. Some were able to maintain limited contacts under communist rule, at least for a while. Eventually, however, the role of opinion research in these countries differed little if at all from its role in the Soviet Union. A few highlights illustrate the difficult and tightly controlled conditions under which opinion research was conducted in communist-governed Eastern European countries.

In 1947, IFOP called an international conference in Paris, attended by some 25 representatives of European opinion research institutes, including Dr. Cenek Adamec from Czechoslovakia, as well as representatives from Poland and Hungary (Riffault, personal communication, 1995). Adamec's description of his background and experience in opinion research provides a measure of the extent to which some eastern and central European social scientists knew of, were interested in, and were active in the developing field of opinion research, as well as the changing status of opinion research under communist rule (Adamec, personal communication, 1995).

Before World War II, Adamec studied in the United States and France (meeting Hadley Cantril, George Gallup, Rensis Likert, and Jean Stoetzel, among others). He also studied opinion research in England where, among other things, he became familiar with sampling and "mass observation" methodology. After having served with the Czechoslovak Armored Brigade in England during World War II, at the war's end, he joined the staff of the newly established Czechoslovak Institute for Public Opinion. The Institute was founded in 1945 under the direction of Joseph Kopta, who had been impressed by the meaning of opinion polling (as practiced in Great Britain and the United States) as a tool for democratic government (Adamek & Viden, 1947). In 1947, Adamek served as vice chairman of the European Commission for Public Opinion Research headquartered in Williamstown,

Massachusetts and became a member of the section, Public Opinion and World Peace. He also published in *Public Opinion Quarterly* and *International Journal of Public Opinion Research.*

As in the the Soviet Union, ideological opposition to opinion research had to be overcome in its satellites in eastern Europe. In the German Democratic Republic (GDR—East Germany), opinion research was justified as a "policy tool employed to ensure the efficient control of society by the party elite … used in decision-making, in the evaluation of already implemented policies or in the manipulation and mobilization of the citizens" (Sieger, 1990, pp. 324-325). The official definition of opinion research was:

> A valuable tool for leadership activity. It serves the purpose of bringing *the party, the state and the people* into closer contact with each other and thus improves their relationships. It facilitates the making of decisions and the preparation of resolutions and policy measures on all levels of socialist society. (Sieger, 1990, p. 325)

The need to overcome ideological resistance to opinion research is also evident in a special 1959 issue of the French journal *Sondages, Revue Francaise de l'Opinion Publique,* which was devoted to Polish studies in sociology and opinion research. The issue's Introduction starts by establishing the ideological bona fides of sociology and opinion research in the face of the "predominate view" that Marxism excludes the use of sociology, sociological research, and public opinion surveys. To validate sociology and opinion research, it was argued that Marxism is a profound sociological theory and that survey research had practical value in helping the builders of a socialist society in the aftermath of World War II. This argument was then used to justify establishing a Center for Public Opinion Surveys. Although "its creation met great difficulties … it started research on practical problems" (Szczepanski, 1959, pp. 9–11).

Ideological justification did not free opinion research from strict party control. In Czechoslovakia, a second opinion research institute had been organized in 1967, during the period leading up to the "Prague Spring" that temporarily liberalized the country. However, after the overthrow of the liberal Dubcek government, the institute was dissolved and its duties transferred to the State Statistical Office (SSO). Because the SSO did not have any staff trained in survey research, six members of the second instutute's staff were initially transferred to it, but they were discharged after one year. A third, communist-dominated research institute was organized in 1972 and continued operations until the communist government was overthrown in 1989. This institute reported directly to the Central Committee of the Communist Party rather than to SSO of which it was formally a division. The head of the institute was always a communist, as were many of its staff. Survey research at this third institute was considered a craft and not a profession. (Adamec, personal communication, 1995).

In East Germany, all opinion research was under the strict control of the Socialist Unity Party (SED), with all survey research carried out by research institutes controlled by agencies of the central government (Sieger, 1990). The Central Office for Statistics controlled the authorization, financing, coordination, and publication of the studies conducted by the four social science institutes. The Scientific Councils of Social Science Research in the GDR, consisting of scientists and party representatives, coordinated and consulted on the research conducted by these institutes. Other survey research institutes reported to the Ministry for Trade and Supply, the State Secretariat for Labor and Wages, and the Ministry of Transportation. In this way, the SED was able to maintain tight supervision over all survey research.

A study of reaction to the lifting of restrictions on East German travel in 1989, just prior to the collapse of the communist government, illustrates how the survey design and interpretation of results of adminstrative studies were shaped by official policy and ideology. The response options to questions were worded to reflect positively on the new arrangements: "a great event, a step toward peaceful co-existence, evidence of sincerity, strengthening trust" (Sieger, 1990, p. 326). The results were interpreted to indicate that identification as a citizen of the German Democratic Republic was so strong that there was little danger of a mass exodus.

In both Czechoslovakia and East Germany, surveys were conducted to serve administrative needs and not to monitor public opinion: The secret police were relied on for the latter. Thus, the studies conducted by the third Czechoslovak institute related to marketing research, public health, culture, and mass media audience measurement. However, even apparently nonpolitical health studies could have political ramifications so that a party consultant was assigned to every study. When asked to participate in a nutrition study being sponsored by the Central Committee of the Czechoslovakian Communist Party, Adamec recommended investigating the relation between nutrition and public health. The reply to this recommendation was that the only research interest was in the adequacy of the food supply. Apparently, the Party was aware of public discontent and was interested in ascertaining whether basic food needs were being met, and nothing more (Adamec, personal communication, 1995).

The expansion and contraction of opinion research in reaction to the relaxing and tightening of totalitarian controls that occurred in the Soviet

Union also took place in eastern Europe. The short tenure of the second research institute in Czechoslovakia and its replacement by the third institute is illustrative. In Poland, the research reported in the special 1959 issue of *Sondages* mentioned above was conducted after the 1956 worker uprisings led to a temporary liberalization of government control. Previously,

> during the period 1948–1955, sociological research, and also public opinion surveys, did not find a favorable climate … the role of the press, like that of the radio, television, or movies, was subordinated to this doctrine: they must combat the effects and influences of hostile ideology and further the spirit of socialist ideology. (Szczepanski, 1959, p. 9)

The administrative use of opinion research in East Germany mirrored what we have seen existed in the Soviet Union, Poland, and Czechoslovakia. Surveys were conducted on such topics as media habits, family and women, education and youth, work and workplace, leisure time, moral preferences, social problems and social policy, politics and ideology, ethnicity and foreign countries, and market research.

The administrative utility to totalitarian regimes of getting feedback on their extensive communications activities explains why audience research was one of the major areas of survey research in Czechoslovakia, East Germany, and Poland. It also explains why, on occasion, researchers from Hungary, Poland, and Czechslovakia visited the Swedish Broadcasting Corporation to learn about western research methodology. These visits took place at least during the period of 1968 to 1972, possibly even earlier, and later as well (Webb, personal correspondance, 1995).

In both the Soviet Union and eastern Europe, periods in which totalitarian controls were eased were also marked by increased, although temporary, direct contacts between survey researchers in communist ruled states and those in western Europe and the United States. Across the years, through Jean Stoetzel, its liaison to UNESCO, the World Association for Public Opinion Research (WAPOR) made repeated attempts to maintain contact with survey researchers in communist countries, with limited, intermittent success. In 1965, WAPOR, under the presidency of Leo Bogart from the United States, participated in a special conference in Dubrovnik, Yugoslavia (Bogart, personal communication, 1995). The initiative for convening and organizing the conference came from Fedor Rocco, a Yugoslav who headed a market research company in Zagreb. The conference was attended by about 100 researchers from communist states including East Germany, Poland, and the host country Yugoslavia, and was characterized by a strong Communist Party presence. A handful of westerners representing WAPOR also attended. Although the conference theme was "Is there a world public opinion?", the focus was on nonpolitical marketing and audience research.

To understand how this conference came to be held, a few points need to be emphasized. Under Tito, Yugoslavia had split from the Soviet bloc on the issue of incorporating market mechanisms into the state economy. As a result, there was considerable interest in that country in learning about marketing research methodology. Also, the conference was held in the mid-1960s, a time when, as we have seen, totalitarian controls over opinion research were being relaxed in many communist countries. During this period, a representative from a Yugoslav marketing-research institute visited a number of research firms in the United States. Extremely important was that the fact the conference's subject matter was almost exclusively methodological.

There was only one paper on a politically relevant research topic, given by an American and it was the target of an immediate, extremely hostile methodological attack (Sharp, personal communication, 1995). The paper reported the result of a study of the reactions of a group of 30 to 35 American students to their contacts with age-peers they met on a Methodist- sponsored tour to the Soviet Union and other communist-controlled countries in eastern Europe. These students were surveyed before and after the trip concerning their expectations and perceptions of the age-peers they met on the tour. The paper reported that these 30 to 35 American students said that the students they met from communist countries only wanted to talk about things like rock music, photography, and other such topics of interest to youth around the world and not about ideological matters such as differences between government in the United States and in communist countries. Although the paper's findings were described as no more than a case study of this one group, all of whom were surveyed, and not as as a representative sample of a larger population, the president of the Yugoslav statistical association immediately challenged it because the so-called "sample" was too small. Only by sticking to aspects of survey research that are adminstratively useful was the conference able to remain harmonious. No subsequent conferences were ever held, despite WAPOR's continued interest.

As in Franco's Spain, polling's role in the Soviet Union and its satellites in Eastern Europe was sharply circumscribed by the limited role the public opinion process had in each, and not by qualities inherent in the methodology. Polls were tolerated primarily during periods of political liberalization and even then only if administratively useful. This leaves us with the question as to whether, in an environment open to the public opinion process, polls can have a democratizing effect.

OPINION POLLS AND DEMOCRACY

The suspicion, distrust, and opposition of totalitarian governments toward opinion research clearly is based on fear of its subversive potential and not of its possible value as information to be used for administrative purposes. It is also clear that polls can be subversive because they are able to document public discontent and even opposition to official policy and practice. That is to say, fear that polls might strengthen the expression of public opinion is what explains the totalitarian response to them. Nevertheless, various social scientists, politicians, journalists, philosophers, and just plain ordinary citizens have all criticized polls as a threat to democracy. A review of their criticisms casts light on the role of polls as a channel through which public opinion might legitimately influence democratic government. For the largest part, critics have had two main targets: the methodological adequacy of polls, and the effect they have on the political process.

Much criticism is directed at the methodological standards of polls, especially the adequacy of the sampling methods used and the wording of the questions asked (Crespi, 1988). The fact is there is considerable room for methodological improvement in most commercial polls, with most falling far short of academic survey research standards. Considering the number of polling organizations that exist, the variability in professional training, background, and experience of their staffs, and the limited budgets that are typically available, it is not surprising that this is so. On the other hand, it must be acknowledged that some employ acceptable methods and try to improve on what they are doing. In any event, although much of the methodological criticisms of how polls are conducted is justified, that does not, in and of itself, mean that the method is inherently flawed. However, there are critics who do take this position, so that even if there were a general raising of standards and the practices of the leading polls were to become the norm, the concerns of those critics would still not be met.

Beyond the matter of sheer technical competence, responsibility, and honesty, many critics have doubts as to the capacity of the polling method as such to capture the complexity and dynamics of public opinion. These doubts are fed and reinforced by the practice of many polls to do no more than report summary percentages ("marginals" in technical jargon) on a limited number of questions as if it were "public opinion" (Crespi, 1989). As has been stressed, this practice indeed distorts the nature of public opinion as process. Some of the leading newspaper polls have tried to deal with this problem by using marginals to enrich analytical news stories (Kagay, 1995; Morin, 1995). Also, the better polls have worked at developing questions that probe the public's thinking and at applying sophisticated analytical techniques that do much more than simply tabulate how many people answered "yes" or "no" to individual questions. Some examples can be found in chapters 2 and 3.

Perhaps the best known examples of polling that is process oriented come from analyses of trends in presidential popularity and in what the public considers to be the nation's most important problems. This type of polling, which attempts to measure collective opinion in dynamic interaction with ongoing political and socioeconomic happenings, contrasts with snapshot polls that report the percentage that favor or oppose some particular proposal as if that were an adequate description of what public opinion is. In its coverage of the 1992 Presidential election, the *New York Times* developed a polling strategy that attempted to track the long-term, middle-run, and short-lived campaign dynamics (Kagay, 1995).

But progress in making polling more process oriented does not answer the criticism that collective opinion cannot be reduced to numbers, that there is a qualitative dimension that is inevitably lost by any quantitative method. The "focus group" method, in which groups of 8 to 10 people gather for an hour or two to dicuss a topic under a moderator's guidance, has been adopted by a number of media polls as a way of probing the qualitative dynamics of opinion (Traugott, 1995). This method has its methodological weaknesses, among which the most prominent are that the groups cannot be considered representative samples of anything, and that analysis is susceptible to highly subjective and biased judgment. Nevertheless, experience is that when used in conjunction with well-designed surveys, focus groups can be a valuable qualitative tool for analyzing opinion dynamics. Although this is the case, using focus groups to study opinion has been sharply criticized by many, including some who decry the limitations of quantitative surveys.

Many critics of polls have an underlying distrust of opinion research that is often couched in methodological terms but is resistant to methodological progress. The roots of this distrust lie in concern over the effects of opinion research on the political process and in assumptions about what is the legitimate role of the public opinion process in a democracy. These concerns have mostly to do with the manipulative uses to which opinion research is often put, what opinion research does to communications between the public and politicians, and elitist suspicion of polls as a populist enterprise.

Polls have become a basic source of information used by politicians and lobbyists in planning election and "public information" campaigns. That is, one of the most important applications of polls has not been to find out what the public thinks in order to serve it better but, instead, to win elections and to influence public thinking on current issues (Crespi, 1989). Polls have become an integral part of an expensive communications technology that has transformed the historical functioning of political parties and that treats the public as its target rather than as its master. Nevertheless, it is also the case that by influencing how politicans select issues on which to campaign, polls have to some degree indirectly increased political awareness of and sensitivity to the public's desires and concerns. Thus, polls have simultaneously contributed to the manipulative efficiency and to the political responsiveness of established power centers. To the extent that the balance of these opposing effects tips in the direction of increased responsiveness, polls can add to confidence in democratic government. On the other hand, if the balance tips toward manipulative efficiency, polls can contribute to the growth of political alienation and anomie.

It should also be recognized that the manipulative use of polls is not inherent in the method but, rather, is a consequence of its application by commercial enterprises serving partisan interests. Hypothetically, one can conceive of polls being conducted for political clients in order to find out how to get their message across and not what to say. Such polls would further communication from the public to politicians, and strengthen democratic linkage. However, few, if any, such polls have ever been conducted and there are few reasons to hope any will be.

Another common criticism of polls is that in order to get elected politicians will merely "follow the polls." Assuming for the moment that the methodological weaknesses of many media- sponsored polls have been remedied (and for our purposes making this assumption is warranted because we are focusing on the distrust of any kind of opinion research), this criticism translates into an elitist criticism of populist democracy. The evident concern is that elected representatives will not rely on their own, presumably superior, knowledge and judgment when making political decisions, but on the presumably ill-considered and uninformed opinions of the general public. Relying on polls is criticized because polls are feared as an agent that enhances the influence of collective opinion, and the more accurately they measure collective opinion the more are they to be feared.

"Following the polls" refers simultaneously to both manipulative efficiency and increased responsiveness, that is, manipulating the electorate by being uncritically responsive to the public's desires. Thus, this criticism is an unexpected combination of two factors—elitist general distrust of the quality of the general public's thinking, and the political alienation that comes when polls are perceived as nothing more than a tool that helps powerful elites rule through manipulating political communications.

Concern with the effects of polls on politics ultimately rests on the fear that they may largely replace elections as the linkage between collective opinion and governments. However, if polls were to improve communications between political leaders and their constituencies, thereby improving the former's sensitivity to, and understanding of, the latter's priorities, needs, and wants, such objections would become difficult to defend. On the other hand, to the extent that polls go beyond improving political communication and become part of the governing process, that would justify many criticisms. The public opinion process includes a complex, continuously evolving set of interactions out of which emerge collective judgments. But we also saw that the process is not a means for governing a people. By the same token, neither are poll reports. Some means would have to be developed for translating poll reports on the public opinion process into government action. Therein lie some serious problems.

If poll results are used as directives that legislatures must follow, they become pseudoplebiscites. That is dangerous, if for no other reason than that in the hands of unprincipled practitioners, polls are susceptible to methodological manipulation. Through the use of biased question wordings and samples, monopolization of communications media, and careful timing, "official" poll results may be distorted to meet desired ends. The existence of competing polls whose results can be compared with each other, rather than relying on a single official poll, is one effective preventive against such manipulation. But competing polls, whose results inevitably will vary to some degree because of sampling error and variations in question wording, cannot serve as a governing body.

At least as important, plebiscites are a favorite tool of totalitarian governments seeking to justify themselves as the true expression of the people's will. Relying on plebiscitarian polls might well undermine democracy and pave the way for totalitarian government. The legitimacy of democracy is enhanced by the effective functioning of communication linkages between collective opinion and government, not by the short-circuiting of those linkages.

THE POTENTIAL CONTRIBUTION OF POLLS
TO DEMOCRATIC LINKAGE

The nature of the public opinion process itself imposes real limitations on what polls can validly accomplish in a democracy. Ignoring those limits would make it impossible for polls to make the kind of contribution to democratic government that they are capable of making. If that were to happen, there is a real danger that polls would contribute to the corruption of democratic governments. If we respect the fact that what polls can do best is improve two-way communications *between* peoples and their governments, and limit its role to that only, then, and only then, polls might function to strengthen democracy.

8

A Kaleidoscopic Process

The idea of public opinion as process has been a persistent theme in the social science literature for at least a 100 years. Nonetheless, this idea has been imperfectly developed as an analytical paradigm—for two reasons. First is the failure to recognize that public opinion is not the end result of a process but exists in the process itself. This failure results in focusing attention on the presumed effects of public opinion instead of on how it functions. A satisfactory theory of public opinion can be developed only by making its functioning as process the object of our attention.

Second, the multidimensionality of the public opinion process, and the implications of that multidimensionality, have not been adequately confronted. The complexity of the public opinion process requires both analyzing its psychological, sociological, and political dimensions and examining their interelationships. Obviously, this cannot be done by reducing the public opinion process to a few summary numbers, as is so often done in news media reports and analyses. But even when that is avoided, the richness of its texture and the complexity of its structure is lost if we treat the public opinion process as a unidimensional sequence. The process model that has been presented here is an attempt to fit these sometimes disparate elements into a coherent whole.

The public opinion process is kaleidoscopic—a variegated, endlessly changing patterning of individual and collective opinions whose meaning and significance exist in those patterns and not only in the content of those opinions. To understand what is happening over time, we have to examine how one complex pattern flows into the next, and the next, and the next. Any one pattern that we may examine, be it the results of an election or a poll, is no more than a "freeze frame," and even that is far too complicated to be encompassed by anything less than a multidimensional analysis.

An obvious question in the study of public opinion as process is, "Where does it come from?" It does not spring full-blown out of thin air. Unquestionably, the process involves the formation and patterning of individual opinions. As we have seen, these are outcomes of an individual's efforts to judge controversial circumstances so as to be able to deal with them. Individual opinions are not merely a mindless parroting of what others have said, although what others say, and who those others are, are significant inputs into opinion formation. When confronted with an issue, the individual's beliefs, values and interests, and emotional state help structure and give meaning to the issue in personally relevant ways. This relevance may be intense, as is the case with strongly held opinions, or it may be weak, as when opinions are unstable and trivial. In all cases, they help define whether and how individuals come to terms with and judge issues.

But, individual opinions are not products of preexisting attitudinal systems acting in isolation from the surrounding world. The formation and persistence of individual opinions is as much a product of the sociopolitical environments in which individuals live as of purely psychological processes. That is to say, individual opinions emerge from the creative interplay between external and internal processes.

Moreover, the public opinion process is much more than a playing out of individual opinions. An individual's position in communication systems—whom one comes into contact with (either face-to-face or indirectly), the control and influence exercised by others over channels of communication that one uses, the extent to which one is (or is not) expected and encouraged to participate in the public expression of opinion—directs the exchange of individual opinions to create an awareness of how one's opinions relates to the opinions of others. The resultant interactive exchange not only affects the formation of individual opinions, of at least equal significance, it leads to the emergence of collective opinions. That emergence sets into motion the social drama wherein a people decide how they, collectively, will deal with issues that, collectively, confront them. In the absence of collective opinions, the larger process is short-circuited.

Once collective opinions come into being, their political significance is a function of how already existing institutions are to accept them as legitimate. Effective democratic linkage to governance depends on participation in a system that activates and mobilizes individual and collective opinions in a manner that leads to identification with the polity and supports the feeling that the polity's functioning includes and reflects those opinions. That requires a system of interactive communications between government and the governed, creating a web of felt interdependence rather than feelings of exclusion and separateness.

Nonlinkage undermines the democratic effectiveness of the public opinion process. The long-term weakening of linkages between collective opinion and governance does more than destroy confidence in particular administrations and embitter partisan competetition. The resultant loss of confidence in one's political efficacy, as an individual citizen and as a member of politically active associations, can undermine confidence in established governmental institutions to express the public's hopes and fears and to serve its needs and wants. Because the political function of collective opinion is fundamental to the legitimacy of the principle of democracy itself, when confidence in existing linkages is weakened, new linkages must be developed if democratic government is to continue.

In the United States, elections and all the paraphernalia of election campaigns are the hub of an interactive network. But, as the experience of a quarter-century in which trust in government has been eroded shows, holding elections is not by itself sufficient to maintain effective linkages between the public opinion process and governance. Radiating from the hub of elections is an intricate web of political and nonpolitical institutions that must supplement and complement elections as linkages between the public and government. The political strands of the web consist of party organizations, government hearings, legislative debates, lobbies, and so on. Significant nonpolitical strands include the news media, voluntary associations, and informal groupings of friends, neighbors, co-workers, and relatives. The existence of a functioning web makes it possible for collective opinion to emerge as part of the linkage between a populace and its government. Public opinion polls are a controversial, sometimes effective, 20th-century addition to this web that in practice can be dysfunctional.

For collective opinion to function as a legitimate political force, nonpolitical as well as political elements of the web of communications must be open to the public and linked to each other. The network can then give voice to the interests of the various sectors of the electorate in the day-to-day functioning of the government, so that governmental responsiveness to the public becomes more than a matter of enacting popularly approved legislation. In addition to that, responsiveness must include a sense of participation and identification. To the extent that the communication network does not function in this way, the public will feel excluded, even those who have the formal right to vote, leading to a concomitant reduction in any sense of political participation, political efficacy, and power that may exist.

On occasion, reduced trust in government may be combined with the perception that political offices and communications media are monopolized or controlled by privileged sectors of society. In the United States, these special interests have, at various times, been defined as social–economic elites or, ironically, disadvantaged ethnic–racial minorities who have been singled out for special, ameliorative attention. To the extent that this combination leads to a decay in the belief that the government is actually functioning responsively to the public, confidence that it is in one's interest to support democracy as well as commitment to the values of democracy can be expected to weaken.

Under such circumstances, simply adhering to the forms of democratic elections could become a ritualistic cloak for authoritarian rule by a privileged oligopoly. Much of the general public would then be transformed into a passive, nonparticipatory mass, forfeiting to privileged elites the right to govern. Alternatively, the majoritarianism associated with democratic elections may generate widespread acceptance of increasing government responsiveness to collective opinion in ways that bypass intermediary institutions like political parties and legislatures. The resultant plebiscitarianism has the potential of evolving into totalitarian movements.

Clearly, the kaleidoscope of individual opinions, collective opinion, and legitimizing institutions cannot be comprehended if we limit ourselves to analyzing discrete elements of the public opinion process. The dynamics of the public opinion process, and whether it will lead to democratic government in preference to authoritarian or totalitarian government, can be adequately grasped only by integrating its component subprocesses into a multidimensional whole.

Although the principle that public opinion exists as process has been the central theme of this work, there are valid reasons for obtaining descriptive measurements of the public's judgments on specific issues at particular points in time. Most importantly, in a democracy, politicians do need to know the wishes of their constituencies. On another level, social scientists need valid, reliable measurements of the level of public support for or opposition to particular issue positions if their analyses of the public opinion process are to be testable. What we need to do when measuring the state of public opinion regarding specific issues is to apply the process model in a way that enriches survey results, avoiding the usually static, frequently superficial, and sometimes even misleading conclusions that a nonprocess model can engender.

At the barest minimum, the process model demands that we recognize that the public's judgments can and do change over time, so that it is never correct to assume that once a judgment has been reached it is immutable. Instead, as Cantril (1944) demonstrated in the first decade of modern public opinion polling, charting the trend in opinion against the sequence of background events makes it possible not only to measure the extent to which opinions change but also to begin to analyze why and how that happens.

But, the process model that has been presented here requires far more than analyses of how and why individual opinions change over time. It also calls for us to relate the collective and legitimating dimensions of public opinion to the individual dimension. Communications research must go beyond conventional "effects" studies of how individual opinions are influenced by what others say, and focus on how individuals become aware of the opinions of others and come to recognize how their individual opinions merge into a collective force. Studies of how the emergence of mutual awareness gives form and direction to collective opinion will make the measurement and analysis of public opinion dynamic, in a way that the election model that now dominates opinion polls and surveys cannot achieve. Our understanding of how public movements—such as women's liberation, right to life, "green" environment, civil rights, and right-wing "militias"—come into being and affect the political climate would benefit greatly from such studies.

Comparably, analyzing the political dimension requires much more than using individual-level variables such as political identification, political efficacy, and participation. Additionally, measures are needed of the extent to which specific alternative viewpoints are accepted, or rejected, as legitimate issues for political debate; which forms of collective and individual expressions of opinion are considered to be politically legitimate for specific issues; and who is considered to be legitimately entitled to participate in, and perhaps even lead, decision making on specific issues. The history of public opinion on issues like segregation, abortion, gun control, Vietnam, affirmative action, health care, and welfare cannot be comprehended if our attention is focused on individual opinions to the exclusion of these issues of legitimacy.

Additionally, applying what we learn about the collective and legitimacy dimensions of the public opinion process to the emergence of individual opinions will strengthen our ability to measure and analyze the latter. The sudden and sharp swings in individual opinions that often occur in polls on presidential performance ratings and candidate preferences will begin to become more comprehensible and less like irrational, random events once we systematically analyze individual opinion as one interdependent part of the public opinion process, and not as its driving force.

The paucity of studies on the emergence of mutual awareness and the legitimacy of opinions is less a methodological than a theoretical issue. Once the need for such studies is recognized, appropriate research designs can be developed readily. A major value of the multidimensional process model is that it makes that need self-evident. Thus, in addition to satisfying the need for a comprehensive theory of public opinion, the process model also provides an agenda for empirical research in areas that have to date been largely neglected.

In summary, the model gives structure, direction, and purpose to the study of public opinion in a way that integrates theory and methodology. The multidimensional process model is not only a theoretical abstraction. It is rooted in reality, and applying it in empirical research enriches both our data collection and our analytical designs.

References

Adamec, C., & Viden, I. (1972). Polls come to Czechoskovakia. *Public Opinion Quarterly*, *11*, 548–552.

Adamek, R. J. (1994). Public opinion and Roe v. Wade: Measurement difficulties. *Public Opinion Quarterly*, *58*, 409–418.

Albig, W. (1956). *Modern public opinion*. New York: McGraw-Hill.

Alexander, H. E., & Margolis, J. (1978). The making of the debates. In G. F. Bishop, R. G. Meadow, & M. Jackson-Beek (Eds.), *The presidential debates: Media, electoral, and policy perspectives* (pp. 18–32). New York: Praeger.

Alinsky, S. (1969). *Reveille for radicals*. New York: Vintage Books.

Allport, F. (1924). *Social psychology*. Boston: Houghton Mifflin.

Allport, F. (1937). Toward a science of public opinion. *Public Opinion Quarterly*, *1*, 23.

Allport, G. W. (1954). The historical background of modern social psychology. In G. Lindzey (Ed.), *Handbook of social psychology* (pp. 3–56). Cambridge, MA: Addison-Wesley.

Allport, G. W. (1967). Attitudes. In M. Fishbein (Ed.), *Readings in attitude theory and measurement* (pp. 1–13). New York: Wiley.

Anderson, L. R., & Fishbein, M. (1965). Prediction of attitude from the number, strength, and evaluative aspect of beliefs about the attitude object: A comparison of summation and congruity theories. *Journal of Personality and Social Psychology*, *3*, 437–443.

Applebome, P. (1993, June 5). The Guinier battle: Where ideas that hurt Guinier thrive. *New York Times*, p. A9.

Arendt, H. (1973). *The origins of totalitarianism*. New York: Harcourt Brace Jovanovich.

Bacalhau, M. (1990). Transition of the political system and political attitudes in Portugal. *International Journal of Public Opinion Research*, *2*, 141–154.

Back, K. W. (1988). Metaphors for public opinion in literature. *Public Opinion Quarterly*, *52*, 278–288.

Bailey, R., Jr. (1974). *Radicals in urban politics: The Alinsky approach*. Chicago: University of Chicago Press.

Barnouw, E. (1975). *Tube of plenty: The evolution of American television*. New York: Oxford University Press.

Bashkirova, E. (1988, June 12–16). *Public opinion in the USSR*. Paper presented at the Gallup International Conference, Helsinki, Finland.

Becker, L. B., Sobowale, I. A., Cobbey, R. E., & Eyal, C. H., (1978). Debates' effects on voters' understanding of candidates and issues. In G. F. Bishop, R. G. Meadow, & M. Jackson-Beek (Eds.), *The presidential debates: Media, electoral, and policy perspectives* (pp. 126–139). New York: Praeger.

Bell, D. (Ed.) (1955). *The new American right*. New York: Criterion Books.

Bell, D. (Ed.) (1964). *The radical right*. Garden City, NY: Anchor Books.

Beninger, J. R. (1987). Toward an old paradigm: The half-century flirtation with mass society. *Public Opinion Quarterly, 51*, 4.

Berelson, B., Lazarsfeld, P. F., & McPhee, W. N. (1954). *Voting: A study of opinion formation in a presidential campaign*. Chicago: University of Chicago Press.

Berke, R. L. (1995, July 4). Change-minded voters of '94 find that unease remains. *New York Times*, pp. 1, 7.

Bishop, G. F. (1982). Effects of presenting one versus two sides of an issue in survey questions. *Public Opinion Quarterly, 46*, 69–85.

Bishop, G. F. (1987). Experiments with the middle response alternative in survey questions. *Public Opinion Quarterly, 51*, 220–232.

Bishop, G. F., Oldendick, R. W., & Tuchfarber, A. J. (1984). What must my interest in politics be if I just told you 'I don't know'?. *Public Opinion Quarterly, 48*, 510–519.

Bishop, G. F., Oldendick, R. W., & Tuchfarber, A. J. (1983). Effects of filter questions in public opinion surveys. *Public Opinion Quarterly, 47*(4), 528–546.

Bishop, G. F., Tuchfarber, A. J., & Oldendick, R. W. (1986). Opinions on fictitious issues: The pressure to answer survey questions. *Public Opinion Quarterly, 50*, 240–250.

Bishop, G. F., Oldendick, R. W., Tuchfarber, A. J., & Bennet, S. E. (1980). Pseudo-opinions on public affairs. *Public Opinion Quarterly, 44*, 198–209.

Blumberg, N. B. (1954). *One party press: Coverage of the 1952 presidential campaign in 55 daily newspapers*. Lincoln: University of Nebraska Press.

Blumer, H. (1939). Collective behavior. In R. E. Park (Ed.), *An outline of the principles of sociology* (pp. 221–240). New York: Barnes and Noble.

Blumer, H. (1948a). Public opinion and public opinion polling. *American Sociological Review, 13*(5), 542–549.

Blumer, H. (1948b). Rejoinder to Woodward and Newcombe. *American Sociological Review, 13*(5), 554.

Blumler, J. G., & Katz, D. (Eds.) (1974). *The uses of mass communications: Current perspectives on gratification research*. Beverly Hills, CA: Sage.

Bogart, L. (1956). *The age of television*. New York: Frederick Ungar Publishing Company.

Bogart, L. (1967). No opinion, don't know, and maybe no answer. *Public Opinion Quarterly, 31*, 331–345.

Bogart, L. (1985). *Polls and the awareness of public opinion*. Hillsdale, NJ: Lawrence Erlbaum Associates.

Bogart, L. (Ed.). (1992). *Project clear: Social research and the desegregation of the United States army*. New Brunswick, NJ: Transaction Publishers.

Boorstin, D. J. (1974). *The Americans: The democratic experience*. New York: Vintage Books.

Brehm, J. (1960). A dissonance analysis of attitude-discrepant behavior. In M. Rosenberg, C. I. Hovland, W. J. McGuire, R. P. Abelson, & J. W. Brehm (Eds.), *Attitude organization and change: An analysis of consistency among attitude components* (pp. 164–197). New Haven, CT: Yale University Press.

Bridgwater, W., & Kurtz, S. (Eds.). (1963). *The Columbia encyclopedia* (3rd ed.). New York: Columbia University Press.

Brinkley, A. (1994). 1936. In A. M. Schlesinger, Jr. (Ed.), *Running for president: The candidates and their mates* (pp. 183–185). New York: Simon & Schuster.

Brosius, H. -B., & Engel, D. (1996). The causes of third-person effects: Unrealistic optimism, impersonal impact, or generalized negative attitudes towards media influence. *International Journal of Public Opinion Research, 8*, 142–162.

Brosius, H. -B., & Kepplinger, H. M. (1995). Killer and victim issues: Issue competition in the agenda-setting process of German television. *International Journal of Public Opinion Research*, 7, 211–231.

Bruneau, T. C. (1981). Patterns of politics in Portugal since the April revolution. In J. B. de Macedo & S. Serfaty (Eds.), *Portugal since the revolution: Economic and political perspectives* (pp. 1–52). Boulder, CO: Westview Press.

Bruner, J. S. (1944). *Mandate from the people*. New York: Duell, Sloan and Pearce.

Bryce, J. (1891). *The American commonwealth*. New York: Macmillan.

Bryce, J. (1921). *Modern democracies*. New York: Macmillan.

Bureau of the Census, U.S. Department of Commerce (1975). *Historical statistics of the United States: Colonial times to 1970*, Washington, DC: Author.

Burnham, W. D. (1978). The appearance and disappearance of the American voter. In American Bar Association (Ed.), *The disappearance of the American voter*. Chicago: Editor.

Campbell, A., Gurin, G., & Miller, W. E. (1954). *The voter decides*. Evanston, IL: Row, Peterson & Co.

Cantor, N. F. (1993). *The civilization of the middle ages*. New York: Harper Collins.

Cantril, H. (1941). *The psychology of social movements*. New York: Wiley.

Cantril, H. (1944). *Gauging public opinion*. Princeton, NJ: Princeton University Press.

Cantril, H. (1958). *The politics of despair*. New York: Basic Books.

Cantril, H., with Strunk, M. (1951). *Public opinion: 1935–1946*. Princeton, NJ: Princeton University Press.

Chaiken, S., Liberman, A., & Eagly, A. H. (1989). Heuristic and systematic information processing within and beyond the persuasion context. In J. S. Uleman & J. A. Bargh (Eds.), *Unintended thought* (pp. 212–252). New York: Guilford.

Chein, I. (1948). Behavior theory and the behavior of attotides: Some critical comments. *Psychological Review*, 55, 175–178.

Childs, H. L. (1937). By public opinion I mean. *Public Opinion Quarterly*, 1(3), 327–336.

Clymer, A. (1993, July 25). Filibuster delays service measure. *New York Times*, p. 21.

Cohen, A. R. (1960). Additional consequences of induced discrepancies between cognition and behavior. *Public Opinion Quarterly*, 24, 297–318.

Cohen, J., Mutz, D., Price, V., & Gunther, A. (1988). Perceived impact of defamation. *Public Opinion Quarterly*, 52, 161–173.

Commission on Freedom of the Press (1947). *A free and responsible press*. Chicago, IL: University of Chicago Press.

Comstock, G., Chaffee, S., Katzman, N., McCombs, M., & Roberts, D. (1978). *Television and human behavior*. New York: Columbia University Press.

Converse, P. E. (1964). The nature of belief systems in mass politics. In D. E. Apter (Ed.), *Ideology and discontent* (pp. 206–261). New York: The Free Press.

Converse, P. E. (1970). Attitudes and non-attitudes: Continuation of a dialogue. In E. R. Tufte (Ed.), *The quantitative analysis of social problems* (pp. 168–189). Reading, MA: Addison Wesley.

Converse, P. E. (1974). Comment: The status of non-attitudes. *American Political Science Review*, 68, 650–660.

Cooley, C. H. (1909). *Social organization*. New York: Charles Scribner & Sons.

Cooley, C. H. (1918). *Social process*. New York: Charles Scribner & Sons.

Crespi, I. (1978). The role of television in declining voter participation. In American Bar Association (Ed.), *The disappearance of the American voter* (pp. 169–176). Chicago: Editor.

Crespi, I. (1981, October/November). Does the public approve of Ronald Reagan? *Public Opinion*, pp. 20, 41.

Crespi, I. (1988). *Pre-election polling: Sources of accuracy and error*. New York: Russell Sage.

Crespi, I. (1989). *Public opinion, polls, and democracy.* Boulder, CO: Westview Press.

Curti, M. (1959). *The making of an American community: A case study of democracy in a frontier county.* Stanford, CA: Stanford University Press.

Dahl, R. H. (1961). *Who governs? Democracy and power in an American city.* New Haven, CT: Yale University Press.

Davis, J. A. (1992). Changeable weather in a cooling climate atop the liberal plateau: Conversion and replacement in forty-two General Social Survey items. *Public Opinion Quarterly, 56,* 261–306.

Davison, W. P. (1958). The public opinion process. *Public Opinion Quarterly, 22,* 91–106.

Davison, W. P. (1968). Public opinion. In D. L. Sills (Ed.), *International encyclopedia of the social sciences,* (Vol. 13, pp. 188–197). New York: Free Press.

Davison, W. P. (1983). The third-person effect in communications. *Public Opinion Quarterly, 47,* 1–14.

Declaration of Independence (1981). *World book encyclopedia.* Chicago: World Book Childcraft Industries.

Delli Carpini, M. X., & Williams, B. A. (1994). Methods, metaphors, and media research: The uses of television in political conversation. *Communication Research, 21*(6), 782–812.

de Toqueville, A. (1954). *Democracy in America.* New York: Vintage.

de Toqueville, A., (1955). *The old regime and the French revolution.* Garden City, NY: Anchor Books.

Deutschmann, P. J. (1962). Viewing, conversation, and voting intentions. In S. Kraus (Ed.), *The great debates: Background–perspective–effects* (pp. 232–252). Bloomington: Indiana University Press.

Donsbach, W. (1994, August). From "How it all began" to ARIMA analysis. *WAPOR Newsletter,* p. 1.

Doob, L. W. (1947). The behavior of attitudes. *Psychological Review, 54,* 135–156.

Doob, L. W. (1948). *Public opinion and propaganda.* New York: Henry Holt and Company.

Duncan, O. D., & Stenbeck, M. (1988). No opinion or not sure? *Public Opinion Quarterly, 52,* 513–525.

Einseidel, E. F. (1994). Mental maps of science: Knowledge and attitudes among Canadian adults. *International Journal of Public Opinion Research, 6,* 35–44.

Eisenstadt, E. N. (Ed.). (1971). *Political sociology.* New York: Basic Books.

Eisenstein, E. L. (1987). *The printing revolution in early modern Europe.* Cambridge, MA: Cambridge University Press.

Elmer-Dewitt, P. (1994). Battle for the soul of the Internet. *Time, 144*(4), pp. 50–56.

Ettema, J. S., Brown, J. W., & Luepker, R. V. (1983). Knowledge gap effects in a health information campaign. *Public Opinion Quarterly, 47,* 516–527.

Evan, W. M. (1959). Cohort analysis of survey data: A procedure for studying long-term opinion change. *Public Opinion Quarterly, 23,* 63–72.

Fascist Grand Council (1972). The charter of labor. In C. Cohen (Ed.), *Communism, fascism, and democracy* (p. 362). New York: Random House.

Festinger, L. (1957). *A theory of cognitive dissonance.* Evanston, IL: Row Peterson & Co.

Fields, J. M., & Schuman, H. (1976). Public beliefs about the beliefs of the public. *Public Opinion Quarterly, 40,* 427–448.

Fishbein, M. F., & Raven, B. H. (1962). The AB scales: An operational definition of belief and attitude. *Human Relations, 15,* 35–44.

Friedgut, T. H. (1979). *Political participation in the USSR.* Princeton, NJ: Princeton University Press.

Friedrich, C. J. (1969). The evolving theory and practice of totalitarian regimes. In C. Friedrich, M. Curtis, & B. R. Barber (Eds.), *Totalitarianism in perspective: Three views.* New York: Praeger.

Gallup, G. H. (1947). The quintamensional plan of question design. *Public Opinion Quarterly*, *11*, 385–393.

Gallup, G. H. (1972a). *The sophisticated poll watcher's guide*. Princeton: Princeton Opinion Press.

Gallup, G. H. (1972b). *The Gallup poll: Public opinion 1935–1971* (Vol. 1–3). New York: Random House.

Gallup, G. H., & Rae, S. F. (1968). *The pulse of democracy: The public-opinion poll and how it works*. New York: Greenwood Press. (Original work published 1940)

The Gallup opinion index/The Gallup poll monthly (1965–1995). Princeton: Author.

Gamson, W. A. (1992). *Talking politics*. New York: Cambridge University Press.

Gans, H. J. (1980). *Deciding what's news: A study of CBS Evening News, NBC Nightly News, Newsweek, and Time*. New York: Vintage Books.

Gentile, G. (1972). The philosophic basis of fascism. In C. Cohen (Ed.), *Communism, fascism, and democracy: The theoretical foundations* (pp. 340–344). New York: Random House.

Gilliam, M., & Granberg, D. (1993). Should we take don't know for an answer. *Public Opinion Quarterly*, *57*, 348–357.

Ginsberg, B. (1986). *The captive public: How mass opinion promotes state power*. New York: Basic Books.

Glazer, N., & Moynihan, D. P. (1963). *Beyond the melting pot: The Negroes, Puerto Ricans, Jews, Italians, and Irish of New York City*. Cambridge, MA: The MIT Press.

Glynn, C. J., & McLeod, J. M. (1984). Public opinion du jour: An examination of the spiral of silence. *Public Opinion Quarterly*, *48*, 731–740.

Goldhamer, H. (1980). The social effects of communiations technology. In H. Lasswell, D. Lerner, & H. Speier (Eds.), *Propaganda, communication and world history* (pp. 349–397). Honolulu: University Press of Hawaii.

Goldner, F. H. (1991). Rhetorical reticence, if you're for it I'm against it, or at least I'll keep my mouth shut: Opinion expression and formation in the context of polarized groups. *International Journal of Public Opinion Research*, *3*(3), 220–237.

Graber, D. (1978). Problems in measuring audience effects of the 1976 debates. In G. F. Bishop, R. G. Meadow, & M. Jackson-Beek (Eds.), *The presidential debates: Media, electoral, and policy perspectives* (pp. 105–125). New York: Praeger.

Green, B. F. (1954). Attitude measurement. In G. Lindzey (Ed.), *Handbook of social psychology* (pp. 335–369). Cambridge, MA: Addison-Wesley.

Greenhouse, L. (1995, June 30). Justices in 5–4 vote reject districts drawn with race the predominate factor. *New York Times*, p. A1.

Haberman, C. (1993, September 21). Pact's fate in hands of Israeli rabbi. *New York Times*, p. A12.

Hagner, P. R., & Rieselbach, L. (1978). The impact of the 1976 Presidential debates: Conversion or reinforcement? In G. F. Bishop, R. G. Meadow, & M. Jackson-Beek (Eds.), *The presidential debates: Media, electoral, and policy perspectives* (pp. 169–171). New York: Praeger.

Hahn, H., & Stout, R. (1994). *The Internet complete reference*. Berkeley, CA: Osborne McGraw-Hill.

Heider, F. (1958). *The psychology of interpersonal relations*. New York: Wiley.

Herrera, C. L., Herrera, R., & Smith, E. R. A. N. (1992). Public opinion and Congressional representation. *Public Opinion Quarterly*, *56*, 185-205.

Hippler, H. J., & Schwartz, N. (1989). 'No opinion' filters: A cognitive perspective. *International Journal of Public Opinion Research*, *1*(1), 77–87.

Horam, M. (1975). *Naga polity*. Delhi: B.R. Publishing Corporation.

Hovland, C. I., Lumsdaine, A. A., & Sheffield, F. D. (1949). *Experiments on mass communications*. Princeton, NJ: Princeton University Press.

Hovland, C. I., Janis, I. L., & Kelley, H. H. (1953). *Communication and persuasion: Psychological studies of opinion changes*. New Haven, CT: Yale University Press.

Hunter, F. (1980). *Atlanta's policy maker's revisited*. Chapel Hill, NC: University of North Carolina Press.

Jahoda, M., & Warren, N. (Eds.). (1966). *Attitudes*. Baltimore, MD: Penguin Books.

Johnston, D. (1995, September 14). Use of computer networks for child sex sets off raids. *New York Times*, p. A1.

Johnston, D. (1996, August 11). The fine print in cyberspace. *New York Times*, p. D4.

Kagay, M. R. (1995). The evolving use of public opinion polls by the New York Times: The experience in the 1992 presidential election. In P. J. Lavrakas, M. W. Traugott, & P. V. Miller (Eds.), *Presidential polls and the new media* (pp. 143–191). Boulder, CO: Westview Press.

Katz, C., & Baldassare, M. (1994). Popularity in a freefall: Measuring a spiral of silence at the end of the Bush presidency. *International Journal of Public Opinion Research, 6*(1), 1–12.

Katz, D. (1960). The functional approach to the study of attitudes. *Public Opinion Quarterly, 24*, 163–204.

Katz, D. (1972). Attitude formation and public opinion. In D. D. Nimmo & C. M. Bonjean (Eds.), *Political attitudes and public opinion* (pp. 13–26). New York: David McKay Company.

Katz, E. (1957). The two-step flow of communication: An up-to-date report on an hypothesis. *Public Opinion Quarterly, 21*(1), 67–78.

Katz, E. (1992). On parenting a paradigm: Gabriel Tarde's agenda for opinion and communications research. *International Journal of Public Opinion Research, 4*(1), 80–85.

Katz, E., & Feldman, J. J. (1962). The debates in light of research: a survey of surveys. In S. Kraus (Ed.), *The great debates: Background–perspective–effects* (pp. 173–223). Bloomington: Indiana University Press.

Katz, E., & Lazarsfeld, P. F. (1955). *Personal influence*. New York: The Free Press.

Kelman, Herbert C. (1961). Processes of opinion change. *Public Opinion Quarterly, 25*, 57–78.

Key, V. O. (1961). *Public opinion and American democracy*. New York: Knopf.

Key, V. O. (1966). *The responsible electorate: Rationality in presidential voting, 1936–1960*. Cambridge, MA: Belknap Press of Harvard University Press.

Kiesler, C. A., Collins, B. E., & Miller, N. (1969). *Attitude change: A critical analysis of theoretical approaches*. New York: Wiley.

Klapper, J. T. (1960). *The effects of mass communications*. Glencoe, IL: The Free Press.

Kolbert, E. (1995, April 23). Prime time snubs Mr. Clinton for reruns. *New York Times Week in Review*, p. 3.

Konner, M. (1995, October 13). A giant leap backward. *New York Times*, p. A33.

Krech, D., & Crutchfield, R. S. (1948). *Theory and problems of social psychology*. New York: McGraw-Hill.

Krosnick, J. A., & Abelson, R. P. (1994). The case for measuring attitude strength in surveys. In J. M. Tanur (Ed.), *Questions about questions: Inquiries into the cognitive bases of surveys* (pp. 177–203). New York: Russell Sage.

Lang, G. E., & Lang, K. (1962). Reactions of viewers. In S. Kraus (Ed.), *The Great Debates: Background–Perspective–Effects* (pp. 313– 330). Bloomington: Indiana University Press.

Lang, G. E., & Lang, K. (1978). The formation of public opinion: Direct and mediated effects of the first debate. In G. F. Bishop, R. G. Meadow, & M. Jackson-Beek (Eds.), *The presidential debates: Media, electoral, and policy perspectives*. New York: Praeger.

Lang, G. E., & Lang, K. (1983). *The battle for public opinion*. New York: Columbia University Press.

Lanoue, D. J. (1992). One that made a difference: Cognitive consistency, political knowledge, and the 1980 presidential debate. *Public Opinion Quarterly, 56*, 168–184.

Lasorsa, D. (1989). Real and perceived effects of 'Amerika'. *Journalism Quarterly, 66*, 373–378, 529.

Lasswell, H. D. (1927). The theory of political propaganda. *The American Political Science Review*, Vol. XXI.

Lazarsfeld, P. F., Berelson, B., & Gaudet, H. (1948). *The people's choice* (2nd ed.). New York: Columbia University Press.

Lewis, N. A. (1993, May 5). Woman in the news: Guerilla fighter or civil rights–Lani Guinier. *New York Times*, A8.

Lewis, P. H. (1995, September 14). Elite Internet address will now cost $50 a year. *New York Times*, p. D1.

Linz, J. J. (1970). An authoritarian regime: Spain. In E. Allardt & S. Rokkan (Eds.), *Mass politics: Studies in political sociology* (pp. 251–381). New York: Free Press.

Linz, J. J. (1975). Totalitarian and authoritarian regimes. In F. I. Greenstein & N. Polsby (Eds.), *Macropolitical theory* (pp. 174–412). Reading, MA: Addison-Welsey.

Linz, J. J. (1976). Some notes toward a comparative study of fascism in sociological historical perspective. In W. Laqueur (Ed.), *Fascism: A reader's guide* (pp. 3–121). Los Angeles: University of California Press.

Linz, J. J. (1978). Non-competitive elections in Europe. In G. Hermut, R. Rose, & A. Rouquie (Eds.), *Elections without choice* (pp. 36–65). New York: Wiley.

Linz, J. J. (1993). Authoritarianism. In J. Krieger (Ed.), *The Oxford companion to politics of the world* (pp. 60–64). New York: Oxford University Press.

Lippmann, W. (1925). *The phantom public*. New York: Macmillan.

Lippmann, W. (1946). *Public opinion*. New York: Penguin Books. (Original work published 1928)

Lippmann, W. (1955). *The public philosophy*. Boston: Little, Brown.

Lipset, S. M. (1963). *The first new nation: The United States in historical and comparative perspective*. New York: Basic Books.

Lipset, S. M., & Schneider, W. (1987). The confidence gap during the Reagan years, 1981–1987. *Political Science Quarterly, 102*, 1–23.

Lowe, F. E., & McCormick, T. C. (1957). A study of the influence of formal and informal leaders in an election campaign. *Public Opinion Quarterly, 20*(4), 651–662.

Lowell, A. L. (1926). *Public opinion and popular government*. New York: Longmans Green.

Luttbeg, N. (1974). *Public opinion and public policy*. Homewood, IL: Dorsey Press.

Lyttelton, A. (1976). Italian fascism. In W. Laqueur (Ed.), *Fascism: A reader's guide* (pp. 125–150). Los Angeles: University of California Press.

McCombs, M. E. (1992). Explorers and surveyors: Exploring strategies for agenda-setting research. *Journalism Quarterly, 69*(4), 813–824.

McCombs, M. E., & Shaw, D. L. (1972). The agenda-setting function of mass media. *Public Opinion Quarterly, 36*, 176–177.

McCombs, M. E., & Shaw, D. L. (1977). The agenda-setting function of the press. In D. L. Shaw & M. E. McCombs (Eds.), *The emergence of political issues: The agenda-setting function of the press* (pp. 1–18). St. Paul, MN: West Publishing Company.

McGuire, W. (1960). Cognitive consistency and attitude change. *Journal of Abnormal and Social Psychology, 60*, 345–353.

McGuire, W. (1967). The current status of cognitive consistency theories. In M. Fishbein (Ed.), *Readings in attitude theory and measurement* (pp. 401–421). New York: Wiley.

McGuire, W. J. (1969). The nature of attitudes and attitude change. In G. Lindzey & E. Aronson (Eds.), *Handbook of social psychology* (2nd ed., Vol. 3, pp. 136–314). Reading, PA: Addison Wesley.

McGuire, W. (1986). The vicissitudes of attitudes and similar representational constructs in twentieth century psychology. *European Journal of Social Psychology, 16*, 89–139.

McLean, I. (1989). *Democracy and new technology*. Cambridge, England: Polity Press.

McNamara, R. (1995). *In retrospect: Tragedy and lessons of Vietnam*. New York: Times Books.

Macpherson, C. B. (1980). *Burke*. New York: Hill & Wang.

Manglapas, R. S. (1987). *Will of the people: Original democracy in non-western societies*. New York: Greenwood Press.

Margolick, D. (1993, June 4). Musty academic speculation or blueprint for political action. *New York Times*, p. A18.

Marwell, G., Aiken, M. T., & Demerath, N. J., III (1987). The persistence of political attitudes among 1960s civil rights activists. *Public Opinion Quarterly, 51*, 359–375.

Mayer, W. G. (1993). Trends in media usage. *Public Opinion Quarterly, 57*, 593–611.

Mayer, W. G. (1992). *The changing American mind: How and why American public opinion changed between 1960 and 1988*. Ann Arbor: University of Michigan Press.

Mayer, W. G. (1994). The rise of the new media. *Public Opinion Quarterly, 58*, 124–146.

Mead, G. H. (1934). *Mind, self, and society*. Chicago: University of Chicago Press.

Mead, G. H. (1968). *Social theory and social structure*. New York: The Free Press.

Mead, M. (1937). Public opinion mechanisms among primitive peoples. *Public Opinion Quarterly, 1*(3), 5–16.

Menache, S. (1990). *The Vox Dei: Communication in the middle ages*. New York: Oxford University Press.

Menzel, H., & Katz, E. (1956). Social relations and innovation in the medical profession: The epidemiology of a new drug. *Public Opinion Quarterly, 19*(4), 337–352.

Merton, R. K. (1949). *Social theory and social structure*. Glencoe, IL: The Free Press.

Meyer, A. G. (1993). Totalitarianism. In J. Krieger (Ed.), *The Oxford companion to politics of the world* (pp. 916–917). New York: Oxford University Press.

Miller, J. C. (1943). *Origins of the American revolution*. Boston: Little, Brown.

Moore, D. W. (1987). Political campaigns and the knowledge-gap hypothesis. *Public Opinion Quarterly, 51*, 186–200.

Morin, R. (1995). The 1992 election and the polls: Neither politics nor polling as usual. In P. J. Lavrakas, M. W. Traugott, and P. V. Miller (Eds.), *Presidential polls and the new media* (pp. 123–142). Boulder, CO: Westview Press.

Mutz, D. C. (1989). The influence of perceptions of media influence: Third-person effects and the public expression of opinions. *International Journal of Public Opinion Research, 1*, 3–13.

Neuman, W. R. (1986). *The paradox of mass politics: Knowledge and opinion in the American electorate*. Cambridge, MA: Harvard University Press.

Nimmo, D., Mansfield, M., & Curry, J. (1978). Persistence and change in candidate images. In G. F. Bishop, R. G. Meadow, & M. Jackson-Beek (Eds.), *The presidential debates: Media, electoral, and policy perspectives* (pp. 140–156). New York: Praeger.

Noelle-Neumann, E. (1984). *The spiral of silence: Public opinion—our social skin*. Chicago, IL: University of Chicago Press.

O'Gorman, H. J. (1975). Pluralistic ignorance and white estimates of white support for racial integration. *Public Opinion Quarterly, 39*, 311–330.

O'Gorman, H. J., & Garry, S. L. (1976). Pluralistic ignorance—A replication and extension. *Public Opinion Quarterly, 40*, 449–458.

Oppenheim, A. L. (1964). *Ancient Mesopotomia*. Chicago, IL: University of Chicago Press.

Ortega y Gasset, J. (1950). *The revolt of the masses*. New York: New American Library.

Osgood, C. E. (1960). Cognitive dynamics in the conduct of human affairs. *Public Opinion Quarterly, 24*, 341–365.

Osgood, C. E., & Tannenbaum, P. H. (1955). The principle of congruity in the prediction of attitude change. *Psychological Review, 66*, 42–55.

Page, B. I., & Shapiro, R. Y. (1992). *The rational public: Fifty years of trends in Americans' policy preferences*. Chicago, IL: University of Chicago Press.

Palmer, P. A. (1950). The concept of public opinion in political theory. In B. Berelson & M. Janowits (Eds.), *Reader in public opinion and communication* (pp. 3–13). Glencoe, IL: The Free Press.

Palmieri, M. (1972). The corporative idea. In C. Cohen (Ed.), *Communism, fascism, and democracy: The theoretical foundations*. New York: Random House.

Pear, R. (1992, November 5). The 1992 elections: Disappointment—the turnout; 55% voting rate reverses 30-year decline. *New York Times*, p. B4.

Perloff, R. M. (1996). Third-person effect research 1983–1992: A review and synthesis. *International Journal of Public Opinion Research, 5*, 167–184.

Petty, R. E., & Cacioppo, J. T. (1981). *Attitudes and persuasion: Classic and contemporary approaches*. Dubuque, IA: William C. Brown Company.

Petty, R. E., & Cacioppo, J. T. (1986). *Communication and persuasion: Central and peripheral routes to attitude change*. New York: Springer-Verlag.

Plato (n.d.). *The republic* (B. Jowett, trans.) New York: The Modern Library.

Ponza, M., Duncan, G. J., Corcoran, M., & Groskind, F. (1988). The guns of autumn: Age differences in support for income transfers to the young and old. *Public Opinion Quarterly, 52*, 441–466.

Popkin, S. (1991). *The reasoning voter: Communication and persuasion in presidential campaigns*. Chicago: University of Chicago Press.

Popov, N. P. (1992). Political views of the Russian people. *International Journal of Public Opinion Research, 4*, 321–334.

Pravda, A. (1978). Elections in communist party states. In G. Hermet, R. Rose, & A. Rouquie (Eds.), *Elections without choice* (pp. 169–195). New York: Wiley.

Price, V. (1992). *Communication concepts 4: Public opinion*. Newbury Park, CA: Sage.

Price, V., & Allen, S. (1996). Opinion spiral, silent and otherwise. *Communications Research, 17*, 369–392.

Price, V., & Tewkbury, D. (1996). Measuring the third-person effect of news: The impact of question order, contrast and knowledge. *International Journal of Public Opinion Research, 8*, 120–141.

Priester, J. R., & Petty, R. C. (1995). Source attribution and persuasion: Perceived honesty as a determinant of message scrutiny. *Personality and Social Psychology Bulletin, 21*(6), 637–654.

Reynolds, D. S. (1995). *Walt Whitman's America*. New York: Knopf.

Rogers, E. M. (1995). *Diffusion of innovations*. New York: The Free Press.

Rogers, E. M., & Shoemaker, F. F. (1971). *Communication of innovations: A cross-cultural approach* (2nd ed.). New York: The Free Press.

Rogers, L. (1949). *The pollsters*. New York: Knopf.

Rojas, H., Shah, D. V., & Fisher, R. J. (1996). For the good of others: Censorship and the third-person effect. *International Journal of Public Opinion Research, 8*, 163–185.

Rojas, H., Shah, D. V., & Fisher, R. J. (1968). *Beliefs, attitudes and values*. San Francisco, CA: Jossey-Bass.

Rokeach, M. (1960). *The open and closed mind*. New York: Basic Books.

Rosenberg, M. J. (1960). A structural theory of attitude dynamics. *Public Opinion Quarterly, 24*, 319–340.

Rosenberg, M. J., & Abelson, R. P. (1960). An analysis of cognitive balancing. In M. Rosenberg, C. I. Hovland, W. J. McGuire, R. P. Abelson, & J. W. Brehm (Eds.),

Attitude organization and change: An analysis of consistency among attitude components (pp. 112–163). New Haven, CT: Yale University Press.

Rosenberg, M. J., & Hovland, C. (1960). Cognitive, affective, and behavioral components of attitudes. In M. J. Rosenberg, C. I. Hovland, W. J. McGuire, R. P. Abelson, & J. W. Brehm, *Attitude organization and change* (pp. 1–14). New Haven, CT: Yale University Press.

Rosenberg, M. J., Hovland, C. I., McGuire, W. J., Abelson, R. P., & Brehm, J. W. (1960). *Attitude organization and change: An analysis of consistency among attitude components.* New Haven, CT: Yale University Press.

Ross, E. A. (1969). *Social control.* New York: Macmillan. (Original work published 1901)

Rossi, P. H., & Freeman, H. E. (1993). *Evaluation: A systematic approach.* Newbury Park, CA: Sage.

Rousseau, J. J. (1952). The Social Contract. In R. M. Hutchins (Ed.), *Great books of the western world* (Vol. 8, pp. 387–484). Chicago, IL: Encyclopaedia Brittanica, Inc.

Rucinski, D., & Salmon, C. T. (1989). The 'other' as the vulnerable voter: A study of the third-person effect in the 1988 campaign. *International Journal of Public Opinion Research, 2,* 345–368.

Sack, K. (1995, September 13). Legislators letting court remap Georgia. *New York Times,* p. A14.

Sanchez, M. -E., & Morchio, G. (1992). Probing "don't know" answers: Effects on survey estimates and variable relationships. *Public Opinion Quarterly, 56,* 454–474.

Sapir, E. (1931). Communication. In E. R. Seligman (Ed.), *Encyclopedia of the social sciences* (pp. 78–80). New York: Macmillan.

Schattschneider, E. E. (1975). *The semisovereign people: A realist's view of democracy in America.* Hinsdale, IL: The Dryden Press.

Schmitter, P. C. (1978). The impact and meaning of "non-competitive, non-free and insignificant" elections in authoritarian Portugal, 1933–74. In G. Hermet, R. Rose, & A. Rouquie (Eds.), *Elections without choice* (pp. 145–168). New York: Wiley.

Schuman, H., & Presser, S. (1978). The assessment of "no opinion" in attitude surveys. In K. R. Schuessler (Ed.), *Sociological methodology* (pp. 241–275). New York: Wiley.

Scott, J., & Zac, L. (1993). Collective memories. *Public Opinion Quarterly, 57*(3), 315–331.

Scott, W. A. (1968). Attitude measurement. In G. Lindzey & E. Aronson (Eds.), *Handbook of social psychology* (Vol. 2, pp. 204–273). Reading, MA: Addison-Wesley.

Shlapentokh, V. (1986). *Soviet public opinion and ideology: Mythology and pragmatism in interaction.* New York: Praeger.

Sherif, C. W., Sherif, M., & Nebergal, R. E. (1965). *Attitude and attitude change: The social judgment-involvement approach.* Philadelphia, PA: Saunders.

Sieger, K. (1990). Opinion research in East Germany—a challenge to professional standards. *International Journal of Public Opinion Research, 2,* 323–344.

Sigelman, L., & Presser, S. (1988). Measuring public support for the new Christian right: The perils of point estimation. *Public Opinion Quarterly, 52,* 325–337.

Simon, H. A. (1957). *Models of man.* New York: Wiley.

Singer, E., & Ludwig, J. (1987). South Africa's press restrictions: Effects on press coverage and public opinion toward South Africa. *Public Opinion Quarterly, 51,* 315–334.

Smith, H. (1990). *The new Russians.* New York: Random House.

Smith, M. B. (1947). The personal setting of public opinion: A study of attitudes toward Russia. *Public Opinion Quarterly, 11*(4), 507–523.

Smith, M. B., Jr., Bruner, J. S., & White, R. W. (1956). *Opinions and personality.* New York: Wiley.

Smith, T. W. (1980). America's most important problem—a trend analysis, 1946–1976. *Public Opinion Quarterly, 44,* 169–180.

Smith, T. W. (1992). Are conservative churches growing? *Review of Religious Research, 33*, 305–329.

Smith, T. W. (1994). Is there real opinion change? *International Journal of Public Opinion Research, 6*, 187–203.

Speier, H. (1951). Morale and Propaganda. In D. Lerner (Ed.), *Propaganda in war and crisis* (pp. 3–25). New York: George W. Stewart.

Speier, H. (1980). The rise of public opinion. In H. Lasswell, D. Lerner, & H. Speier (Eds.), *Propaganda and communication in world history* (Vol. 2, pp. 147–167). Honolulu: University Press of Hawaii.

Stevenson, H.N.C. (n.d.). *The economics of the central Chin tribes.* Bombay: The Times of India Press.

Stimson, J. A. (1991). *Public opinion in America: Moods, cycles, and swings.* Boulder, CO: Westview Press.

Swain, C. M. (1993, June 3). Black majority district a bad idea. *New York Times*, p. A23.

Szczepanski, J. (1959). Introduction: Etudes polonaises de sociologie et d'opinion publiques [Introduction: Polish studies of sociology and public opinion]. *Sondages: Revue Francasise De L'Opinion Publique*, No. 1, pp. 7–11.

Tannenbaum, P., Greenberg, B. S., & Siverman, F. J. (1962). Candidate images. In S. Kraus (Ed.), *The great debates: Background–perspective–effects* (pp. 271–288). Bloomington: Indiana University Press.

Thomas, W. I., & Znaniecki, F. (1958). *The Polish peasant in Europe and America.* New York: Dover Publications.

Thurstone, L. L. (1928). Attitudes can be measured. *American Journal of Sociology, 33*, pp. 539–554.

Tichenor, P. J., Donohue, G. A., & Olien, C. N. (1970). Mass media flow and differential growth in knowledge. *Public Opinion Quarterly, 34*, pp. 159–170.

Times Mirror Center for the People and the Press. (1995, October 16). *Technology in the American household: Americans going online … explosive growth, uncertain destinations.* Washington, DC: Times Mirror.

Trager, J. (1992). *The people's chronology.* New York: Henry Holt and Company.

Traugott, M. W. (1995). The use of focus groups to supplement campaign coverage. In P. J. Lavrakas, M. W. Traugott, & P. V. Miller (Eds.), *Presidential polls and the new media* (pp. 51–66). Boulder, CO: Westview Press.

Tripothi, R. (1942). *History of ancient India.* Delhi: Motilal Banarsidass.

Uleman, J. S., & Bargh, J. A. (Eds.). (1989). *Unintended thought.* New York: Guilford.

Wanta, W., & Hu, Y. -W. (1994). Time-lag differences in the agenda-setting process: An examination of five news media. *International Journal of Public Opinion Research, 6*, 225–240.

Weber, M. (1961). Types of Rationality. In T. Parsons, E. Shils, K. D. Naegle, & J. R. Pitts (Eds.), *Theories of society* (Vols. I and II, pp. 1063–1065). New York: The Free Press.

Weber, M. (1968). *Economy and society.* New York: Bedminister Press.

Weimann, G. (1991). The influentials: Back to the concept of opinion leaders? *Public Opinion Quarterly, 55*, 267–279.

Weimann, G., & Brosius, H. -B. (1994). Is there a two-step flow of agenda setting? *International Journal of Public Opinion Research, 6*, 323–)341.

Wiebe, G. D. (1951). Merchandizing commodities and citizenship on television. *Public Opinion Quarterly, 15*(4), 679–691.

Wiebe, G. D. (1952). Responses to the televised Kefauver hearings: Some social psychological implications. *Public Opinion Quarterly, 16*(2), 179–200.

Wiebe, G. D. (1953). Some implications of separating opinions from attitudes. *Public Opinion Quarterly, 17*, pp. 328–352.

Will, G. (1995, October 21). Why should voters demand secrecy? The Times (Trenton), p. A17.

Willnat, L. (1996). Mass media and political outspokeness in Hong Kong: Linking the third-person effect and the spiral of silence. *International Journal of Public Opinion Research, 8*, 187–212.

Wolfinger, R. E., & Rosenstone, S. J. (1980). *Who votes?* New Haven, CT: Yale University Press.

Wood, G. S. (1992). *The radicalism of the American revolution.* New York: Knopf.

Young, K. (1954). Comments on the nature of "public" and "public opinion." In D. Katz, S. Eldersveld, & A. M. Lee (Eds.), *Public opinion and propaganda: A book of readings* (pp. 62–69). New York: Dryden Press.

Zajonc, R. B. (1960). The concepts of balance, congruity, and dissonance. *Public Opinion Quarterly, 24*, 280–296.

Zaller, J. R. (1992). *The nature and origins of mass opinions.* New York: Cambridge University Press.

Zhao, X., Zhu, J. -H., Li, H., & Bleske, G. L. (1994). Media effects under a monopoly: The case of Beijing in economic reform. *International Journal of Public Opinion Research, 6*, 95–117.

Author Index

Subject Index

A

Advertising, *see* Broadcast media; Newspapers
Agenda-setting, 40–42, *see also* Communication effects
  cognitive input, 41–42
  issue saliency, 40
  by type of audience 40–41
  by type of medium, 40
Ambiguity, tolerance of, 31,
Attitude, *see also* Attitudinal systems; Individual opinion
  behaviorist definition, 18
  functionalist definition, 19
  verbalized opinion, 18
Attitudinal systems, 19–24
  affective component, 21–23
  behavioral intention component, 23–24
  cognitive component, 20–21
  perception, role in, 19, 162
  setting priorities, 20
  value and interest component, 20
Attitudinal change, 25–36 *see also* Individual opinion change
  cognitive processing, 43
  direct experience, 33–36, 43,
  information processing, 32–33
  learning theory, 26–27
  systemic processes, 27–28
Authoritarianism, 97–104
  contrast with totalitarianism, 104

legitimacy of collective opinion, 98–101, 108–109
  in medieval Europe, 101–103
  philosophy of, 98–99
  Portugal under Salazar, 103–104
  types of authoritarian regimes, 98–101
Audience size and structure
  broadcast media, 83
  Internet, 91–93
  mass audiences, 85
  nonbroadcast media, 86
  priestly readings and disquisitions, 77
  print media, 80–81

B

Balance theory of attitude change, 28–29
Belief systems, 123–124
Broadcast media, *see also* Audience size and structure; Literacy
  advertising, 84
  entertainment vs. news, 84
  institutional developments, 83, 84
  mass audience, 84–85
  mutual awareness, effects on, 84–85
  political use, 84–86
  publics, social structure of, 85
  technological development, 83

C

Climate of opinion, *see* Collective mood
Cognition and agenda setting, 41–42

About The Author

Dr. Irving Crespi has 40 years experience in public opinion research. He is a past president of the American Association for Public Opinion Research (AAPOR), and also of the World Association for Public Opinion Research. He has served on the editorial board of *Public Opinion Quarterly*, and on its AAPOR Advisory Committee. He is a former executive vice president of The Gallup Organization, vice president of The Roper Organization, and senior vice president of Mathematica Pollicy Research. He was polling consultant to the *New York Times*, and has directed opinion surveys for NBC, CBS, and *Newsweek*.

In addition to his 20 years on the Gallup Poll's research staff, Dr. Crespi has directed or consulted on opinion surveys on an extensive range of public policy issues including teen-age smoking, abortion, retirement, domestic violence, school desegregation, public transportation for persons with disabilities, energy conservation, pollution, and effects of early election-night forecasts on turnout.

Dr. Crespi is author of *Public Opinion, Polls and Democracy*, and of *Pre-Election Polling: Sources of Accuracy and Error*, and co-author of *Polls, Television and the New Politics*, as well as numerous articles on public opinion.

AEC0940

JE